"*Then* **Bud** *Said to* **Barry,** *Who Told* **Bob...**"

"*Then* **Bud** *Said to* **Barry,** *Who Told* **Bob...**"

The Best Oklahoma Sooners Stories Ever Told

Jeff Snook

TRIUMPH
B O O K S

This book is available in quantity at special discounts for your group or organization. For further information, contact:

Triumph Books
542 South Dearborn Street
Suite 750
Chicago, Illinois 60605
(312) 939-3330
Fax (312) 663-3557

Printed in U.S.A.
ISBN: 978-1-57243-997-9
Design by Patricia Frey
Editorial Production by Prologue Publishing Services, LLC

Photo Credits:
All photos courtesy of AP Images unless otherwise indicated.

To Amy—you may not know a zone blitz from a screen pass, but thank you for allowing me to continue my relationship with the other love of my life: the game of college football.

table of
contents

Preface   xiii

Acknowledgments   xvii

Chapter 1: The Early Years: Bennie the Great   1

**Chapter 2: George Lynn Cross:
A President Who Didn't Punt**   9

**Chapter 3: The 1940s:
Tough Times, Tougher Men**   19

Big Stage for the Army Game   22

The Hollis Connection   23

The Record Punt Return   24

The Buddy-and-Darrell Feud   25

Walker and Royal   26

The Biggest Upset of the Era   27

**Chapter 4: Bud Wilkinson: Legendary Coach,
Honorable Man, Loving Father**   29

The Early Days   32

As an Assistant   33

He Wasn't One to Berate You   35

As a Motivator   37

He Did Have Some Fire   39

And He Knew His Football   41

As an Educator   43

His Sense of Humor   46

As a Beloved Father   46
A Coach Adjusts After Football   48
A Final Tribute   49
Bud Wilkinson by the Numbers   50

Chapter 5: The 1950s:
Oklahoma Builds a Dynasty   **51**
Arnold Was an "Old" Quarterback   54
Crowder Makes History, Somewhat   55
A Sooner on the Longhorns' Bench   55
They Call It "The Streak"   56
"Which One Is the Legend?"   60
Krisher the Hitting Machine   60
The One and Only Tommy McDonald   61
Ol' "Ski-Jump Nose"   63
Bud: Why Did I Vote for That Rule?   64
The Food-Poisoning Incident   65
Say "Hey" to Gomer   66

Chapter 6: Prentice Gautt:
OU's Jackie Robinson   **67**

Chapter 7: The 1960s:
Losing, Transition, and Heartbreak   **73**
From 0–5 to 5–5   76
The Ol' Rugged Cross   77
There Will Never Be Another Joe Don Looney   77
Bud's Final Farewell   81
Awful Season, But Help Is on the Way   82
The Chief's Practical Joke   83
Jim Mackenzie: Gone Too Soon   85
The "Big Kid" Becomes a Legend   87
Riley the Strong One   89
The Fairbanks Era   90
Attack of the Oranges   91
Owens Carries the Load   94

Chapter 8: Bob Kalsu:
An Oklahoma Legend, An American Hero   **95**

Chapter 9: The 1970s:
From Chuck to Barry, Good Times Ahead   **111**

The Game of the Century   *115*
The Year of the Forfeits   *117*
No Tube-Time, No Bowls, No Problem   *119*
Steve Davis: Simply a Winner   *120*
A Weighty Matter   *122*
The Selmons: Men Among Boys   *122*
Joe's Famed Silver Shoes   *124*
Where Did "Tinker" Come From?   *126*
Nice to Meet You, Joe!   *126*
Who Was That Iowa Defensive Back?   *127*

Chapter 10: The 1980s: From J.C. To Jamelle,
Another Title for Barry's Boys   **129**

Elway's Big Day   *132*
Barry Calls Off the Dogs   *133*
LT's Forgettable Appearance in Norman   *133*
The Name's "Dick"   *134*
"Don't Touch Me, Doc"   *135*
Marcus's Huge Day, Wasted Talent   *135*
Keith Jackson, the Tight End   *136*
Aikman Once Was a Sooner   *137*
The 1985 "Ice Bowl"   *138*
National Champions Once Again   *139*

Chapter 11: Two Sides of "The Boz"   **141**

Chapter 12: Port Robertson: If You Needed
Discipline, He "Loaned" You Some   **149**

Chapter 13: Barry Switzer: From Crossett to the Hall Of Fame 167

A Coach Who Loved His Players 171

As a Recruiter 172

A Huge Heart 174

His Motivational Speeches 175

He Had His Share of Critics 176

The NFL Calls Him 178

Loyal to the End 180

Barry Switzer by the Numbers 181

Chapter 14: 1989–1998: The Dreadful Years 183

Mister Gary Gibbs 185

The 11 Months of Schnellenberger 187

John Blake's Miserable Three Years 188

Chapter 15: Bob Stoops: The Sooners' Savior 191

Bob Stoops by the Numbers 201

Chapter 16: OU Potpourri: Was "Sooner Magic" Real? Just Ask Nebraska 203

Famous Voices 206

The Notre Dame Jinx 207

Those Alumni Games Were Tough 208

Merv Johnson Makes a Home in Norman 209

OU Family Rallies to Help Katrina Victim Oubre 210

Clayton, McGruder Are Heroes 214

The Oregon Officiating Fiasco 215

What's in a Name? 217

Chapter 17: Texas: The Team Oklahoma Loves to Hate 219

1947: Was His Knee Down? 227

1974: A Hard-Hitting Slugfest 227

1976: "Are You Spying on Us?" 228

1980: "Hold onto the Ball!" 229

1984: Kiss Your Sister Again 229

1996: First Overtime Game 230

2000–2004: Stoops Takes No Prisoners 230

Chapter 18: Sooners in the Bowls **233**

Bud's First Bowl 235

The LSU Spying Scandal 237

The Bear Bites Back 237

OU Befriends OB—The Orange Bowl, That Is 238

JFK Attends Orange Bowl 238

The Vols Miss a Field Goal 239

Two Sugar Bowls, One Year 239

The Revenge Game 240

Just Who Is the Underdog? 240

A Rose Is a Rose 242

The Debacle Loss to USC 242

An Amazing, Remarkable Game...But Still a Loss 243

**Chapter 19: Oklahoma and the
Heisman Trophy** **245**

Billy Vessels 247

Steve Owens 248

Billy Sims 250

Jason White 252

Others Sooners Who Received Heisman Votes 253

**Chapter 20: The Best to Wear the
Crimson and Cream** **255**

Position by Position 258

The Biggest Victories (In No Particular Order) 267

The Most Disappointing Defeats 268

Chapter 21: Oklahoma Traditions **271**

The Sooner Schooner 273

The RUF/NEKS 275

Memorial Stadium 275

The Sooners Name   276
"Boomer Sooner"   277
The OU Chant   278
Crimson and Cream   278

**Chapter 22: The Oklahoma Sooners
by the Numbers   279**

Bibliography   285

Preface

As you read this book on Oklahoma Sooners football, I want you to remember the legacy of three men, what they stood for, and how they worked and lived.

One was famous.

Another was not.

And one became a prominent hero posthumously.

One was a sliver-haired legend with an impeccable persona, a polished public speaker with a soft voice and an even softer manner.

The other was coarser than an armadillo's hide.

And the third gave his life for his country.

One signed autographs by the thousands and posed for pictures with babies throughout the state.

The other worked in obscurity.

The third just wanted to be one of the guys, even though he did the work of five men and displayed the leadership and courage of 10.

These three men symbolize the heart and soul of a century of Sooners football.

Bud Wilkinson, Port Robertson, and Bob Kalsu.

The former, as you know, was a legendary football coach and author of the NCAA-record 47-game winning streak, three national championships, and 14 conference championships from 1947 to 1963.

Robertson was an academic counselor and former wrestling coach, giving more than 40 years of his life to ensure hundreds of Sooners athletes would receive the education they were promised.

Wilkinson and Robertson knew each other well and shared common beliefs that education, not football, was the way to prosperity for a young man.

Their tools were discipline, respect, and hard work.

There are times I wished I could go back in time, if only to meet great men like Bud, Port, and Bob; to interview them, perhaps to get to know them a little and discover what made them so great.

Their attributes remind me at times of my father's, he of the same generation.

I have always preached about the importance of college athletics, but I know there are times that the coaches of today's game need to know about men like Bud and Port, and the players of the game need to know about Bob Kalsu.

Today's coaches are paid salaries that men like Wilkinson, Paul "Bear" Bryant, and Woody Hayes never would have dreamed of, yet possess only a portion of their class, loyalty, and integrity, and that is a shame.

Port probably never earned more than $40,000 in any year of his lifetime.

Yet, if a man's life is measured by the contribution he made or the friends he counted, both Bud and Port surely died as much richer men than most.

After reading this book, I'll bet that you'll agree.

To all Sooners fans, I implore you to honor the legacy of Kalsu, an All-American in 1967 who was killed in Vietnam three years later after leaving the Buffalo Bills to serve his country. He put this country before himself, as thousands have done, and made the ultimate sacrifice. Let him never be forgotten.

Same goes for Jack Mildren, the "Father of the Wishbone" and former Oklahoma lieutenant governor. Jack died of cancer on May 22, 2008, at the age of 58. He was one of the most-memorable quarterbacks in college football history and one of my favorite people this game has ever produced.

I will never forget watching the "Game of the Century," and I have never doubted Jack's long-held belief that he would have led the Sooners down the field to beat Nebraska if he had had another minute or two on the clock. I also will always remember sitting with him through book-signing sessions for *What It Means to Be a Sooner* a few years ago as he greeted OU fans warmly, as if he personally knew each and every one of them. God bless you, Jack. You will be missed.

Through all the stories of Oklahoma football over the past 100 years or so weaves a common thread.

It has to do with men like these.

Success on the field originated with the four Bs: Bennie, Bud, Barry, and Bob, not that I need to use their last names. Coaches Owen (1905–1926), Wilkinson (1947–1963), Switzer (1973–1988), and Stoops (1999–present) have orchestrated 63 of the Sooners' most celebrated seasons.

Already their legacies are secure in history.

The football field at Memorial Stadium is named after Bennie Owen. One of the most popular coaches the game has ever known, Wilkinson is an American legend who won three national championships and authored the longest winning streak (47 games) in college football history. Switzer won three more national titles, while current coach Bob Stoops resurrected a program that had fallen on hard times, winning yet another national title for the school before maintaining a perennial championship contender.

Combined, those four coaches have won 521 of Oklahoma's 779 victories.

And amazingly, they lost only 134 games in those 63 seasons.

They arrived in Norman as natives of Kansas, Minnesota, Arkansas, and Ohio, and became integral parts of the Sooners family.

"Wilkinson set a standard that I think Barry carried on and Bob is doing now, that coaching is best done if it complies with the greatest definition of love," said Eddie Crowder, the Sooners' quarterback from 1950 to 1952, who later became head coach of Colorado.

"Love is patient and love is kind. And Wilkinson had patience and kindness toward his players. He wasn't temperamental. I think Barry did the same thing, And I think Bob is doing it. And it has been proven through three of the greatest records in college coaching.

"That's one of the reasons the Oklahoma Sooners have been so successful."

It is men like these, and men like Port Robertson and Bob Kalsu, who have made Oklahoma's football history so glorious. I hope you enjoy their stories…

—Jeff Snook

Acknowledgments

I want to thank all the Sooners who contributed stories for this book.

You are the men who realize that the University of Oklahoma's rich football history is special and unique and that it can be saved and preserved for future generations in the form of a book.

Thanks for your time and effort in telling your stories.

I want to especially thank Leon Cross, a Sooners All-American and lineman from 1960 to 1962.

Like me, Leon believes that the tradition and history of college football, and especially that of the Oklahoma Sooners, should be told. He was a huge help in prodding fellow Sooners to contribute to this project.

I also want to thank Jay Wilkinson, son of the legendary Bud Wilkinson. Bud handled everything in his life with the utmost class and dignity, from his unmatched success as a collegiate football coach to a failed run for the U.S. Senate and a tough two-year period as an NFL head coach. Remarkably, I can still hear his supple voice as it filtered through my parents' television during my adolescent Saturday afternoons.

In the game of life, Bud Wilkinson was a true champion.

And it is easy to see that the apples didn't fall far from that tree when it comes to Jay, a vice president of a major company in Houston, and Pat Wilkinson, one of the country's foremost eye surgeons, who lives in Baltimore.

I want to also show my appreciation for the Kalsu family: Jan, Jill, and Bob Jr. They opened their hearts to share wonderful stories, memories, and thoughts about Bob, the Sooners' All-American tackle who was killed in Vietnam on July 21, 1970. I wrote Bob's chapter with tears in my eyes, but I can only imagine the heartbreak his family has endured for almost four decades. It is a daily pain that will never fully disappear.

And thanks to Barry Switzer, a coach who won three national championships, one Super Bowl, and the hearts of hundreds of Sooners players.

What I like about Barry is that he continues to serve his former players in many ways, from simple friendship to a helping hand when they need it most, long after they are done serving his needs.

"When you recruit 'em and sign 'em," he told me, "I tell 'em I got 'em for life. And I always meant it."

I believe him.

chapter 1

The Early Years:
Bennie the Great

Bennie Owen, shown here kneeling with Bud Wilkinson on the Sooners practice field in the late 1940s, worked for the OU athletics department from 1905 to 1937, first as head football coach, then as athletics director, and finally as intramural athletics director. Following retirement, he was one of Oklahoma's biggest fans. Photo courtesy of University of Oklahoma.

The new University of Oklahoma football coach arrived in Norman, having been raised elsewhere and having played his football in another state, at another school, and immediately became beloved by his players.

He certainly was innovative for his era, introducing new offensive formations and plays that took defenses years to adjust to. And his teams scored quickly, won games by lopsided scores, and played hard from start to finish.

Naturally, by coaching an undefeated, championship season soon after his arrival, it did not take long for the Sooners faithful to cherish their new head coach.

Bob Stoops?

Barry Switzer?

Bud Wilkinson?

Bennie Owen?

If you had guessed any, or all, of the above OU head coaches, you would be accurate. It is simply remarkable and astonishing and yet somewhat coincidental that these three Oklahoma legends, and one in the making, had so much in common.

There will be plenty about Bud, Barry, and Bob later in this book, but it was Owen who became Oklahoma's first and foremost coaching legend.

Born in Chicago in 1875, Owen and his family moved to St. Louis, Missouri, when he was 12 and then to Arkansas City, Kansas, following high school graduation. He enrolled at Kansas University at the age of 23 to pursue medical studies, but soon he fell in love with this relatively new game that was captivating America from coast to coast: football.

He blossomed into the star quarterback for Fielding Yost's undefeated Kansas team in 1899.

Following his graduation from KU, Owen received his first head coaching job at Washburn College. Then he moved east to become Yost's top assistant at the University of Michigan, where he helped his mentor develop the famous point-a-minute teams that captivated the early sportswriters.

From there, Owen moved on to become head coach at Bethany College in Kansas, with his primary job as a chemistry professor. The Bethany Swedes, then a regional football power, defeated Oklahoma 12–10 in 1903 in Kansas and 36–9 on November 25, 1904.

That day is significant, for it was the first time Owen laid eyes on Norman and the University of Oklahoma.

For the next 33 years, beginning with the 1905 season, it is where he would build his legacy as one of the game's most successful pioneers. Owen would become one of the nation's most well-known football coaches for 22 seasons, before serving as the school's athletics director.

Before his arrival, the university had dabbled in the sport from 1895 to 1905 but had not taken it too seriously, as many schools in the East did at the time. OU didn't spend much money on its football budget and played a limited schedule of local teams until a first meeting with Texas in 1900.

Five years later, after 10 years and only 49 games (29 wins, 15 losses, five ties) played in front of few fans, the Sooners started to regard the sport in earnest.

Owen replaced Fred Ewing, who lasted only one season, which ended with a 4–3–1 record. Ewing's final game, ironically, had been that 27-point loss to Owen's Bethany team.

Owen immediately turned the Sooners into winners, coaching OU to its first win over the Texas Longhorns on the way to a 7–2 season.

Instantly, Owen's players loved him. Due to a tiny athletics budget, Owen remained on campus during the football season and commuted from Arkansas City. In 1907 Owen lost his right arm in a hunting accident and was soon fired by the Oklahoma legislature, which stated that his salary of $3,500 was too high for something as peripheral as football. They also cited the loss of his arm as another reason for his dismissal following a 4–4 season.

However, when the OU president heard of this news, he quickly reversed the decision, and Sooners players and fans rejoiced.

Owen was innovative and progressive with his ideas, becoming known as the forerunner in the Southwest region of the country for utilizing the forward pass. He also built his teams around speed and quickness, rather than size and strength.

To open the 1911 season, the Sooners walloped Kingfisher College 104–0. It was the first of eight games in which Owen's wide-open team would score more than 100 points in a game, including a record 179–0 win over Kingfisher in 1917. There were 26 more games in which his teams scored 50 or more points.

So when Barry Switzer, who arrived as an assistant coach in Norman 61 years after Owen's arrival, introduced the term "hang a half a hundred on 'em," or "score 50 points" in layman's terms, history shows it was Owen who first accomplished the feat with regularity.

In fact, the 1911 team finished 8–0, averaged 35 points per game and allowed only 15 points all season, which included a 6–3 win over Texas in the final game.

Owen's explosive teams are the primary reason the Sooners today rank number one in NCAA history in points scored, because it was not commonplace for collegiate teams to score more than 30 points pre-1930.

To be exact, 5,026 of those 29,772 points the Sooners have scored throughout history (through the 2007 season) were scored during Owen's 22 seasons.

During Owen's tenure, the Sooners became a charter member of the Southwest Athletic Conference (SWC) during its debut season in 1914, finishing second to Texas in the inaugural season due to a 32–7 loss to the Longhorns. OU finished 9–1–1 that season, but took no prisoners the following year.

The 1915 Sooners won all 10 games, scored more than 50 points in its first three, and beat Texas 14–13. That team, OU's first conference championship team, was widely regarded as Owen's best.

Five years later, OU departed the SWC and joined the Missouri Valley Intercollegiate Athletic Association (MVC). (As a side note, the conference split two years later, and Oklahoma remained aligned with the teams that formed the new Big 6 Conference. Naturally, it later became the Big 7, then the Big 8, where it stood through 1996. When the former SWC disbanded, Texas, Texas A&M, Baylor, and Texas Tech were added to form the current Big 12 Conference.)

By 1920 the sport was growing rapidly throughout the United States and was no longer considered an intramural hobby—and the state of Oklahoma was caught up in its increasing popularity. Owen realized that a new, larger stadium was needed and stated he wanted to begin raising the $340,000 to build the Sooners a new home.

The first game at Memorial Stadium was played October 20, 1923—Owen's team dismantled Washington, Missouri, 62–7. At the time, the new stadium was called Boyd Field. It later was renamed Owen Field, in honor of the coach who began Oklahoma's winning tradition.

His teams won three conference titles (two SWC and one MVC), Owen's teams never won the MVC championship, and he retired from coaching in 1926, following a 5–2–1 season, to become OU's athletics director. His record was an impressive 122–54–16.

National champions were not named during his coaching era by the wire services (Associated Press started the practice in 1936) or surely he would have produced one, if not two, for the Sooners.

Furthermore, Owen coached the Sooners' first four All-Americans, including Forest "Spot" Geyer, a running back who was known as one of the finest passers the growing sport had ever seen. Hence, his nickname originated from his pinpoint accuracy. Geyer had a spectacular season for the 1915 SWC championship team, which averaged 37 points per game.

Owen wasn't one-dimensional, either. He knew basketball almost as well as football, and served as the Sooners' head hoops coach for 13 years, orchestrating two undefeated seasons and having only two losing seasons.

As OU athletics director from 1927 to 1934, Owen oversaw construction of a new field house, golf course, tennis courts, baseball field, and other facilities that have been expanded and modernized over the years but remain today. He then became director of intramural athletics before retiring in 1938.

A charter member of the College Football Hall of Fame (Class of 1951), Bennie Owen died on February 26, 1970, in Houston, Texas, at the age of 94.

So while Bud Wilkinson is considered the author of Oklahoma's dynasty during the 1950s, Switzer the caretaker of the ultimate success in the '70s and '80s, and Bob Stoops the current-day savior, Bennie Owen has to be considered the patriarch of the Sooners football program.

chapter 2

George Lynn Cross: A President Who Didn't Punt

Dr. George Lynn Cross created what some Oklahomans now call the "Monster," otherwise known as the Sooners football program. Cross, the longtime OU president, brought Bud Wilkinson to Norman and helped build a national powerhouse. He frequently attended practices as well as games and matches of most Sooners sports. Photo courtesy of University of Oklahoma.

"We want to build a university our football team can be proud of."

Of course, George Lynn Cross was joking, although today's critics of the enormity of intercollegiate athletics would have you believe he was dead serious.

Nevertheless, Dr. Cross, the University of Oklahoma's longest-serving president (1943–1968) had a vision when he was hired that was ahead of his time, realizing that college football could serve as a centerpiece for camaraderie, pride, and enthusiasm among students, alumni, and all residents of the state.

And he realized this more than 60 years ago.

Cross, born May 12, 1905, the same year in which Bennie Owen arrived in Norman as head football coach, served in the U.S. Navy following World War I and became OU's president at the height of World War II.

By the war's end in 1945, when thousands of servicemen returned to the country to begin college in their early- to mid-twenties, many universities were beginning to build their athletics programs with the bounty of great athletes.

Likewise, Cross's foresight was for a strong OU football team in which not only all students and alumni could rally around, but one that would make all Oklahomans proud.

"I remember how all of it started here," Cross said during the 1980s. "It was 1945, and the war had ended, and here in Oklahoma, we were still feeling very depressed from those tough days that Steinbeck wrote about in *The Grapes of Wrath*.

"Then, during a board of regents meeting, it was suggested to me that I try to get a good football team. It would give Oklahomans a reason to have pride in the state."

Even Barry Switzer, who made a point to study Oklahoma history when arriving in Norman as an assistant in 1966, later marveled at how and why the football program was revived in the 1940s.

"After the war, maybe when Oklahoma didn't have much to be proud of, George Cross and some other people said, 'Let's create something good, something that Oklahoma can be proud of,'" Switzer said recently. "The time was right. The war was over. Lots of guys coming out of the service. I know their stories well. One day I went into Dr. Cross's office, and he told me the whole story."

Until World War II, the bulk of the Sooners' success in football came during the 22 years under Bennie Owen, but that had been more than two decades earlier. Since Owen's 1920 team, OU had won only one conference championship (1938) in more than a quarter of a century.

By the end of the 1945 season, what Owen created was floundering in poor health. It was on life support, at least as far as beating rival schools, capturing conference championships, and earning revenue. Since the national wire services started awarding national championships in 1936, the Sooners' cupboard was empty. What football trophies it had were old and dusty.

Coach Dewey "Snorter" Luster's teams had lost five straight games to Texas during his 1941 to 1945 tenure. Even worse, his last two teams had lost to Oklahoma State. And as Sooners coaches have learned from Owen to Bob Stoops, Commandment 1 in the OU coaching handbook is that one does not lose to Oklahoma State and keep the masses happy.

Following a 5–5 season in 1945, Luster was fed up with the intense pressure, the losing and not being able to satisfy the Sooners faithful. He also was having some health problems, so he resigned.

This was two years into Dr. Cross's tenure as president, and it left him facing his first hiring for the coveted position of head football coach. During a board of regents meeting to discuss the matter, several regents realized that the thousands of returning veterans would include top-notch football talent.

Two questions dominated the agenda: How to find them? And how do you recruit them to the University of Oklahoma?

OU's athletics director, Jap Haskell, formed a list of names as head-coaching candidates, including Jim Tatum, the head coach of the Iowa Pre-Flight Seahawks, the top-flight Navy team. They agreed on an interview, and Tatum asked if he could bring one of his assistants along for the meeting. Haskell agreed. During the meeting, the regents, as well as Dr. Cross, fell in love with Tatum's assistant.

His full name was Charles Burnham Wilkinson, but he went by "Bud."

Tatum was loud-mouthed, cocky, and boisterous, and next to the stately Wilkinson, he came off as the immature pupil rather than the seasoned mentor. And, as the state of Oklahoma would come to discover over the next few decades, Bud Wilkinson was mannerly, eloquent, and a 6′3″ walking testament to dignity.

Plus, he knew a little about football, as well.

After some negotiating, Cross secured Tatum—and Wilkinson—in a package deal to lead the Oklahoma football program into the future, but it didn't happen easily. Tatum was peeved that Cross and the regents made the offer contingent on Wilkinson's inclusion.

The initial season, 1946, under Tatum proved successful—the Sooners finished 8–3 and won the Gator Bowl. Tatum knew his football all right, but the main reason for OU's turnaround was a boatload of new talent in players such as linemen Buddy Burris, Plato Andros, John Rapacz, and Wade Walker, as well as quarter-back/running back Jack Mitchell, who once played for the University of Texas.

What Tatum ultimately proved, and perhaps Dr. Cross realized even during the interview, was that he didn't have the ideal temperament or personality to fit perfectly for Oklahoma. He also figured correctly that his top assistant, however, did.

Plus, there was this little matter of Tatum giving the Sooner players more than $100 each on the trip to the Gator Bowl, just days after Cross ordered him not to do so. That insubordination infuriated Cross. And Tatum suddenly wanted more control, including the firing of some athletics department personnel.

Rather than fire the new coach on the spot—remember, he just had produced an 8–3 season—Cross created a new contract offer he predicted the combative Tatum would refuse. His plan worked perfectly, as Tatum turned down the offer, left in a huff, and became the University of Maryland's new coach. That opened the door for Cross to hire Wilkinson, who had planned to quit coaching and return to work for his father's business in Minnesota.

It was as if Cross were a master chess player, making all the right moves for the future of the Oklahoma football program. And over the next 17 years, Wilkinson's Sooners would become a dynasty unlike any other in college football before—or since.

It was checkmate for Dr. Cross.

As the years progressed over his tenure, Cross was intimately involved in many facets of the program, including the hiring and resignations of head coaches and assistants, rare for a collegiate president. Remember, no head coach was fired under his tenure: Wilkinson (1963) and Gomer Jones (1965) each resigned; Jim Mackenzie died of a heart attack following the 1966 season; and Chuck Fairbanks resigned to take an NFL job following the 1972 season.

Thus, he never had been forced to endure a task collegiate presidents deem as pleasant as root canal—firing a football coach.

Still, Cross, like most every university president in America, didn't want athletics to overshadow or interfere with academic achievement. His academic background was in botany, and he knew the tail was not to wag the dog, no matter his infamous aforementioned quote.

Cross actually made this statement in 1951, following the Sooners' first national championship season. He stated it to the Oklahoma legislature during a presentation asking for more money in which to run the university. He admitted during several interviews over the years that it was just a wisecrack, growing from his frustration over having to beg for money to run the state's largest and most prestigious university.

For more than an hour, Dr. Cross thoroughly explained the specifics of his request, backed up by detailed analysis and data. When he finished, one "sleepy old senator," as Cross later labeled him, raised up in his seat.

"Yes, that's all well and good," the state senator said, "but what kind of football team are we going to have this year?"

Cross then replied, *"We want to build a university our football team can be proud of."*

Years later, he admitted, "It was a cynical remark because I thought my whole presentation had been wasted, but the quote was picked up all across the country."

In reality, it made him sort of famous, or infamous to others.

If anything, it proved he had a great sense of humor, as well as a great sense of how crucial football and athletics could become for a university the size of the University of Oklahoma.

During his quarter of a century as OU president, Cross was one of the Sooners' biggest fans through all the championships, wins, and losses. He often stood on the sideline during games, and even practices, especially during the early days, and made most of the road trips and bowl games. He knew all the players by name.

"George Cross had a lot to do with our football success back then," said Buddy Burris, an All-American lineman from 1946 to 1948 who died at the age of 84 in November 2007. "He was *for* the program. He was *for* the men. He was *for* all the players out there on the football field. I remember him at most all of the practices. He would be out there taking pictures…the Texas game, the bowl games, the was right there with us."

Former All-American lineman Leon Cross said Dr. Cross (no relation) truly loved the game and the Sooners players.

"Many days Dr. Cross showed up at football practice. It was impressive to us players that the president would take time from his busy schedule to show such interest," he said. "He had been an athlete in college at South Dakota State, which I'm sure contributed to his keen interest in athletics. He always sat at the scorers table at the home wrestling matches, and he really admired [former OU wrestling coach and athletics counselor] Port Robertson.

"I once asked Dr. Cross how he survived 25 years in such a political climate like that of the university. He smiled and said to me, 'I survived some four-to-three votes [there were seven board of regents].'"

Dr. Cross even penned a book about the football program in 1977, titled *Presidents Can't Punt.*

Fortunately for the Sooners faithful, not only did Cross not punt back in the '40s, but he threw deep and scored a touchdown by seeing the potential in a man named Bud Wilkinson.

George Lynn Cross died in 1998 at the age of 93.

Before he died, Cross mentioned in several interviews, however, that the millions of dollars that college football generated, through television contracts and bowl payouts, wasn't necessarily a good thing. In a sense, he admitted he came to hate the commercial aspect of the monster he created.

He also cringed when OU athletes ran into serious trouble off the field, leading to Switzer's resignation in the spring of 1989.

"It all makes me sick to my stomach," Dr. Cross told *The New York Times* at the time. "But it's not just Oklahoma's problems. What's happening here at the moment symbolizes with specifics what's wrong with big-time college athletics, particularly football."

He also mentioned that the Oklahoma president, or any collegiate president for that matter, who doesn't make decisions about the direction of the athletics department is doomed to face serious problems. He pointed to that ultimate truth as the downfall of several of his successors, who utilized a hands-off approach and let their athletics directors handle the monster.

"Football players became separated from the rest of the student body and didn't participate in other activities," Dr. Cross said. "In the end, the president must assume responsibility for the entire school. The buck must stop there."

And the buck always stopped with Cross, who loved the essence and purity of the game of football.

Today, George Lynn Cross Hall houses OU's department of botany and microbiology, the department's administrative offices, labs, and the university greenhouses. It also is where he maintained an office well into his nineties.

A statue of Cross is located in front of Evans Hall, the main administration building on the Oklahoma campus.

Surely, proponents and fans of the football program and college athletics in general will say the Sooners' tradition and success over the past seven decades is Cross's greatest legacy. However, the vocal critics of college athletics' unparalleled growth and well-publicized scandals will say it was his greatest flaw.

chapter 3

The 1940s: Tough Times, Tougher Men

Head coach Bud Wilkinson and assistant coach Gomer Jones shout directions to the Sooners from the sideline in November 1949. The architect of Oklahoma's 47-game winning streak that still stands as a record a half-century later, Wilkinson left an indelible mark on the record books.

Remember that back in the 1940s Army and its pair of Heisman Trophy winners, Felix "Doc" Blanchard and Glenn Davis, were the talk of college football. The Cadets had the best of everything, especially when it came to reputation, publicity, and even equipment.

Before the Sooners' 1946 season-opening game at Army, keeping up with the Joneses took on a whole new meaning.

Jim Tatum had just been hired by Oklahoma president George Lynn Cross and the board of regents, and suddenly, the new coach had recruited dozens of talented players to Norman.

Tatum and offensive coordinator Bud Wilkinson had introduced the new talent to the split-T formation, the run-oriented offense featuring the option, something Wilkinson had learned from Missouri legend Don Faurot.

Nobody in 1946 had the slightest idea that this new offense of Oklahoma's would give opponents fits for the next 18 seasons, as the university would build the greatest dynasty the game has ever seen.

But first things first, Tatum wanted his new team to look as good as the best teams in the country.

"We had practiced in those old leather helmets," quarterback Jack Mitchell recalled, "and everybody knew that Army wore those modern Riddell helmets. Well, Tatum had made up his mind that he would order the Riddell helmets for the entire team. He told us that we would have helmets just like the Army team. They were much better helmets that offered you more protection, and once word got out on those helmets, that's all anyone talked about.

"We kept after our equipment man, Sarge Dempsey, always asking, 'Sarge, when are those helmets coming in? When are those helmets coming in?'"

Mitchell recalled that one day Tatum was nowhere to be found at the beginning of practice when suddenly a big truck was seen heading toward the practice field.

"Guess who is sitting on top of the truck?" Mitchell asked. "That's right, Tatum. He was sitting up there going through those helmets as the truck came down the road.

"He then tossed all of those helmets out for us, and all of the big ol' linemen got up there first and got theirs. Finally, I got mine, and it was so big. By the end of practice, it had pivoted around and slid down and cut my nose. I still have a scar there.

"I walked up to Sarge and said, 'My helmet is too big for my head.'

"Tatum was standing there at the time, and he said, 'No, Jack. Hell, there's nothing wrong with that helmet—that's just like the helmet Davis and Blanchard wear.' I guess he didn't care about the size of it, but I'll bet Davis's and Blanchard's fit their heads."

Big Stage for the Army Game

Led by Blanchard and Davis, Army was riding a 19-game winning streak into the meeting with Oklahoma. But Blanchard, who won the Heisman Trophy the previous season, had injured his leg in the Cadets' opening game a week earlier and would miss the game against the Sooners.

The game had been billed as the most important in Oklahoma history to that point, considering the opponent, the new coaching staff, the influx of talent, and the fact that President Truman would be a special guest at the game, as well.

"Come game time, Tatum was so nervous," Mitchell recalled. "He was taping ankles just to keep focused."

Sporting their new helmets, the Sooners got off to a great start as Stan West and Norman McNabb fell on the football in the end zone for a 7–0 lead.

But the more experienced Cadets tied the game 7–7 at the half and went on to win 21–7.

"We just screwed up every time we turned around that day," All-American tackle Buddy Burris recalled. "We could make three to five yards every running play, but we couldn't pass. Darrell [Royal] threw a couple of bad passes that day, and they took one of his fumbles back for a touchdown."

The key play of the game was the fumble return, which occurred after the Sooners drove to the Army 15-yard line while trailing 14–7.

"It was a lateral play, and somehow the ball got knocked up into the air, and [Arnold Tucker] picked it off and ran 85 yards for a touchdown," Royal said recently. "I would like to see that play on film today just to see exactly what did happen on that play."

During the game, especially as things turned worse, Tatum didn't settle down much, either. He cussed and fretted and did some strange things as his players wondered just what made their new coach tick.

Burris couldn't believe his eyes.

"That was Jim Tatum's first game, and he got all excited on the sideline," Burris recalled. "He was complaining about some illegal plays and screaming at the officials.

"At one point, he wanted some water to drink, but they didn't have any nearby. So one of the guys was over there [on the bench] soaking his feet in water. Jim went over and picked up the bucket and drank it. I thought he had just about lost his marbles."

It was a crushing loss, but yet it was a game of firsts—the first time a U.S. president attended an OU football game and the first time the Sooners traveled by airplane to a game.

For the record, Davis managed only 19 yards on 12 carries against Oklahoma's defense, his lowest career output. Nevertheless, he would go on to win the Heisman Trophy that season.

The Hollis Connection

The tiny town of Hollis, Oklahoma, has produced quite a few Sooners over the years. Four of them—Olin Keith, J.R. Manly, Alton Coppage, and Marvin Whited—played together in the late 1930s and early '40s, inspiring a young hometown boy named Darrell K. Royal.

"I'll never forget this," Royal said. "Those were four guys from Hollis who lettered in football. They would come back home with those big lettermen jackets with the big white 'O' on them. From that point on, after seeing them, that was my ambition."

Royal achieved his goal, becoming an All-American for the Sooners. He still holds the career interception record of 18.

Ironically, Royal ended up spending most of his career (1957–1976) as the head coach of the Sooners' biggest rival— the Texas Longhorns. He is a living legend in the Lone Star State while most of the younger generation does not realize that he was born and bred a Sooner.

Royal had a 6–1 record coaching against his beloved mentor, Bud Wilkinson, and was 12–7–1 overall against his alma mater. In the 1970s he feuded openly with OU coach Barry Switzer.

As of 2008, he has lived in Austin, Texas, for 52 years.

"It is really hard for some people to believe you can have feelings for both Texas and Oklahoma," he said. "My alma mater is where I got my formal education, where I played, and where I knew all of my teammates. Some people cannot understand my feelings for both, but it is not a complicated matter for me. It never has been."

The Record Punt Return

Royal still holds the school record with a 96-yard punt return, recorded against Kansas State in 1948. There is an excellent chance it will never be broken for the simple reason that punt-returners are instructed repeatedly never to field a punt inside their own 10-yard line.

And to his day, Royal has no idea of why he did just that.

"All I can say is that I never should have fielded it," he admitted. "You never field punts inside your 10-yard line, let alone inside your own 5. When I got into coaching, we would put our punt-returners on the 10 and tell them, 'Now, if it's a high kick, fair-catch it. If it's over your head, let it go.'

"But for some reason, I did field it that day, and I got behind the wall. It wasn't clear sailing, but it was pretty close to it."

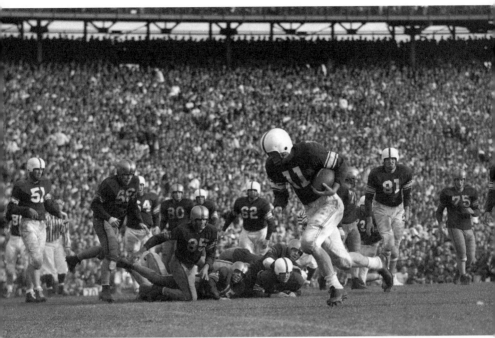

Darrell Royal (11) sweeps left on his way to a touchdown in the fourth quarter of the Sugar Bowl in New Orleans on January 1, 1950. Other Oklahoma players include Stan West (64), Dee Andros (62), and Jim Owens (81).

The Buddy-and-Darrell Feud

It was no secret that two of OU's best players from the 1940s didn't care for each other. Burris, a three-time All-American lineman, loved needling Royal, whom he regarded as an egotistical player who never accepted any blame when things went wrong.

The Sooners lost to Santa Clara 20–17 at the beginning of the 1948 season. At a key point in that game, Royal took a sack on a called screen pass, which infuriated Burris.

"He just froze up," Burris recalled. "We didn't get along too well after that. When the newspapers came out, someone bad-mouthed him about it. Well, my locker was right next to his, and I heard him say that he didn't play that badly."

I said, "Hell, Darrell, you've played a lot worse…"

"He didn't like that too much," Burris added.

Burris also blamed Royal for that fumble that led to Army's win in the '46 opener. Years later, at a team reunion, Burris spent the night getting under Royal's skin.

"Once the party was over, I was leaving and I said something to Darrell, and he gave it to me—knocked me out with a punch," Burris said. "I was mad over it for a long time, but I finally got over it."

They recently made up.

"We had a little run-in once a long time ago, but when I saw him recently, I stuck my hand out to shake his hand," Royal said. "Buddy said, 'The heck with that—give me a hug!' You forget those old grievances as time passes on."

Walker and Royal

Wade Walker and Royal never had such problems. They became the best of friends—and remain so more than a half-century later.

Royal named his son Darrell Wade Royal.

"I will always love Darrell Royal, I promise you," Walker said.

"When Darrell and I graduated, we made a bond. The first one to be a head coach would bring the other as an assistant. Sure enough, he got the job at Mississippi State [in 1954] and he called me. At that time, we always felt that if you made $10,000, you were really cutting it. Darrell told me, 'I can't get you $10,000, but I can get you $9,500.'

"I said, 'I'll be there.'"

Walker replaced Royal as head coach at Mississippi State when he left to become head coach at Texas. Walker also later served as the Bulldogs' athletics director before returning to Norman as OU's athletics director before retiring in 1986.

The Biggest Upset of the Era

That aforementioned 1948 season-opening loss to Santa Clara in Norman ranks as one of the greatest upsets of the decade, especially considering the Sooners ran off 10 consecutive victories to cap a brilliant season.

Royal saw it differently than Burris did, of course.

"We just had an off day, a real bad day," he said. "Plus, Santa Clara had a good football team."

"We ran out of gas in the fourth quarter that day," Walker said.

Remarkably, the Sooners did not lose again until the 1951 Sugar Bowl—a 13–7 defeat to Paul "Bear" Bryant's Kentucky Wildcats. In between was a span of 31 consecutive victories.

"I never dreamed [at that time] that we would never lose another football game in my career," Royal admitted.

But that's exactly what happened—the Sooners put together a winning streak that was the envy of college football. The amazing thing is, when it came to winning streaks, that 31-game stretch would pale in comparison once the Sooners of the 1950s got rolling.

chapter 4

Bud Wilkinson:
Legendary Coach,
Honorable Man,
Loving Father

Bud Wilkinson is shown with his 1949 Coach of the Year
plaque at a dinner of the American Football Coaches
Association in New York on January 12, 1950.

You cannot describe Oklahoma's 13th football coach with only one chapter. After all, there have been several books written about Charles Burnham "Bud" Wilkinson, and even those tomes run out of pages before thoroughly describing the essence of the man.

For starters, he was the ultimate winner as a coach, the architect of *the* longest (47 games) and one of the longest (31 games) winning streaks in college football history. His 11 seasons, from 1948 to 1958, produced a record—107–8–2—that had not been accomplished in the six decades of college football before or the five decades since.

"Nobody will ever come close to that again," said Claude Arnold, the starting quarterback on the Sooners' 1950 national championship team. "Ever."

Wilkinson was educated, having earned a master's degree, and he did everything he could to make sure his players earned their college degrees as well. He was classy, a football coach who could fit in perfectly at a state dinner—of which he attended numerous—and he knew many of the U.S. presidents and congressmen very well from the 1950s until his death in 1994.

He was worldly with a firm grasp of history. And for a man who would become so famous, he had virtually no ego. He was deeply religious and a wonderful father to two boys, who grew up to be successful adults.

Most of all, Bud Wilkinson was the definition of a perfect gentleman. He treated everyone with respect, even those who may not have deserved it. His compassion for his fellow man, whether he knew you for years or just met you moments ago, was one of his biggest attributes, all his friends, players, and colleagues say. He dealt with fame—and he was famous not only in the state of Oklahoma, but nationwide as the age of television dawned on America—as flawlessly as he did everything else in his life.

"He was such a good man that I never saw him walk away from an autograph request," said Bill Krisher, a Sooners All-American in the 1950s. "He would stand there outside of our bus until the last person....I've never known a bigger gentleman."

There were times, too, that he was so revered in the state of Oklahoma that even his younger players wanted his John Hancock, realizing they were in the presence of greatness. "I, like everyone else, was completely in awe of Coach Wilkinson," said Jerry Thompson, an All-American from the 1950s. "He was a Godlike figure, very much a gentleman and very intelligent. He always shook your hand and wanted to know how you were.

"As I knew him for the rest of my life and later coached with him, he never changed."

Perhaps Lou Holtz had one of the best lines ever to describe Bud.

"In a game played by amateurs," he wrote in the foreword for Jay Wilkinson's biography of his father, "he came to stand for what professionalism was all about."

Perhaps those are a few reasons that Wilkinson attracted people from all facets of society. He became close friends with John F. and Robert Kennedy and Richard Nixon. He knew celebrities like Bob Hope and company CEOs like Lee Iacocca. At the same time, he chatted extensively with his car's mechanic and a restaurant waitress as if they were the most important people in the world.

"He attracted everyone," said Leon Cross, one of Wilkinson's former players and assistant coaches. "He knew JFK back when he was a senator. One day Bud was walking around with this gentleman, and he introduced him, and it was Ben Hogan. That always impressed me, the type of people who associated with him. They just seemed drawn to him, like we all were."

The Early Days

Wilkinson played at the University of Minnesota and learned much of what he later taught at Oklahoma—motivation, organization, and the game's fundamentals—from the Gophers' head coach, Bernie Bierman.

Those Minnesota teams won the first official wire-service national title when AP named them champions in 1936 and also claimed titles from the National Championship Foundation in the previous two years, amounting to essentially three consecutive national championships. Wilkinson played guard as well as quarterback on those three teams.

Amazingly, Wilkinson also excelled at golf in college and was the goalie on the Minnesota hockey team.

Following graduation, he became an assistant coach at Syracuse, where he earned his master's degree in English. He then coached one season at Minnesota, in 1941, before enlisting in the U.S. Navy the following year as World War II arrived in full bloom after Pearl Harbor was attacked.

Wilkinson was assigned to the Iowa Pre-Flight School where he met Don Faurot, the famous Missouri coach, who had developed many of football's new formations at the time. That is where he learned the split-T, which would propel the Sooners' offense to unparalleled heights.

By 1944 Bud was assigned to the USS *Enterprise* and saw action in the Pacific during the war's final two years. As Jay Wilkinson wrote, his father was nearly killed one time when a Japanese kamikaze pilot slammed his airplane into the ship's deck. Fourteen men were killed, but Bud stood behind a steel beam on deck, saving his life.

As an Assistant

Wilkinson first arrived in Norman in 1946 as George Lynn Cross and athletics director Jap Haskell interviewed Jim Tatum for the job. At the time, Tatum and Wilkinson were friends from their Navy days, but the OU powers-that-be were so impressed with Bud that he almost became the head coach right then and there.

"I had heard that when the school interviewed Tatum, that they were more impressed with Coach Wilkinson than they were with Tatum," said Darrell Royal, who would be a freshman in 1946.

At the time, Wilkinson had planned on coaching only one season in Norman as a favor to Tatum and then he would return home to the family business in Minnesota. But those who studied Wilkinson's work especially knew he would someday become an excellent head coach.

"There was no question even then that Bud Wilkinson would become a great head coach," said Jack Mitchell, the Sooners' quarterback from 1946 to 1948.

Wade Walker will never forget meeting Bud. On his original trip to Norman as a recruit, he went to Haskell's house to meet Tatum.

"When I walked in there to see him, a tall, younger-looking man was with them," Walker recalled. "I asked him, 'What position do you play?'

"He looked at me and said, 'Why, I am one of the coaches. My name is Bud Wilkinson.'"

Just months into the 1946 season, Sooners players realized Wilkinson would make an outstanding head coach, someday, somewhere. They just didn't figure it would be at Oklahoma so soon.

"I knew Coach Wilkinson would become the head coach," Walker said. "He was the epitome of grace. He was an English major and he spoke properly. He was a wonderful offensive coach. Bud—I never called him Bud back then—was a great organizer, and his teams were going to win."

Of course, it didn't hurt that thousands of veterans were returning following the war, and Tatum had stockpiled some talent that would benefit Wilkinson.

"Jim recruited me hard," lineman Buddy Burris recalled. "One day I was on a tractor in the field when a big, old car pulled up at the other end of the field. Jim took me off that plow and put me in that car, and that was the end of it. I was going to Oklahoma.

"That first year, the team was full of discharged veterans like me. I think we had 175 uniforms checked out at one time. It was simply a case of survival. They would line you up and run you as long as you could make it."

The Sooners had lost the much-anticipated opening game to Army 21–7, played in front of President Truman in New York, but as the season progressed, the Sooners won eight of 11 games. Along the way, however, Tatum was making his share of enemies. Many players mimicked his Southern accent and most said he played favorites with the starting lineup.

After the Sooners whipped North Carolina State 34–13 in the Gator Bowl, a perfect storm led to Tatum's departure.

"Tatum was a real charmer who was a very good coach, but he played favorites," Burris said. "He played all of those Navy guys over other players who should have been playing. Homer Paine and I were very good friends on that team, and we agreed that if Tatum stayed for another season, we would leave and sign pro contracts."

Tatum had blown past his assigned budget for the Gator Bowl, and part of the money had gone as a payment to his players. The OU administration was not happy. Following a confrontation about the issue and a subsequent contract offer he deemed insulting, Tatum bolted for Maryland.

Most Sooners were ecstatic.

"At the time, all of the players loved Bud Wilkinson, and he was a very good assistant coach," Burris said. "We all wanted him to be the head coach, too. I don't know of a player on the team who didn't like Bud. So once Tatum left, it was a natural that they would name Bud head coach.

"And, boy, were we happy about it."

He Wasn't One to Berate You

Wilkinson was extremely popular from the beginning because he treated everyone the same—with class and dignity.

"He wasn't like Tatum, who was a wild man," Mitchell said. "Bud was just a real nice guy. He kept his cool and treated you well. He really was ahead of his time. He had things so organized. He had a practice schedule that was down to the minute."

Wilkinson never verbally abused players, either, setting him apart from other legends of his era like Alabama's Paul "Bear" Bryant or Ohio State's Woody Hayes, even though they were as revered by their players as Wilkinson was by his. He just took a softer, almost unfootball-like approach.

"The worst I ever heard him say to a player is, 'Son, it just looks like you don't want to play,'" Walker recalled. "You think about that. How can you put it any better to motivate someone?"

"I think one of the things he realized [was that] what was most important to each player was his pride," Royal said. "Coach would never take away a player's pride by yelling or cursing at him in front of his teammates."

Tommy McDonald, halfback and College Hall of Famer, added, "I have never seen that man raise his voice at anybody, and I have never seen that gentleman grab a player by his jersey and start shaking him or something like that. The only way he would do anything was to call you into his office and, if he wanted to dress you down or anything like that, he would do it by himself and with the door shut. The great thing about Wilkinson was that he would not embarrass you in front of the other players. He wasn't a show-off that way."

"He would never criticize you in front of your peers," said center/linebacker Wayne Lee. "It was always on a one-on-one basis."

Wilkinson's main weapon of discipline was manipulating the team's depth chart. If you were not motivated or had not practiced well or not played well on the preceding Saturday, you may have found your name sliding lower on the depth chart. And it worked both ways, too.

Guard J.D. Roberts saw his depth-chart method work perfectly with his roommate.

"One time my roommate was the starting guard one week and on the sixth team the next week because of a bad game," Roberts recalled. "He went to see Coach one day to confront him about not playing. He came back to our room, and I asked if he saw Coach Wilkinson.

"Yeah, I saw the silver-tongued, gray-haired coach," he said.

"How'd it go?" I asked.

"Oh, the hell with it...," he said. "Boomer Sooner!"

"That's how good Coach Wilkinson could make you feel," Roberts concluded.

As a Motivator

While Notre Dame's Knute Rockne and others are well-known for their rah-rah speeches, Wilkinson motivated quietly, through reasoning and storytelling. He rarely used a speech in which he raised his voice, the halftime of the 1956 Colorado game being one of the few exceptions.

Take the week of the 1954 Orange Bowl as an example.

"It was the first bowl game for all of us," Roberts, a team captain, explained. "Quite a few guys on that team were married, and their wives made the trip to the Orange Bowl. The night before the game they always had the Orange Bowl parade, and some of the guys asked me if I would say something to Coach Wilkinson about maybe all of us going to the parade.

"I told them, 'I think everybody knows the answer to that one.' I knew damn well that wasn't in the game plan, but I went up to Coach Wilkinson anyway."

For starters, the Sooners were playing Maryland, now coached by Tatum, and Wilkinson knew Tatum wanted to beat his former team badly.

Following dinner that night, the coach recapped the entire season, game to game. He talked about how hard his team had practiced, prepared, and played each week. Then he mentioned the parade.

"I understand a lot of you want to go to the parade," he told his players. "All I can say is that if you think going to this parade will help us win this ballgame, I am all for it."

However, he then proceeded to present several reasons why it wouldn't. Then he left the room, leaving it to a team vote.

"The captains said, 'Let's vote. Raise your hands if you want to go to the parade,'" Roberts said.

"Not one hand went up."

The Sooners beat Maryland and Tatum 7–0 to conclude a 9–1–1 season.

"As you can tell from the parade issue," Roberts added, "you could say we believed in Coach Wilkinson."

Beloved by his players, Bud Wilkinson discusses the game plan with three of his squad, (left to right) Dick Bowman, Darlon Hearon, and Kurt Burris in December 1953, prior to the Orange Bowl in Miami.

One of the most revealing motivational stories involving Wilkinson came before the 1951 game against Texas. The Sooners had just won the national title the year before and had lost to Texas A&M a week earlier, mainly because they were playing many new players since most of the starters had graduated.

On the flight down to Dallas, the coach observed his younger players laughing and joking. Once they landed, they were besieged for autographs from dozens of children. Then they continued in good spirits as they reported to receive their 75 cents to gain entry into the Friday night movie, a road-game routine.

As the players gathered for what was supposed to be a defensive meeting, Wilkinson called off the X's-and-O's chalk talk and delivered a major life lesson for many in the room.

"You people aren't ready to play," he started. "You think you're really something big. You remind me of a great American story called 'Shirt Sleeves to Shirt Sleeves in Three Generations.'"

He proceeded to tell the story of how a family had immigrated to America with the goal of earning a living simply to raise a family in this new country. The second generation then grew up more prosperous, attending college and earning more money than their parents. Finally, the third generation was "driven to school, had hot lunches, and expected an education," and had more money and material possessions than their grandparents had ever dreamed of.

Following college, the third generation returned to run the family business because they figured that was what was owed to them. With that attitude and no work ethic, they ran the family business into the ground and suddenly their lifestyles returned to that of the first generation.

Then he reprimanded his players for getting big-headed over signing autographs, even though some had never played much for OU before.

"You have not earned the right to sign an autograph for anyone," he said. "You haven't done anything yet. You are living off the work of those who came before you. Good night!"

By the end of the lecture, most of his players sat in the room stone-faced and ashamed, having been verbally slapped back to reality. OU lost 9–7 to Texas the next day, but then won the next seven games to finish the season 8–2.

He Did Have Some Fire

McDonald loves to tell the story of how Bud got fired up during the 1956 Colorado game, in which the Sooners trailed 19–6 at halftime.

"He came in there and shut the door. He just stood there and he looked as if he was ready to jump into a jersey," McDonald said. "Then he said: 'It has taken Oklahoma so many years to build that reputation up, and you are letting that reputation down. You are letting it down. That jersey on your back—you have let that jersey down against Colorado today. It has taken so many great players ahead of you to start this streak and to get this streak going. Everybody wants to be the team to beat us. And you are letting every one of those ballplayers who have played in that jersey down. Now what in the heck are you guys going to do about it? Are you going to show these people in the stands that you deserve to be in that jersey? You have not earned it this first and second quarter. Please let me see you go out there and show me in the third and fourth quarters that you deserve to be in that jersey. Go get them!'

"And that's what we did. I don't think we even opened the door. I think we ran right through the wall."

Oklahoma rallied to win 27–19, to extend the record-winning streak to 36 games.

After the game, he came in and said, "Guys, I think I have said enough today. I'll talk to you on Monday or Tuesday in the meeting room."

"On Monday in the meeting he told us that he was so proud of us and we were family," McDonald recalled.

"He said, 'This is my family, and I am so proud of you guys. I am absolutely lost for words. You showed me something on Saturday that has probably been the greatest experience of my life, seeing you behind 19–6 and you came back and you ran them in the ground. It has been the greatest experience of my coaching career up to this point. I want to compliment each and every one of you. You have reached down and told yourself that this is for pride. This is what winning is all about.'

"It was marvelous," McDonald added.

Walker loved his pregame speeches as well.

"One philosophy he used to say: 'We will pour the pine to them for three quarters. It will be so fierce for three quarters that come the fourth quarter, they will give up. We will win the fourth quarter.' That got you ready to play your best that day," Walker recalled.

Still, no matter how worked up he became, Wilkinson got his point across without invoking common-speak in the coaching industry: profanity.

"Maybe once or twice a year did I ever hear him cuss," Leon Cross recalled. "And those words were minor compared to today's standards."

"He never used harsh words against you, but he would use psychology," running back Leon Heath added. "He had one rule: if you didn't hustle, you didn't play."

And He Knew His Football

Being as smart as he was, it was only natural that Wilkinson knew the intricacies of the game as well as any other coach. He knew fundamentals and he knew how to stay a step ahead of the opponents' coaching staffs.

"I would have to put him in the same category as Vince Lombardi because he was not only a great, great motivator, but also an excellent X-and-O guy as far as calling plays," McDonald said. "Plus, he could judge talent. He had a keen eye for talent just like Lombardi did. Wilkinson was ahead of his time."

"I thought I knew a lot about football until I met Bud," quarterback Jimmy Harris once said. "He spent so much time on so much detail—it was like going to school with the greatest professor in the world."

Wilkinson's most important axiom was what he labeled "the will to prepare."

He used to tell his team that everyone on both teams had the will to win on game day, when the bands were playing, the cheerleaders were on the sideline, and the parents and girlfriends were in the stands. But it was the "will to prepare"—to get out of bed at 5:00 AM when the body aches from the previous day's practice— that would determine Saturday's victor.

"The will to prepare is the key ingredient to success," he often said.

On the field, for the most part, Wilkinson's teams ran the split-T that Don Faurot had invented at Missouri. Defensively, the Oklahoma coach is given credit for perfecting the 5–2 defense, which was flexible enough to convert to what today's analysts would call a 3–4, simply by dropping its two ends a few yards off the line of scrimmage.

Lee, a cocaptain and All-American in 1962, said that although Wilkinson's Plan A was usually good enough to win, he always had a Plan B just in case.

"Coach Wilkinson and his staff always had two or three trick plays ready for every game," he said. "Sometimes we used them, sometimes we didn't."

One time, during the game against Army at Yankee Stadium in 1961, Wilkinson had noticed that Army's defense always huddled tight but far away from the line of scrimmage. He noticed at times they were not ready when the offense approached the line of scrimmage.

"We had warned the referees ahead of time that we might do this," Lee explained. "If a play ended on the right hash mark, we had designed a play where we would have several players remain on the left hash mark."

During a close battle that day, the Sooners' offense set quickly and casually snapped the ball as a receiver ran free, resulting in an easy touchdown which had surprised the Cadets, still huddling some 20 yards away. That play resulted in a 14–8 win.

Royal, who was very close to Wilkinson when he played at OU, became his chief rival from 1956 to 1963, when the two crossed paths as head coach of Texas and Oklahoma, respectively. And Royal, who was 6–1 against Wilkinson in those games, said he hated coaching against his beloved mentor because one of them had to lose.

"The things I learned from Coach Wilkinson—like trying to make first downs, then make another first down instead of trying to break one for a touchdown on every play—stuck with me," he said. "He wanted to break the game down into a series of downs, and it worked well for him."

Wilkinson's mantra, having the will to prepare is more important than having the will to win, was illustrated in how prepared he was for each game, Eddie Crowder said.

"Let me give you an example," said the former OU quarterback and Colorado head coach. "Each day, he would spend time with the quarterbacks on a one-on-one basis. He would set up the checkerboard-like display with miniature football players that looked like little soldiers on a board that represented a football field.

"He'd give you the game situation, the down and distance, and have you call the play. You'd get a result and go through the process all over again. During the week of the game, you'd go over at least 13 possessions with him."

Why 13? Because during a game in the early '50s, there were an average 13 possessions per team per game. That is how well-prepared Bud Wilkinson was for a football game.

As an Educator

"If it weren't for Bud, I don't know what I would have been in life. I really don't," Mitchell said recently. "I went into coaching because of what he taught me and what I learned while at Oklahoma."

Highly educated himself, Wilkinson demanded his players earn their degrees as well. He lectured them constantly about the benefits of education and stressed that they would not miss a single class or they would be punished severely. Said punishment was running the stadium steps enough to satisfy Port Robertson, the former OU wrestling coach who became the athletics department's academic counselor.

Wilkinson wanted his players to be well-rounded, not just jocks.

"When we went out socially, he insisted that we not talk about football," Jerry Thompson said. "He would say, 'Don't talk football.

Talk politics. Talk history. Talk about anything, but don't talk about football."

Dale Perini (1960–1961) tells the following story, illustrating how genuine Wilkinson was in his desire for his players to receive a college education:

> As a freshman in 1958, I had pretty good balance and quickness and started both freshman games that year. We mainly just held dummies for the varsity and assisted in their drills. Our real "try-out" for the varsity started in spring football where we were first evaluated as potential football players. On the first day of spring football in 1959, I was listed on the second team.
>
> In those days, the second team was a "playing team," as two-platoon was not existent. I think we switched teams every seven minutes. By the second day of spring practice, I was on the fifth team. I never got above that level and most practices I was listed as an "AO," which stood for "all others." I was not even a "prospect" of becoming a player at Oklahoma. I was also from out of state [Carlsbad, New Mexico], so that didn't help matters.
>
> At the end of spring football, we all met with Coach Wilkinson on a individual basis, and normally he invited each player back for the next year since the NCAA only allowed a football scholarship to be awarded on a year-to-year basis. You can imagine my fear of being sent back to New Mexico as an out-of-state, 18-year-old, an "AO" without a chance of playing.
>
> When my appointment date with Coach Wilkinson arrived, I was scared to death he would tell me to go home. But he was very kind to me and he made me believe that my poor performance in spring football was something I could overcome. Basically, he told me I had gained about 10 pounds, had lost a step or two, and that I didn't quite have the strength to keep blockers off of me.
>
> He said if I would get a little quicker and stronger, I could play at Oklahoma. I walked out of his office that day

singing "Boomer Sooner." I knew I was ready to make a commitment of improving my strength and quickness and I would come back next year ready to play.

When a junior-college coach from Lawton tried to talk Perini into transferring so he could play immediately, the player went to see Wilkinson again.

Imagine my surprise when he replied, "I think that's a horrible idea. He went on to explain that he had given permission to the junior-college coach to talk to me, but that he didn't think it was a good idea for me leave OU for two reasons:

First of all, I could learn more football on OU's practice field than I could playing 30 games at a junior college. Secondly, and most importantly, when I changed from one school to another, he pointed out that I would lose college hours. Then he said, "Don't ever forget why you're here!"

I walked out of his office singing "Boomer Sooner" for the second time that day.

I guess I never really realized what Coach Wilkinson had done for me until many years after I had graduated. He was truly interested in me as a person and not just one of his players. In the end, I finally worked my way to the second team as a junior due to an injury to our starting end and then became a starter as a senior. I am still thankful I went to the University of Oklahoma and had the opportunity to play for a coach like Coach Bud Wilkinson. He really had a tremendous influence on my life.

He was exactly the type of man George Lynn Cross had figured him to be during that interview that led to Tatum's hiring.

"Bud was a class act," Cross said in 1989. "'Over 90 percent of the football players graduated. Now, it's well under 50 percent. One year, our starting quarterback flunked out, but he was technically still eligible for the Orange Bowl game. Bud refused to let him play. That's the type of coach he was."

His Sense of Humor

Bud was not widely credited with having a great sense of humor, but those who knew him well know that he did. It may have been a bit of a dry wit, but it usually was delivered in his typical good-natured manner.

"The only time I witnessed Coach Wilkinson being embarrassed occurred during the halftime break of our 1955 game with Kansas State," said lineman Byron Searcy. "We were leading 40–0, and the atmosphere in the dressing room was unusually relaxed. Players were in a happy mood, drinking Cokes, throwing a few orange slices, and generally behaving like the game was over.

"When Coach Wilkinson came into the room, the atmosphere returned to normal, and everyone was working their best on having a good game face. Coach seemed to be relaxed also and had little to say. He did mention that our corners needed to be attentive to the very small Kansas State halfback on his curl routes.

"He said something like, 'He was wide open once, and if one of the officials hadn't been in the way, it could have amounted to a substantial gain.'

"He did not realize that one of the officials had come into the dressing room to notify us for the start of the second half and was standing behind him as Bud said it. The team responded with a roar of laughter. We all loved him."

"Dad really had a great sense of humor," Jay Wilkinson said recently, "but I think he felt he had an image to uphold. He felt it was important to uphold a solid reputation as head coach of the University of Oklahoma. He didn't go around joking with everybody.

"People used to ask me what he was *really* like, and I would say, 'He's just as he is on TV.'"

As a Beloved Father

By all accounts, Bud was a loving, caring father just as he was a loving, caring football coach.

Jay wrote his father's biography, detailing his life and career in glowing terms, even though Bud was often absent from home as most collegiate football coaches have been and continue to be.

Interestingly enough, Jay wrote that his father did not give him and brother Pat special access to team functions or practices, and that they rarely hung around the Sooners' locker room.

"As little kids, Pat and I were given Oklahoma jerseys with the numbers 26 and 44, which were the numbers of Jack Mitchell, the great Oklahoma quarterback, and Myrle Greathouse, the outstanding linebacker," Jay wrote. "That was about as close as we got to them. Neither Pat nor I had special privileges regarding the team. We weren't permitted to sit on the bench or act as water boys because Dad felt the father-son relationship should be separate from practice and game conditions."

Bud always loved it, of course, when his boys achieved top grades in school, and especially when Pat became his high school's co-valedictorian.

Legendary Ohio State coach Woody Hayes, a close friend of Wilkinson's, was visiting at that time. When he heard of Pat's accomplishment, he returned to Columbus and mentioned to his son Steve, "Why can't you make straight A's like Coach Wilkinson's son?"

To which Steve Hayes quipped, "Dad, I'll make straight A's when you win 47 straight games."

Steve Hayes is now a circuit court judge in Columbus, Ohio, and often tells that story.

"Steve and I laughed about it, as well," said Jay, who lived in Columbus for 14 years and got to know Steve Hayes. "It's a great quote."

As you would expect from "Bud's boys," Jay and Pat turned out to be highly successful in their own right. Jay, who became an All-American quarterback at Duke, is a vice president of AIG Retirement in Houston, while Pat is one of the country's foremost retina surgeons in Baltimore.

While at Duke, Jay often received letters from his father, several of which he published in his biography of Bud. They offered advice on academics and football, detailed what was happening back in Norman, but most of all, conveyed the love and pride that only a father could convey to his son.

One letter, sent during a tough time in Jay's career, read: "Do your total, all-out best on every single play. Never be discouraged if you don't do too well nor overly elated when you make a good play. I know you are hot, tired, and probably sick of football and practice, but this discipline—putting up with totally tough, unhappy situations is one of the greatest lessons of the game that you'll appreciate as time goes on. Life has some rugged hills for all of us—and this training enables you to climb them with a song in your heart.

"We miss you and think of you each day. I pray for your happiness, growth, and development, and love you with all my heart and soul. I love you, Jay. No father can ever be more fortunate than I in having sons like you and Pat."

He concluded every letter the same way, telling Jay how much he loved him and how much he missed him. If they would have awarded national championships for fatherhood, the Sooners head coach would have been a candidate for those, too.

A Coach Adjusts After Football

Soon after Wilkinson left OU following the 1963 season, he announced a run for the U.S. Senate.

Then, shockingly to some, he lost the election to Democrat Fred Harris.

"He ended up losing the election to Fred Harris because a lot of Oklahomans in those days would just automatically push the Democratic button no matter who was running for office," Leon Cross stated.

Wilkinson's defeat in politics, something of which he experienced so little in college athletics, didn't diminish his legend as far as most Sooners fans contend. They loved him just as much.

He later proved his versatility by becoming quite good at handling the microphone duties, too, as one of ABC's lead college football television analysts. His soft voice, easy manner, and knowledge of the game made him a natural in the broadcast booth. His only fault was he hated to criticize fellow coaches.

He did fail in a brief comeback as head coach of the St. Louis Cardinals, but that's a testament to the inept ownership of the Cardinals back then rather than an indictment of Wilkinson's coaching ability.

"I made a statement one time and I stick by it: Bud Wilkinson represented everything that is good about college athletics," Leon Cross stated. "We had a good graduation rate. We looked at him as a man who set a good example for us. He had the utmost respect of anybody who ever played for him.

"He conducted his business like a real pro. We held him in such high esteem. He taught us so much more than football. He taught us how to get along in this world."

Which will be Bud Wilkinson's legacy among those he coached, taught, and to whom he became a second father.

He coached three national championship teams, 14 conference champions, and compiled a 145–29–4 record for a .826 winning percentage. But it was 17 years as a head coach and one year as an assistant in which he mentored University of Oklahoma football players about football and more about life and how to live it successfully.

The class and dignity in which he did it all will set him apart as a true American legend.

A Final Tribute

Fortunately, the Sooners family received the chance to thank Wilkinson one final time during a testimonial dinner on September 13, 1991. Curt Gowdy, the legendary broadcaster and former voice of the Sooners on radio in the 1940s, was the master of ceremonies, and hundreds of Bud's former players and assistant coaches attended.

"His health had declined rapidly at that time," Jay Wilkinson said. "The divorce of my mom and dad made it awkward for a lot of people, including us. There was never an appropriate time in the early years to hold it. But with his congestive heart problem, and his illness, the time was right. He did appreciate it. I know it meant a lot to him."

Bud Wilkinson died February 9, 1994, at the age of 77, two years after suffering a severe stroke. His second wife, Donna, and son Jay were at his bedside.

"He was my father," Jay Wilkinson wrote, "but he was also, and remained until his death, my best friend."

Recently, Jay said, "I don't think a week goes by that somebody doesn't mention him to me. Fortunately, in my adult life, I always knew how respected he was, how much he was revered. He was a great father. He was a great guy.

"And I miss him every day."

Bud Wilkinson by the Numbers

Born: April 23, 1916, Minneapolis, Minnesota
Died: February 9, 1994, St. Louis, Missouri
Married: Mary Shifflett, 1938–1975 (divorced); Donna O'Donnohue, 1976–1994
Education: Bachelor's degree, University of Minnesota; master's degree, Syracuse University
Assistant Coach: Syracuse University 1937–1941, Iowa Pre-Flight 1945; University of Oklahoma, 1946
Head Coach: University of Oklahoma, 1947–1963; St. Louis Cardinals, 1977–1978
Record: 145–29–4 (.826 winning percentage) at Oklahoma; 9–20 at St. Louis
Bowl Record: 6–2

chapter 5

The 1950s: Oklahoma Builds a Dynasty

Carl Dodd runs downfield, leaving Notre Dame defensive back Nick Pietrosante (49) and Oklahoma blocker Dennit Morris (51) upended in his wake on November 16, 1957, in Norman. Notre Dame's 7–0 win ended the Sooners' record 47-game winning streak.

If the 1940s belonged to war heroes, the Army football team, and Joe DiMaggio's hitting streak, the '60s to the Beatles and Elvis, and the '70s to Watergate, campus unrest, and disco music, then the 1950s surely belonged to Bud Wilkinson's Oklahoma Sooners.

They entered the decade riding a 21-game winning streak but were ranked sixth in the 1950 preseason poll only because they had been decimated by graduation. Almost every starter from the undefeated '49 team had moved on.

By the time the '50s were over, the Sooners would be featured in *Sports Illustrated*, *Time*, and *Newsweek*.

From 1950 to 1959, the Sooners were the kings of college football, winning 93 of 105 games (they had lost 10 and tied two). They rolled to national championships in 1955 and '56, and had another undefeated team in '54, but undefeated Ohio State was voted the champions of the AP Poll and undefeated UCLA were named the champions of the UPI poll (and the critics complain of today's system?).

The Sooners produced 23 All-Americans in the 1950s and one Heisman Trophy winner—Billy Vessels in 1952.

The state of Oklahoma was now known for its beloved Sooners, not for being "Okies" or for the uncomplimentary image its citizens were portrayed with in John Steinbeck's *The Grapes of Wrath*.

Sooners suddenly was synonymous with *winners* and *champions*, and those titles brought Oklahomans together like never before. The OU campus, and Memorial Stadium specifically, had become the gathering point for the abundance of pride and fellowship.

The heights the football program reached had exceeded even George Lynn Cross's wildest imagination.

"It was," Cross said, "a time for all Oklahoma people to be very proud. We had a coach and a football team that were winners on and off the football field."

Arnold Was an "Old" Quarterback

Claude Arnold seems to be the forgotten man in a string of Wilkinson's great quarterbacks that included Jack Mitchell, Darrell Royal, Eddie Crowder, Gene Calame, and Jimmy Harris.

For the record, Harris was 25–0 as a starter, while Calame was 15–0. Royal was 15–1, and Crowder was 16–3–1 and an All-American.

"Well, we only passed a few times each game," Arnold recalled. "I, of course, wanted to throw the ball more, but that was Bud's offense."

The few times he did get the chance to air it out, however, Arnold usually led the Sooners from behind.

Take the 1950 game against Texas A&M, for example. The Sooners fell behind 28–27 and were left with a little more than a minute remaining and 69 yards to go.

"It was the most spellbinding game," said Crowder, a backup quarterback at the time. "Here was a football game that was lost, then it appeared it might be a tie, and then we ended up winning the game. Claude hit four of five passes on the last drive. We had a running offense, but it had the flexibility to pass when we needed to."

"We went 69 yards in about a minute," recalled Arnold, who had two four-touchdown passing games in his career. "On the final play, I pitched it out to Leon Heath, and he ran over somebody [to score the winning touchdown]. I remember people just sat there for 15 minutes. The fact we won the game was so astounding that the crowd just sat there after the game."

The win extended Oklahoma's winning streak to 23 games (it would end at 31 games).

Arnold, who graduated from high school nine years earlier, was 26 at the time of his senior season. He had played two years in the intramural league at OU.

"I had been on the football team at Oklahoma in 1942, then went into the service," he said. "Then, after the war, I spent two years in intramurals, but it wasn't as if I was discovered there."

Crowder Makes History, Somewhat

Crowder, too, was an excellent quarterback and one of Wilkinson's favorites during his tenure at OU.

He was named All–Big 7 in 1951 and All-American the following season, before becoming an assistant coach for the Sooners from 1956 to 1962. He later became head coach at Colorado, using many techniques and philosophies he learned from Wilkinson.

Crowder says the 1952 game at South Bend, Indiana, a 27–21 Notre Dame win over the Sooners, was remarkable for another reason. He passed 28 yards for a touchdown to Billy Vessels, who won the Heisman Trophy that season. Later, he was intercepted by Johnny Lattner, who won the Heisman in 1953.

"Over the years, I have told the story of being the only quarterback in college football history to throw a touchdown pass to two Heisman Trophy winners in the same game," he said.

However, there's just one problem.

"It's really a flawed story, because one of our guys pulled down Lattner at the 1-yard line, and Neal Warden scored on the next play," Crowder admitted. "But let the record stand that I am the only guy who completed a pass to a Heisman winner on each of the two teams in the same game."

Anyway, Eddie, it's still a good story.

A Sooner on the Longhorns' Bench

Following OU's 8–1–1 season in 1952, the team did not play in any bowl game, the second consecutive bowl-less postseason after three consecutive Sugar Bowl appearances.

"I was back home in Dallas for the holidays," Sooners guard J.D. Roberts said. "Texas was playing Tennessee in the Cotton Bowl, and I wanted to go to the game in the worst way. Texas was staying at the Melrose Hotel, so I went down there and ran into one of their coaches and asked him for a pass.

"He said, 'Come sit on our bench.'

"So I did. I was a Sooner who actually sat on Texas's bench during that Cotton Bowl. And they kicked Tennessee's butt all day long."

They Call It "The Streak"

As in 47 games.

Baseball has Joe DiMaggio's 56-game hitting streak. The NBA has the Boston Celtics' eight-season championship streak. College basketball has John Wooden's UCLA dynasty.

But the most renowned streak in college football belongs to Bud Wilkinson's Sooners.

From October 3, 1953 (a 7–7 tie at Pittsburgh), through November 16, 1957, the Sooners never lost or tied, compiling a winning streak that likely never will be broken in major-college football.

The week before the tie with Pitt, the Sooners lost 28–21 to Notre Dame in the '53 season opener.

"We had lost quite a few people from the 1952 team and had only seven or eight seniors," guard Roberts said. "It was primarily sophomores. They had Johnny Lattner, who was one heck of a football player. Lattner went on to win the Heisman Trophy, and rightfully so. He deserved it.

"We had a chance to tie at the end of the game, and had a receiver wide open, but ended up losing."

Following the tie, the streak started with a 19–14 win over Texas in Dallas, a game that evened the Sooners' record at 1–1–1.

Nobody had an inkling what was ahead of Oklahoma over the next four-plus seasons.

As the streak mounted, here are some interesting facts: Texas, Kansas, Colorado, Kansas State, Missouri, and Iowa State each accounted for five of Oklahoma's wins, or 30 total, while Oklahoma State and Nebraska were beaten four times each, which accounts for eight more.

The Buffaloes came the closest to ending the streak, losing by only seven points in 1953 and '54, by eight in '56, and by one in '57.

Remarkably, the Sooners recorded 23 shutouts during the streak. That's right—23!

"We never knew how many games it would reach at the time," All-American lineman Bill Krisher said. "We just went out and took care of our business and never thought about losing. We were beating our opponents so much that I really feel some of the toughest football we played was in our scrimmages.

"Teams got so frustrated that they couldn't beat us, they resorted to anything. Iowa State was biting and kicking us under the pile, and I remember asking the referee, 'Can't you call these penalties?'

"He said, 'Bill, if I start calling these penalties, we'll be here all night.'"

On October 27, 1956, the Sooners' streak reached 35 games with a 40–0 walloping of Notre Dame in South Bend.

"They had Paul Hornung," Krisher recalled. "Well, Jerry Tubbs—we called him 'Tubby'—went in there and hit Hornung. In all my years of football, even in the pros, I have never seen a harder hit. You could have heard that hit two blocks from Notre Dame Stadium. I would really like to see that one on film."

Throughout the streak, Wilkinson had warned his players not to get too full of themselves.

"One of these days you will face defeat," he said. "You don't know when it will happen, but it *will* happen."

Apparently, Bud wasn't talking to Jimmy Harris, Jay O'Neal, Jerry Tubbs, or the class that played in 1954, '55, or '56. (In fact, Tubbs' high school team never lost a game, either.) O'Neal goes one better—he never played on a losing team in junior high, high school, or college, essentially nine seasons of football with a big, fat zero in the loss column.

"Can you imagine that?" said Jerry Thompson, a lineman from 1957 to 1959. "Never knowing what losing feels like?"

As Wilkinson had warned, the '57 Sooners did learn.

On November 16, Notre Dame brought a 4–2 team to Norman and entered the game as an 18-point underdog. The Irish had been 2–8 the season earlier, including that pasting delivered by the Sooners in South Bend.

So, obviously, many of OU's players may not have taken Notre Dame too seriously. The streak was now just three games shy of 50. That week, *Sports Illustrated* featured the Sooners on the cover with the title, "The Team That Can't Be Beaten."

"I don't think it ever entered anybody's mind that we would get beat," center Bob Harrison said. "It was like being on a fast train. You just hopped on it and enjoyed the ride."

At the same time, the Sooners could tell that opponents were giving that extra effort as the streak mounted, wanting to be known as the team that stopped the insanity.

"Anytime you are the best, everybody wants to beat you that much more," Krisher said. "And Notre Dame surely did, since we had beaten them so badly the year before."

The Irish surely were motivated, while the Sooners likely were complacent and overconfident.

At halftime, the score was 0–0.

"I couldn't believe we couldn't score on them," Harrison said. "We couldn't make anything."

As the fourth quarter wore on, fans at Memorial Stadium were in disbelief the game was tied but figured the Sooners would somehow figure out a way to win. After all, they always had.

But when Notre Dame halfback Dick Lynch cut around the right end after taking a pitch and scampered untouched into the end zone with 3:50 left in the game, full panic suddenly set in.

"On Notre Dame's touchdown, I hit the quarterback as he let the ball go," Krisher said.

"When they scored that touchdown on the sweep, I was in the middle and I knew if somebody turned him inside, I could have gotten him," Harrison said.

But no defender maintained an outside lane, and Lynch reached the end zone standing up.

The Sooners did threaten, but a series of incompletions killed their hopes of extending the streak, with their first scoreless effort in 12 years and first loss in four years.

"We didn't have any offense that day and ran out of time," Harrison added. "My old roommate, David Baker, had a friend who had put all of those old game films on tape, and he gave me some of them. I looked at the tape recently and still can't imagine why we couldn't beat Notre Dame."

The day the streak ended signaled a period of mourning in the state of Oklahoma. It was shocking, surreal, and unbelievable to many. As Krisher dressed and exited the locker room after the game, he recalls seeing fans still sitting in their seats, stunned by the loss.

"We didn't leave the field right away because we were so stunned, and our fans stayed, too," Thompson recalled. "It was very traumatic for all of us."

As a side note, Arkansas had played SMU in the Cotton Bowl that day at the same time. As the Razorbacks' charter flight was heading back to Fayetteville, a Hogs linebacker by the name of Barry Switzer was reading the *Sports Illustrated* article about the "unbeatable" Sooners.

"As I was in the middle of the article, the pilot came over the audio system and said, 'I have a college football score that may interest you: Notre Dame 7, Oklahoma 0.

"And that started the *Sports Illustrated* jinx. It was the greatest streak in college football history."

(Actually, the *SI* jinx may have started two years earlier when Olympic skier Jill Kinmont was featured on the cover. By the time the magazine hit the newsstands, she was paralyzed in a nasty spill.)

Had Notre Dame not ended it, the streak surely would have surpassed 50 since the Sooners easily disposed of Nebraska, Oklahoma State, and then Duke in the Orange Bowl to finish the '57 season with a 10–1 record, but the national title went to Woody Hayes's Ohio State team.

What many people forget as time passes is that the Sooners had a 31-game winning streak from 1948 to 1950. Over the years, it became simply a forgotten, second-fiddle string of wins to the famed streak of 47.

"That's right—Oklahoma did have a string of 31 wins before that," Tommy McDonald said. "That just goes to show you that Wilkinson was such an outstanding judge of talent. It really points to what a marvelous coach he was. What other coach has ever had a winning streak of 31 games and then a 47-game winning streak? It really shows that this guy had a magic wand."

"Which One Is the Legend?"

This funny story comes from Byron Searcy, a lineman from 1955 to 1957.

"It occurred on the practice field and involved a walk-on freshman from California," he said. "I believe his name was Lindsey, who was a hard worker but had poor vision. During the first week of practice, he was told to go to Coach Wilkinson's group session to assist the varsity backs with a drill. He was eager to respond, but he seemed confused, so he asked one of the assistant coaches, 'Which one is Coach Wilkinson?'

"That was good for a great many laughs throughout the year, and at the end of the season, Lindsey received an autographed copy of a Coach Wilkinson photograph from the team."

Krisher the Hitting Machine

Guard Bill Krisher (1955–1957) may have been one of the most underrated linemen in college football history. He was named All-American during his senior season and finished as the runner-up to Iowa's Alex Karras for the Outland Trophy.

And he was OU's fiercest hitter.

"I liked to hit people," he said. "That was the fun part of the game. A distinction I had at OU was that my shoulder pads kept breaking. I would always break my pads, and they had to ship new ones in for me quite a bit. Then they developed a lever-pad that wouldn't break."

The One and Only Tommy McDonald

Given the fact that he played most of his NFL career for the Philadelphia Eagles, it's probably safe to say that Tommy McDonald is "an odd bird."

McDonald, a halfback, was a key player during the 47-game winning streak for Bud Wilkinson's teams. He won the Maxwell Award in '56 and was a two-time All-American. During the '55 season, he became the first Sooner to score a touchdown in every game of the season, while his 20.2-yard average on punt returns remains second-best in school history.

He finished his career with 1,696 yards rushing, 3,108 all-purpose yards, and 36 touchdowns.

"Everybody always told me I was too little to play football (I weighed about 146 pounds at Oklahoma)," he said. "But Bud knew I could catch real well and I was fast, so he devised plays to get me the ball."

McDonald was a great football player, but the truth be known, he was not the most popular Sooner among his teammates.

"He had a bit of an ego," Krisher admitted. "He was always telling everyone how great he was. Some of us linemen got together and told him, 'We don't want to hear you telling us how great your are, so we may open the gates on you.' That meant we wouldn't block anybody for him. We did that about four times in practice one day and he said, 'Okay, okay. I got the message.'"

McDonald was inducted into the College Football Hall of Fame in 1985 and is one of only two Sooners (Lee Roy Selmon is the other) to be inducted in the College Hall and the Pro Football Hall of Fame.

During his 12-year NFL career as a wide receiver, he helped lead the Eagles to a 1960 NFL Championship and was selected to six Pro Bowls. He also led the league in touchdown receptions

Halfback Tommy McDonald was a key player during the 47-game winning streak for Bud Wilkinson's teams. He finished his stellar career with 1,696 yards rushing, 3,108 all-purpose yards, and 36 touchdowns.

twice (1958 and '61), and led the NFL in receiving yards once (1961).

By the way, as a good trivia question, McDonald was the last non-kicker to play in the NFL without a face mask.

McDonald retired after the 1968 season with 495 receptions for 8,410 yards and 84 touchdowns, the second-highest total of touchdown receptions in NFL history at the time.

Here's an interesting coincidence following his career. He operated Tommy McDonald Enterprises, a company that produced the official Heisman Trophy portraits of the award's winners.

"I don't paint them myself," McDonald said. "I have two artists who work for me, and they do all the painting. We've done portraits for schools that include Oklahoma, Nebraska, and Maryland. We also used to do it for the baseball All-Star Game. It was a fantastic business.

"By chance, I lucked into it. A guy did a portrait of me. In the old days, the club would furnish you with pictures so you could send it out to fans. So I sent a picture out to this guy. After one of my games, I came out of the dressing room, and this guy was standing out there with a box and he pulls a painting. He tells me that he wants me to have it because he's a big fan of mine and he appreciated me sending him out an autographed picture. I wanted to pay him for it, but he wouldn't let me. I pulled out a picture of my wife from my wallet and asked him if he could do a portrait of her because her birthday was coming up in a couple of months. I said he had to let me pay him, and he said he would.

"The portrait was magnificent. Then I thought about it and of all the rings, watches, trophies, and silver trays, but nobody gives something like these. Then it just became a great business for me."

Ironically, McDonald finished third in the 1956 Heisman balloting—the year Notre Dame's Paul Hornung won the award in spite of the Fighting Irish's 2–8 record.

These days, you can catch McDonald on ESPN's annual college football award show on the Thursday following each regular season as he presents the Maxwell Award. Before he presents the award, he gives the winner a ceremonial chest bump.

"I am still a Sooner through and through," McDonald said recently. "I still take my phone off of the hook when they lose."

Ol' "Ski-Jump Nose"

Thompson had a way of sticking his nose into matters on his way to becoming an All-American and one of OU's finest-ever two-way players.

During his first game in an OU uniform, in 1957, he broke his nose against Pittsburgh.

"I'll never forget the first guy I lined up against in a game—his name was Jim McCusker," he recalled. "Those big ol' coal miners were a lot larger than us country boys from Oklahoma. One time I fired off the line of scrimmage—and remember that we did not have face masks back then—and McCusker hit me in the face so hard that my nose was sticking out the other side of my face.

"The next play, I thought I would get even with him. So I fired out and he hit me again and straightened it back up. He knocked me out cold. The next thing I remember was waking up on the airplane and Bud was sitting next to me."

"How do you feel?" the coach asked. "Don't worry, it only hurts when you laugh."

Thompson recalled, "I must have looked awful, but I broke my nose a few more times after that. They used to call me 'ski-jump nose,' and it remains pretty flat against my face like a boxer's nose. Anyway, that was my introduction to college football!"

Bud: Why Did I Vote for That Rule?

The NCAA, as it frequently has done as the game of football has developed over the years, has tweaked the rules here and there. One of the most significant rule changes came in 1958, when coaches voted to allow two-point-conversion attempts following touchdowns.

It may have cost the Sooners the '58 national championship, which would have been Wilkinson's fourth.

Former OU star and Wilkinson protégé Darrell Royal, in just his second season as head coach at Texas, called for a two-point conversion, and his Longhorns converted it to beat the Sooners 15–14 in the third game of the season.

It was Oklahoma's only loss of the season.

"I was on the rules committee, and when the suggestion came up, I felt like it was something that would make the game more interesting, and it would make it easier to come from behind," Wilkinson said later. "I obviously wasn't very satisfied with my vote."

The loss dropped OU from No. 2 in the nation to No. 11, the first time the Sooners had not been ranked in the top 10 since 1953.

It also marked Royal's first win against his mentor, and he said it made him sick to his stomach—literally. It was reported that he threw up before meeting reporters following the game.

"I still don't like it," he said, referring to the new rule, "even though it enabled us to win today. It makes it unfair on the coaches."

The Food-Poisoning Incident

The Sooners entered the 1959 season firmly entrenched as a dynasty, having won 60 of their past 62 games, and were ranked as the nation's No. 1 team but faced a difficult opening game at Northwestern.

"Coach Wilkinson always liked to take us to nice places on the road, so we went to Chicago on that Thursday and ate at The Chez Paris," Thompson recalled. "When we started eating the fruit salad, almost three quarters of the team got sick instantly. They were throwing up and laying all over the parking lot that night, but I never got sick for some reason. I was eating everyone else's fruit salad and their steaks, too. I always told everyone that they just poisoned the good players.

"As we later found out, it was related to the bookies and gambling. Somebody wanted to make sure that Oklahoma didn't play very well in that game. We had several guys in the hospital the night before the game."

Sure enough, Ara Parseghian's Northwestern team demolished the Sooners 45–13 on a rainy, messy day in which the Sooners lost five fumbles.

"To this day, I don't know what that drug was, but it worked," Thompson said. "When we got back home, Bud downplayed the whole thing. He told us they had put a drug in our food, but that was all that was said about that. He didn't want to make too much stink about it."

One report stated that the Sooners went from being a six-point favorite to a three-point favorite two days prior to the game.

In the end, there was no definitive cause or origin, and the Chicago police never issued a report.

Say "Hey" to Gomer

Gomer Jones was Wilkinson's most trusted and loyal assistant, working with him for more than 25 years (1947–1963). He later became head coach in the 1964 and 1965 seasons, as OU stumbled to a 9–11–1 record, before serving as athletics director.

As an assistant to Bud, he served as the defensive coordinator and line coach.

"We always had a great defense," Thompson said. "And I always believed the one man who never received enough credit was Gomer Jones. Gomer ran the defense, while Coach Wilkinson ran the offense. It was as if they were partners.

"Gomer also was my mentor because he was the line coach. He was so far ahead of other line coaches in the game of football at that time. He taught footwork and used boards to teach you your steps, and we had sled drills—things that no other coaches were doing at that time."

chapter 6

Prentice Gautt:
OU's Jackie Robinson

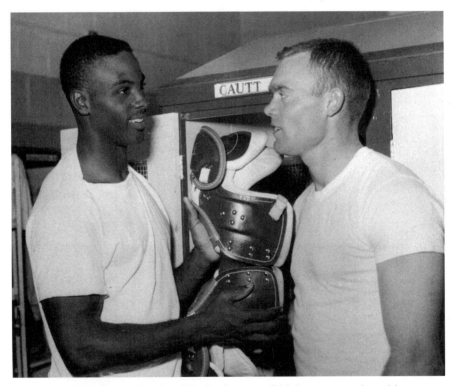

Prentice Gautt, the first black player at Oklahoma, speaks with teammate Brewster Hobby in September 1957. In 1956 Gautt became the first black football player at Oklahoma and went on to play in the NFL.

Prentice Gautt was a true All-American in every category: as a running back, as a teammate, as a student, and later as a graduate student, as a Ph.D. candidate, as an administrator, and as a family man. Perhaps no Sooner was as respected as Gautt.

What he didn't want to be known for was as his role as the Sooners' first African American football player. In other words, he probably wouldn't care much for the title of this chapter, but there is no denying his crucial part in Oklahoma's history.

"The only thing that I knew was that I wanted to play football for Oklahoma and for Bud Wilkinson," he once said of his teen-aged days. "I didn't think of it as being a pioneering kind of thing. I didn't go to Oklahoma for that reason."

Gautt, an all-state running back at Oklahoma City's Douglass High, truly was a pioneer, however, breaking the color barrier when he enrolled as a Sooner football player in 1956.

OU's student body had not been integrated until 1950, and Bud Wilkinson knew it was time for progress on his football team some six years later. After researching Gautt's character and temperament, he calculated that he had what it would take—and that he could handle all the scorn that would come his way during the process.

Of all the major decisions he had to make from 1947 to 1963, none turned out to be more correct or more important.

"Everybody knows that Coach Wilkinson hand-picked him to become the first black player at Oklahoma," teammate Leon Cross said. "I once told Jay Wilkinson, who was writing his father's biography, that either Coach Wilkinson was a genius in picking Prentice or he was very lucky.

"Prentice, who had the same major as me, zoology/biological sciences, was very helpful to me as a freshman, and I will never forget him for that."

Wilkinson had been pressured not to offer an athletic scholarship to Gautt, but made arrangements so a group of doctors and pharmacists paid his way into OU. Within a year, he had a full scholarship, so the donated money then went to another black student. He went on to become a two-time All–Big 8 player and an academic All-American.

"It seems to me that doors opened for me without my thinking about it," he said a few years ago. "Bud Wilkinson was a blessing to me. Without him, things would have been a lot different. His philosophies and his values rubbed off on me. He treated all of his players the same way—with dignity."

Gautt said that during the spring of his freshman year, Wilkinson gave him a thorough lecture that changed his approach. He did it as only Bud Wilkinson could do it—honest, straightforward, to the point, without ever raising his voice. To that point, Gautt later admitted he was not giving 100 percent on the practice field.

"It was like he wanted me to do well," Gautt said. "He wanted me to improve. I would spend Wednesdays talking to him as if it were my time on the couch. Bud was so supportive of me. He didn't let me sink. He was constantly telling me, 'You've got to be smart, you've got to work hard, you've got to be tough, and you've got to be powerful.'

"In many ways, I saw myself as just another football player trying to make it at a great program. It was never about setting a trend or writing history. It was about football and school and teammates."

While he would succeed wildly in the first two categories, the third grew to love him like a brother.

"I'll always remember that incident when our freshman team returned from that game at Tulsa," lineman Jerry Thompson recalled. "We stopped by a restaurant to eat, and they had a nice dinner set up for all the players, but they wouldn't let Prentice eat in the restaurant with us.

"[Freshman coach] Port Robertson stood up and told all of us, 'Boys, we're leaving.'

"We all marched out of there in unison. I think we ended up eating hamburgers on the way back to Norman."

It was an easy decision for the Sooners, no matter how much their stomachs growled at the time. Once they got to know him, they would do anything for Prentice.

"Prentice was a great human being," Thompson said. "He was a good student, very humble and very easygoing. I don't know anybody who didn't like Prentice Gautt."

Gautt once reflected on the trip to Dallas to play Texas in 1957. The team walked into the President's Hotel in Forth Worth, while he was ushered to a cab to be taken to a nearby house owned by a black family to stay the night.

"Going through those things was a knock at one's self-concept," he once recalled. "It was difficult at that age to just say, 'That's their problem, not yours.' It was difficult, but I had supporters encouraging me, telling me, 'Hey, you're bigger than that.'

"At the time, I didn't see myself as a pioneer because I was too caught up in the excitement and mystique of playing Texas. Now that I look back on it, I am pretty proud that I was the first. I am glad I went through the things I did when I was younger, because they made me a better person. I had maybe five or six negative things happen to me, but I was at Oklahoma for four years. Just look at all the positive things that happened to me. That is what I always tried to do."

Gautt took that positive approach to the playing field, where he became one of OU's best players in the late 1950s. He rushed for 94 yards on only six carries, including a 42-yard touchdown on the second play of the game, to be named MVP of the 1959 Orange Bowl—a 21–6 win over Syracuse.

After playing eight seasons in the NFL, he became an assistant coach at Missouri and earned his doctorate degree. He later joined the Big 8 Conference as an assistant commissioner in 1979. Seventeen years later, he was named senior associate commissioner of the Big 12.

When he was informed in 1999 that OU would name its athletic academic center "The Prentice Gautt Academic Center," he shed tears of joy.

"I was overwhelmed!" he said.

On the day that OU honored Gautt, he stood on the 50-yard line of Memorial Stadium "and received the longest ovation I have ever witnessed in the stadium," athletics director Joe Castiglione said. "And it went on and on. All of us were standing there, and the tears were running down our cheeks. I get kind of choked up thinking about it."

Nobody at Oklahoma knew Gautt better than Jakie Sandefer, who became his roommate on the team's road trips. It was the beginning of a lifelong friendship.

"Prentice asked me to introduce him into the Oklahoma Sports Hall of Fame, and I was very honored that he asked me," Sandefer said. "My statement there was, 'Was Prentice different? Yeah, Prentice was different. He had more class than the rest of us, and he was a better student!'"

Before he died, Wilkinson once stated that his biggest accomplishment wasn't coaching the 47-game winning streak or orchestrating all those national championship teams and building the Oklahoma dynasty. It was having Gautt become a Sooner when he did.

"It was the most significant thing I did when I was coaching; there's no question in my mind," he is quoted in his biography, *Bud Wilkinson, An Intimate Portrait of an American Legend*. "But all the credit belongs to Prentice, believe me. It was so damn tough for him that anything I could do was after the fact. The rapid change in the segregation situation is one of the marvelous things that has happened in America in my lifetime."

Gautt died unexpectedly March 17, 2005, at the age of 67 from flu-like symptoms. He was posthumously given the 2005 Outstanding Contribution to Amateur Football Award by The National Football Foundation & College Hall of Fame (NFF) two months later.

"I saw him three months before he passed away, and I was very, very saddened by his death," Thompson said. "He was a great Sooner."

chapter 7
The 1960s: Losing, Transition, and Heartbreak

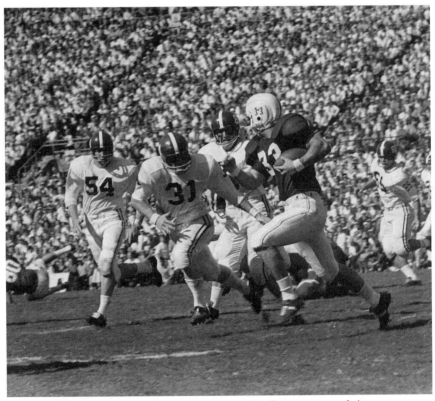

Joe Don Looney gains two yards in the first quarter of the Orange Bowl against Alabama on January 1, 1963. Oklahoma lost 17–0.

As the decade of the 1960s began, the Sooners had to put to rest the most successful decade in college football history.

Not living off of the laurels of 10 consecutive conference championships (eight Big 8 titles from 1950 to 1957 and two Big 8 titles in 1958 and 1959 once Oklahoma State joined the conference) and three national champions is a difficult thing to do.

The football program suddenly was surrounded by controversy, having been placed on NCAA probation over an assistant coach's recruitment of a lineman from Nebraska some two years earlier. The details are varied depending on which report you read, but none implicated any wrongdoing by Bud Wilkinson, who had encouraged the recruit to attend his home-state Nebraska.

The recruit, Monte Kiffin, did just that, becoming one of the Cornhuskers' better players. Kiffin later had a successful career as an assistant coach, and as of the 2007 season, was the defensive coordinator of the Tampa Bay Buccaneers.

The imposed infractions for OU: no bowl games and no games on television.

The probation didn't help recruiting much, either.

Coincidentally or not, the Sooners stumbled to a 3–6–1 record in 1960, by far the worst season in Wilkinson's 17 seasons as OU's head coach.

"None of us ever thought about having a season like that when we arrived at Oklahoma," center/linebacker Wayne Lee said.

"We probably didn't have the talent in 1960 that we had in the past," lineman Leon Cross admitted. "The leadership wasn't there. I know Bud was very frustrated with that team. He tried several different things to motivate that team, but not much worked.

"We had a lot of bad luck that season. I think we lost seven starters to injury, and Bud was always searching for a quarterback."

Another factor could have been Wilkinson's schedule, which was taxed to the limit given that he was now President Kennedy's executive director of the Youth Fitness Council.

From 0–5 to 5–5

The 1961 season was a tale of two seasons.

The first was a shocking 0–5 start, which meant the Sooners had lost nine of their last 10 and had a 3–11–1 record over the past season and a half.

"There were two reasons for [the poor start]," Lee explained. "I think Bud was getting a little tired of coaching. Second, I think OU had gotten a little casual in recruiting. There just wasn't the talent on campus there had been in the '50s. The newspapers, the alumni, and the players were in shock after that 0–5 start. We were losing sleep and losing weight because we were frustrated."

After a 22–14 loss to Colorado dropped OU to an unprecedented 0–5, Wilkinson publicly predicted his team would not lose again that season.

Amazingly, he was right.

"Having an 0–5 record in Norman, you can imagine what it was like," Cross said. "Most people said that 'Bud Wilkinson has seen his day.' However, he never lost confidence in us. He told us in a meeting that we would win our next five games, and we did."

The Sooners ripped off wins over Kansas State, Missouri, Army, Nebraska, and Oklahoma State to finish at .500.

Wilkinson was ecstatic, as his team had made a complete turnaround from the doldrums of losing.

"From the standpoint of effort and courage, this team is as good as any I have ever had at Oklahoma," he told the press. "This team has just refused to quit at any time, and there have been plenty of times it could have."

Many observers of OU football firmly believed it was Wilkinson's finest coaching job, even better than all of his undefeated seasons and national championship editions. He took a downtrodden team, defeated mentally and physically, and turned it into an undefeated team.

It also gave Oklahoma hope that a return to glory lay ahead in 1962.

The Ol' Rugged Cross

It seemed as if Leon Cross spent a lifetime at the University of Oklahoma.

The New Mexico resident followed the Sooners in the 1950s because New Mexico native Tommy McDonald was a big star. Cross arrived in Norman in 1957 as a freshman guard/linebacker, watching Notre Dame end the famed 47-game winning streak from the stands of Memorial Stadium. Then he broke his foot working his summer job, requiring surgery and a year of recovery. Once he was healthy, he blew out a knee during a spring scrimmage. Another surgery. Another year.

"Here I was, a junior in college, and I had never played a down," Cross recalled.

One day, he was limping out of the dorm following surgery, and teammate Joe Rector said, "There's the 'Old Rugged Cross.'"

"Then they started calling me 'Rugged' for short, and it stuck," he said. "They still call me that around Norman."

Cross became a starting guard in 1960 and later won an extra season of eligibility because of his injuries.

"By the 1962 season, it began to feel like I had been there forever," he recalled. "I was 23 and the oldest guy on the team."

Cross was named a cocaptain and All-American that season. He later became an assistant coach for Wilkinson and an OU assistant athletics director from 1973 to 1993.

There Will Never Be Another Joe Don Looney

Joe Don Looney had the type of rare talent about which they write books and make movies.

A native Texan, Looney was a superb athlete who had failed to stick first with the Texas Longhorns before he attended Cameron Junior College simply because of his off-field behavior.

To be precise, he was rebellious, a certified smart aleck and an All-American hell-raiser. His is one of the greatest names in sports history—and he was one of the most-talented players ever to wear a Sooners uniform—but there never has been a surname which fit an individual so perfectly.

Somehow, he wound up in Norman before the 1962 season.

"We had rebounded from 3–6–1 to 5–5, and now it was time to take the next step," center/linebacker Wayne Lee said. "Coach Wilkinson came to us before the season and told us about a player who had superior talent, but had been problematic in other areas. He had a meeting with Leon Cross and me, the cocaptains, and told us, 'Listen, this player wants to play for us, but he can be a problem. Do you want him or do you want to stiff-arm him?'"

"We made a special effort to make Joe feel welcome," Cross explained. "We all new what a great talent he was and knew he could help us win the Big 8 championship."

Lee added, "We talked and decided we had the leadership to deal with a problem like this. We could handle Joe Don Looney. That season, Joe Don made some phenomenal plays and led the nation in punting, too."

His legend in Norman began during the season opener in '62 against Syracuse. The Sooners trailed 3–0 late in the game and had just stopped the Orangemen at their own 40-yard line.

Bold and cocky, Looney told Wilkinson, "Just put me in the game, and I will win it for you."

Wilkinson, desperate because the offense was going nowhere fast, did just that. On his first career carry, Looney appeared stopped near the line of scrimmage, but busted free and ran 60 yards for a touchdown that, true to his word, won the game for the Sooners.

"In our season opener," Jim Grisham recalled, "we beat Syracuse 7–3 on a 60-yard run by Joe Don Looney on his first career carry for Oklahoma."

Looney truly had the strength of most linemen and better speed than most running backs and receivers in college football. Many who saw him run said he reminded them of the great Jim Brown, a football and lacrosse star at Syracuse who later became an NFL legend.

Looney rushed for 856 yards and scored 10 touchdowns that season. He also averaged 42.4 yards per punt.

"He had just amazing strength and speed," Lee added.

But Wilkinson and his team leaders could take only so much of Looney once the 1963 season started.

"Yes, the '63 season was a different story," Cross recalled. "Coach Wilkinson hired me as one of his assistants and recruiting coordinator. We started the year with a 31–14 win over Clemson followed by a 17–12 upset of the then No. 1–ranked USC Trojans. Suddenly, we were the new No. 1.

"Joe had good success in those first two games but had become a problem to the coaches with lack of effort in practice and his bad behavior off the field. He had a run-in with some high school kids at a local drive-in food hangout."

Many media accounts simply said that Looney "beat up" an assistant coach. It really wasn't exactly correct, since graduate assistant John Tatum, who also had been a member of the '62 team, held his own.

"The story has been greatly exaggerated over the years," Cross recalled, "but here's what happened:

"John was holding a dummy during a blocking drill for the backs. Joe apparently didn't like the way Tatum was holding the dummy and the force that he used while thrusting it during the drill, so he grabbed Tatum's T-shirt and ripped it off. Tatum threw him to the ground, pulled off his helmet, and was about to sock it to him when the coaches stopped the action."

But Wilkinson did not dismiss Looney then. It took another week and another incident.

"He was kicked off the team the week after the Texas game because of his disruptive behavior before and after the game," Cross explained. "Coach Wilkinson went the last mile with Joe, even trying to get Joe to go to a psychologist for help. Joe refused every effort that Coach Wilkinson made to help him. That resulted in his dismissal from the team. And I believe that Joe was the only player that Coach Wilkinson ever dismissed from any of his teams."

However, that didn't stop the New York Giants from wasting their first pick of the '64 draft on him.

Once he got to the NFL, Looney continued to be loony.

On his first night with the Giants during summer camp of his rookie season, he missed bed-check. Coach Allie Sherman left a note under Joe Don's door that read, "When you get in, please come see me."

Looney took the note and wrote on it, "Coach, I'll see you in the morning. I'm tired," and slipped it under Sherman's door.

Sam Huff, the Hall of Fame linebacker, said, "Joe Don never had both shoes tied. His whole life made no sense. He always had a smart answer for you, and he was very clever."

The Giants actually paid Huff extra to room with Looney, with strict orders to keep him out of trouble. Huff tells countless stories in which dozens of women showed up at their door at all hours of the night, trying to see the rookie.

"Just give me five minutes," Looney would beg his roommate.

Once, Sherman saw Looney didn't have his ankles taped and he ordered it done. Looney refused, telling him, "I know more about my ankles than you do."

After an argument, Looney gave in and taped his ankles over his socks. He was traded to Baltimore after only 28 days as a Giant.

"I wanted him," then-Colts coach Don Shula said. "He had all this fantastic natural ability."

But when he was 15 minutes late to a meeting, Shula fined him $100.

As always, Joe Don had the last word—and it was a good one: "Okay, but how come you didn't give me $100 for being 15 minutes *early* last night?"

While playing for Detroit in 1966, coach Harry Gilmer turned to Joe Don, gave him the next play, and told him to go to the huddle. Looney refused, telling the coach, "If you want a messenger, call Western Union."

For that, he was suspended.

Dan Devine, the former Notre Dame coach who was head coach of the Green Bay Packers, once said, "Joe Don Looney may have been to football what Mickey Mantle was to baseball," meaning he had that much talent.

Following one year serving in Vietnam and one year on a failed comeback with the New Orleans Saints, Looney traveled Europe a bit before settling in tiny Alpine, Texas, about 80 miles north of the Mexican border. He lived there just as strangely as he had acted: in a solar-powered house with no electricity. He experimented with religions, drugs, and different philosophies. To call him eccentric would be to give him the benefit of the doubt.

By the 1980s, by most accounts, it seemed that Joe Don had gotten his act together somewhat. He even once told the *Dallas Times-Herald*, "It's funny. When I played football, I couldn't play life. And now that I can play life, I can't play football."

It remains one of the greatest quotes in sports history. It would serve as a great lesson for many of today's professional athletes.

Looney died September 24, 1988, eight miles north of Study Butte, Texas, when his motorcycle missed a curve on State Highway 118. He was discovered face-up under a mesquite bush, wearing a helmet. The highway patrolman's report says Looney never hit his brakes.

He was 45 years old.

In the end, someone, J. Brent Clark, did write a book about Looney's life, titled *3rd Down and Forever: Joe Don Looney and the Rise and Fall of an American Hero*. There was even talk that a Hollywood producer wanted to make a movie about him.

The book and the would-be script, however, justifiably didn't include much about Looney's exploits on the field, and that was the saddest ending to his legacy.

Bud's Final Farewell

Nineteen sixty-three had to be one of the most difficult years in Wilkinson's life.

To know Bud Wilkinson was to know that he was much more than a football coach. He knew politics and he knew politicians.

He knew President John F. Kennedy very well, having been named by JFK as the head of the Youth Council on Physical Fitness in 1961.

After dealing with the Looney distraction, the Sooners regrouped and won their next five games heading into a show-down with Nebraska on November 23 in Lincoln.

At about the time the Sooners were having a light practice at Nebraska's Memorial Stadium on Friday, Wilkinson was given the news that his good friend had just been assassinated in Dallas. Most all of the scheduled games for that Saturday were cancelled, but after speaking with members of the Kennedy family, Wilkinson was told to go ahead and play the OU-Nebraska game. JFK would have wanted it that way, he was told.

Played on a day of mourning in which the crowd cheered rarely, and the players appeared listless, the Cornhuskers won 29–20.

The next week, OU rebounded to beat Oklahoma State 34–10 to finish the season with an 8–2 record. It would be Wilkinson's final game as the Sooners' head coach.

"I knew he loved politics and he had been good friends with JFK, but I was surprised at our staff meeting one day when he said he was retiring to pursue something else," said Cross, then on OU's staff.

"Then I was surprised after he had announced he was running for the Senate and that he was running as a Republican. Oklahoma was a Democratic state."

Awful Season, But Help Is on the Way

Nineteen sixty-five was perhaps one of the most miserable seasons in Oklahoma football history.

Bud Wilkinson had retired two years earlier, and following a 6–4–1 season in Gomer Jones's first season in 1964, the Sooners fell to 3–7.

They lost their first three games and last three games of the season and were shut out a remarkable four times. They beat only lowly Big 8 teams Kansas, Kansas State, and Iowa State, and averaged only 10.6 points per game. Jones resigned.

"The Sooners team of 1965 was best noted, I think, for being the catalyst that brought so many great coaches to Norman in the following spring of '66," said Bob Flanagan, a defensive end on that team. "We needed a change."

Jim Mackenzie was then hired from Arkansas, bringing assistants named Barry Switzer (offensive line), Chuck Fairbanks (defensive backs), and Galen Hall (receivers) with him.

"On January 3, 1966, I flew on a DC-3 to Oklahoma City, and Jim met me at the old Will Rogers Airport," Switzer recalled. "I became a Sooner for the next 23 years."

The Chief's Practical Joke

However, Flanagan noted, the '65 team did "have some great athletes: Carl McAdams, Ben Hart, Mike Ringer, Larry Brown, Jim Riley, Carl Schreiner, Gordon Brown, Granville Liggins, Bob Kalsu, and many others who would play two years later in the Orange Bowl."

Another was an undersized linebacker/safety named Thurman Pitchlynn.

"Pitchlynn was a senior during my sophomore year, and a really good athlete," Flanagan recalled. "He 'lockered' next to me that year, so we saw a lot of each other during those months…and laughed, cried, and cussed a lot, too! Now, Thurman was known as 'Chief'…a nickname for his heritage and his wildness."

As the story goes, he was the great grandson of Peter Pitchlynn, the great chief of the Choctaw Nation. Flanagan will tell the rest of the story:

> I was also a bit nervous around "Chief," just because he was
> a *real* Indian. Until I got to OU, I was never around any real
> Indians much, so around him I was always on edge. I guess
> I was ready for him to scream, pull out a hatchet, and scalp

me. It never happened, of course, but being a sophomore, and not knowing any better, I was always on the alert.

Getting ready for practice one afternoon, Chief comes into the locker room, sits down on the bench next to me, with this huge grin and a gleam in his eye, and asks, "Wanna see something special?"

Being curious of course, I said, "Sure, what is it?"

He reaches into his shirt pocket slowly, pauses a few seconds for drama's sake, and pulls out a paper towel. Holding it in the palm of one hand, he slowly begins to unwrap it. He's not showing this to anybody else, just me. So now I'm really interested, as you can imagine. I can see hidden down in his palm, on top of the white tissue, something that was light-gray colored.

Chief puts it up close to my face and I smell some kind of chemical stink...and then it hits me what this thing is. An ear! A human ear!

I had a quick thought that Chief has gone wild, somewhere, and cut an ear off somebody. Maybe he scalped them or even worse.

"Where in the hell did you get that thing?" I asked, lurching back away from his outstretched hand.

"I cut it off a body in my biology class," he answered.

Later I found out it was "taken" from a cadaver the class was dissecting, although I don't think you were allowed to take any of the body parts home with you. Well, I thought it was weird, so I asked him, "Why?"

"I'm going to put it in Carlyle's locker for him," he told me.

Bill Carlyle had gotten into a scrape the previous summer with another player while working at Lake Tahoe. This other guy chomped down on Bill's ear during the fight and removed a perfectly curved-out section of the top of Bill's ear. (Bill became kind of a Beatle-looking dude after that.)

Anyway, we all got a great laugh when Carlyle opened the tissue-wrapped present in his locker that afternoon. And we all needed a laugh every once in a while that year. I mean, winning three games and losing seven was no fun.

By the way, during the following spring, Pitchlynn was named the MVP of the Alumni Game.

Jim Mackenzie: Gone Too Soon

Given time, Jim Mackenzie may have become a Sooners coaching legend, almost everyone who knew him agrees. But what Mackenzie didn't receive was enough time.

He was a former player for Paul "Bear" Bryant at Kentucky in the 1950s and tough as nails, yet he knew how to relate to his players. He could recruit, he could coach with the best of them, and he was progressive in his approach.

So on the surface, when Oklahoma chose him as its new coach, hiring him off of Frank Broyles's staff at Arkansas, it appeared to be the right move.

And nothing that Mackenzie did in 1966 would betray that opinion. He laid a solid foundation during a 6–4 season, bringing in young, bright assistants as the Sooners revamped their program.

They even had a new look, replacing their white helmets with the crimson helmets adorned with the interlocking "OU."

One of the best offensive linemen in Sooners history, Ken Mendenhall, says Mackenzie was an excellent, if not polished, recruiter.

"I was going to sign with Arkansas because they had a really strong program," he recalled. "They had won the national championship the year before [1964] and I liked it there. One night I get a call from Jim Mackenzie, and he asked me where I was going to college."

Soon as Mendenhall uttered the word "Arkansas," Mackenzie asked, "Has your mother started dinner yet?"

Not yet, Mendenhall said. The coach told him to sit tight, that he would be there to take the family out to dinner.

"Look," Mackenzie told him, "we need the best players in Oklahoma to go to Oklahoma. The program has been down and out, but that is about to change. We will build a winner here, and it will be better for you to stay in-state."

"He was a great recruiter, and I could tell he knew what it took to win football games," Mendenhall said. "Jim wasn't what you would call a smooth operator. He had his shirt-tail out a little, but you could tell he was very genuine. He convinced me."

The Sooners had started 4–0 in 1966, including an 18–9 win over Texas. But they finished with four losses over their final six games, including a 38–0 loss to Notre Dame in Norman.

One of Mackenzie's final decisions as head coach, admirable as it was, backfired when he ordered a two-point conversion while trailing Oklahoma State 15–14 with 1:29 remaining during the final game of the season. Bobby Warmack completed a pass to Ron Shotts, but he was tackled at the 2-yard line, and the Cowboys held on to win the game.

"We came up here to win," Mackenzie said, explaining his decision, "not to play for a tie."

It would be his final game.

Less than five months following his first season, on April 28, 1967, Mackenzie took a trip to Amarillo, Texas, to recruit quarterback Monty Johnson. He returned home near midnight, spent a few minutes with his wife Sue in the living room, and excused himself to go to the bathroom, telling her he was not feeling well.

Their daughter Kathy found him face-down in the bathroom later. He had died suddenly of a heart attack.

He was only 37 years old.

"We were all shocked. Just stunned," Mendenhall remembered. "You lose your coach like that and you feel lost."

Barry Switzer, brought to Norman as an assistant under Mackenzie, related what Pat James told him once. James coached at Kentucky under Bryant and knew Mackenzie as well as anyone. He also came to Oklahoma that year with Mackenzie, Switzer, and Chuck Fairbanks.

"One night, I was over at Pat's house," Switzer recalled, "and he said, 'Now let me tell you something. I coached for Bear Bryant, and Jim is the best football coach I have ever been around. He's *better* than Bear Bryant.'

"Pat knew what a great coach Jim was, and I recognized it, too."

Switzer often thinks of Mackenzie and wonders how Sooners history would have been altered if he had not died.

"I often regretted that Jim didn't have the opportunity to enjoy long-term success at Oklahoma," he said. "Jim would have had that great success, trust me. Sure, I know my career probably would have turned out different. I probably would have ended up in pro football."

A few days following Mackenzie's funeral, OU named Fairbanks as his successor.

"It was devastating to the entire team when Jim Mackenzie died," All-American nose guard Granville Liggins recalled. "Chuck Fairbanks replaced him for my senior season, meaning I had three head coaches in three seasons at Oklahoma."

When Fairbanks left OU following the 1972 season, it would be Switzer's turn.

The "Big Kid" Becomes a Legend

Eddie Lancaster, a lineman in the 1960s, loves the story of the day the "big kid" overslept.

"He was from Columbia, South Carolina," Lancaster said, "and his name is Byron Bigby. Byron was a free spirit in every sense of the word. He had a great heart, but just couldn't seem to get with the program early on. He lacked organizational skills. I believe he is the only player in the history of OU to miss a practice completely with no medical or personal reason: *he slept through practice!*"

This is what happened, as Lancaster recalled:

> In 1964, when we started spring drills, it was a very rainy—we practiced on a field that was east of our dormitory because the coaches didn't want to destroy the main practice fields.

Every day we walked past the track facilities to the east to a field to practice, and it was muddy every day.

Keep in mind there were now about 80 freshmen, along with the upperclassmen which was about 40 to 50 more, so the coaches had to manage about 120, 130 kids. At times, it was chaotic.

One day as we were returning from yet another two-hour spring practice, we walked past the dorm to return to the dressing room, and one of our other freshmen said, "Bigby wasn't there today!" Here we were all covered in mud, wet, and now we were upset that Byron wasn't there.

Someone else said, "I bet he slept through it!" We all started to laugh as we started yelling at the dorm windows, "Hey, Bigby, you missed practice." The coaches were nowhere around, so we knew he couldn't get in trouble, and we also knew he couldn't possibly sleep through practice. No one does that.

Lo and behold, as we screamed at the dorm, Byron's curtains parted on the fourth floor and there was Byron—in his underwear with the most astonished look on his face I have ever seen. I must tell you that everyone took a nap before practice. You had to in order to make it through, but Byron had slept through the alarm.

We were all amazed, but the look on his face was so incredible that we just died laughing right there. We continued to walk to the dressing room, thinking Byron was not long for the team. After all, this was inexcusable. As we returned to the dressing room, we saw a blur come in, put on his practice gear, and run outside.

Byron had gotten out of bed, run around the south side of the stadium, snuck in the dressing room—which was about a mile run—dressed, run out of the dressing room on to the adjoining practice field, found a mud puddle, rolled around in it, and then taken a seat on a bench at the entrance of the practice field before the coaches arrived. He had mud all over him and had wet his hair as mock sweat, and he sat there, trying to appear very tired. As the coaches arrived to enter the dressing room, one of them patted Bigby on the shoulder and said, "Good practice, son!"

Byron became a legend that day.

During his junior and senior seasons of 1967 and '68, Bigby became a starter at offensive tackle on the line as fullback Steve Owens was emerging as a star.

"He played next to me and he played his ass off. He was good," Lancaster recalled. "He remains one of the favorites of anybody on our team. We called him the 'big kid,' because that's what he was—just a big kid with a great heart."

In January 2008 several of his former teammates visited Bigby at his South Carolina home.

"He hasn't changed one bit," Lancaster said soon after the visit, "still the 'big kid.'"

Just days later, Bigby died.

Riley the Strong One

Perhaps there never has been a stronger lineman at Oklahoma than Jim Riley, who opened many holes for the Sooners from 1964 to 1966, even though the offense wasn't consistent in those years as OU struggled to a 15–15–1 record.

"Let me tell you how strong big Jim is," Barry Switzer said. "Derland Moore was in the NFL [during the '70s], and he went to Las Vegas and won the NFL arm-wrestling tournament. Well, one night during spring practice, the night before a Red-and-White game, a few of us were sitting at the bar with a bunch of former players, and Derland came in there and was telling everybody about his arm-wrestling championship.

"Big Jim is sitting over there, watching a pool game and listening to this. Derland is talking about how he did this, and he was coaching up the other players on how you arm-wrestle. Big Jim said, 'Look at them, just a bunch of kids…'

"Mike Reilly is sitting there and he asks Jim, 'Do you really think you can whip Derland?'

"Jim looked at me and snapped his fingers and said, 'Just like that.' So I walked over to the bar and I said, 'Derland, you remember Jim Riley, the old gray-haired guy here? He said you couldn't put him down.'

"'Well, bring him over here,' Moore told me.

"They put the hands up there and started, and Jim went *boom*. Won easy. Derland then said, 'Wait a minute! Wait a minute! Let's do that again!'

"To which Riley asked, 'Left-handed or right-handed?'

"Again, Riley whipped Moore easily.

"Then he went back over there and finished his beer.

"All of those young football players looked at Jim, and said, 'Who is he?'"

The Fairbanks Era

Fairbanks was a Michigan State man, having played for the Spartans' 1952 national championship team under coach Clarence L. "Biggie" Munn. He had a great eye for talent, he could recruit and X-and-O with the best of them, and, mostly, was all business.

It was no picnic for the Sooners during his six years as head coach.

"Our coaches were really tough on us," tight end Steve Zabel recalled. "During that season, we would come out of a film session and ask each other, 'Did we win that game? I thought we won that game?'"

The Sooners won all but one in Fairbanks's first season of 1967. In fact, his first team came within three points of winning a national championship. The only blemish was a 9–7 defeat to Texas in the season's third game.

Zabel tells the story following a 23–0 win over Colorado on November 4 of that season, a night in which he and several teammates celebrated into the wee hours. On that Monday morning, he bumped into Fairbanks as he headed to class.

"What time did you get in Saturday night?" Fairbanks asked Zabel.

As Zabel stammered for an answer, the coach snapped, "Don't lie to me! I know you did not get in until 2:00 in the morning!"

"Knowing that I did not come home at all, I thought that sounded pretty good, so I just said, 'You're right, Coach.'"

The next day, Fairbanks ordered the curfew-breakers to report to the stadium at 5:00 AM to run sprints.

"We figured that he wouldn't come out to run us, but he would send some assistant," Zabel recalled. "Then out of the dark comes this yellow, four-door Olds 88 that Coach Fairbanks drove. He yelled at us to get over to the stadium, but the gates were locked, so we started climbing the fence. Then he told us to climb down and to run all the way around the stadium to the other entrance. As we jogged, he was chasing us in that car, honking his horn and screaming, 'Sprint! Run!'"

Zabel said he could tell that Fairbanks watched his players run for the entire three hours that morning, by noticing his lit cigarette in the darkness of the southeast ramp of the stadium.

"We had played and we had paid and we were all scared to death of Chuck Fairbanks," he added.

Attack of the Oranges

The November 18 game against Kansas at Memorial Stadium was the biggest of the '67 season. The Sooners entered the game with a 6-1 record and would earn a trip to the Orange Bowl with a victory. OU had not been to the New Year's Day game in five years.

"Kansas had a great team," quarterback Bobby Warmack recalled. "They had Bobby Douglass, John Riggins, John Zook, and those guys. We hadn't moved the ball all day, and we trailed

The 1969 Heisman Trophy winner, workhorse running back Steve Owens had 4,041 career rushing yards and 57 touchdowns for the Sooners.

them 10–7 late in the game. We hold them, and they punt, and the punt rolls out of bounds at our own 4-yard line.

"I am standing on the sideline and I look across the field and see Kansas coach Pepper Rodgers throwing an orange up into the air and catching it."

Warmack then engineered a drive to advance the Sooners to Kansas's 30-yard line before he made the play of his life with little more than a minute remaining.

He play-actioned and threw deep to Zabel, who had run by a Kansas defensive back.

As Zabel sprinted by him, he heard the beaten defensive back utter, "Oh, shit."

"Then I saw the ball coming, and I said, 'Oh, shit.'"

He caught it in stride near the rear of the end zone. Immediately, delirious OU fans pelted the field with oranges.

"As a matter of fact, we got a penalty for it," Warmack said. "That was a game that allowed the coaches there to go recruit a lot of great athletes for years to come."

The 14–10 win over Kansas led to the Sooners' 26–24 win over Tennessee in the Orange Bowl, in which Volunteers kicker Karl Kremser missed a 43-yard field goal with only seven seconds remaining.

"Those Orange Bowl practices were the most difficult practices of the year," Zabel recalled.

"That 1967 team was a very good team," said Steve Owens, who rushed for 869 yards and 13 touchdowns as a sophomore that season. "But we did it because of the way the guys felt for Jim Mackenzie. We all dedicated that season to him. Looking back, I can say that team was a special team, and we played for the memory of Coach Mackenzie.

"I loved coach Fairbanks, too. He was all business. Everything he did was to the tee."

Zabel agreed.

"As far as Coach Fairbanks, I thought he was a terrific coach. I respected him. I feared him," he said. "To this day, I don't think he's received the credit he's due for building the OU program for what it is. He was very, very organized, and he knew his football."

Fairbanks had a good 30–13–1 record during his first four seasons as head coach, but he was not the most popular man in Norman. "Chuck Chuck" bumper stickers and signs were everywhere.

"At that point, Chuck was kind of depressed," Switzer once said.

Meanwhile, assistant coaches Pat James and Switzer were studying the wishbone, and once they convinced Fairbanks to switch to the new offense, the Sooners' fortunes were about to change as the decade of the '60s came to a close.

Owens Carries the Load

Over the final three seasons of the decade, Owens became the Sooners' workhorse like no other workhorse in college football history. The Sooners fed him the football as if he had an unrelenting appetite.

And time after time, he delivered. He finished with 207, 393, and 358 carries from 1967 to 1969, giving him more than 200 carries more than the next OU player on the rushing attempts list.

The capper, of course, was his 55-carry day for 261 yards in his final game—a 28–27 win over Oklahoma State that helped save Fairbanks's job.

At one point on the final drive of the game, Owens carried 12 consecutive times.

"The offense was built around me, and it was a basic ball-control type of offense," he said. "We knew we could wear defenses down in the second half. It was a burden at times, but any running back loves getting the ball as much as I did. I was conditioned for it. [Running backs coach] Switzer made sure of that."

Even as he was becoming one of the biggest stars in college football history on his way to the 1969 Heisman Trophy, Owens was beloved by his teammates because he never changed along the way to 4,041 career rushing yards and 57 touchdowns.

"I remember being in the locker room, and Steve would walk in with bruises all over him after carrying the ball 35 times the previous Saturday," said offensive tackle Eddie Foster, who was then a freshman. "He would get in the whirlpool, get taped, and go back out to practice like it was no big deal. He never missed a day.

"He would be in there talking to the freshmen, asking us about classes, girlfriends, and regular stuff, and I was thinking, *Gosh, you are the whole offense and always carrying the load for the entire team, and you are talking to me?*"

chapter 8

Bob Kalsu: An Oklahoma Legend, an American Hero

Jill Kalsu-Horning, left, and Bob Kalsu Jr., right, pose with their mother, Jan Kalsu, and pictures of Bob Kalsu Sr. and his medals in April 2004 in Edmond, Oklahoma. Kalsu Sr., an All-American lineman with the Sooners who played pro ball for the Buffalo Bills, was one of three NFL players to serve in Vietnam and the only one to die in that conflict.

Jan Kalsu stared at her husband in adoring silence, his 6'3", 240-pound frame sprawled out on the bed of the Ilikai Resort in Honolulu. Their 17-month-old daughter Jill napped beside him as a breeze blew off the blue Pacific and into their room.

She couldn't help notice he slept so deeply that bubbles blew out of his mouth with every breath.

"I couldn't believe how exhausted he was," she recalled. "He just wanted to sleep so much. Each afternoon, he would take a nap and fall into a deep sleep."

It was just another quiet afternoon in paradise, perfectly suited for taking a nap. Suddenly, as harmless fireworks exploded in the atrium of their hotel, her husband sprang to life and dived for cover. It took several moments before he realized he was still on R&R, safe with his family more than 6,000 miles away from the jungles of Southeast Asia.

Jan realized then, that even though her husband never talked about it, "he must have faced that fear of dying all the time, every day of every week."

If only she could have stretched that week of May 1970 into a lifetime. She and the only man she ever loved had strolled the beach with their beautiful toddler in hand, playing in the sand and waves, soaking up the sun as families have done since the Hawaiian islands were discovered.

"I still have the cutest pictures of him and Jill walking the beach," Jan explained.

It was pure bliss, and yet, they all knew it was only temporary. Here she was, seven months pregnant, with their whole lives ahead of them. They were in love, with one child and another on the way.

But the Vietnam War wouldn't wait, summoning First Lieutenant James Robert "Bob" Kalsu, one of the greatest offensive linemen the Oklahoma Sooners ever produced, back to combat duty in a matter of days.

When the week of R&R came to an end, Jan's airplane was scheduled to leave for the mainland before Bob's flight would head west across the Pacific. His massive hand held hers as she sat on the final car of the tram that would take her to the airport terminal, as she held Jill in her arms. Suddenly, the tram jerked forward and they lost their grip on each other.

"Bob!" she shouted. "Please be careful! Please come home to us."

"No," he answered, as the tram pulled his wife and daughter away. "You be careful! You are going to have our baby!"

Bob stood there alone, watching his family disappear into the distance.

It was the final time his wife would ever hear his voice. It was the final time she would ever touch his hand, or see his face, or hear his laugh. More than anything, Jan loved her husband's gregarious laughter, which was matched only by the size of his heart—and as it would be proven over the next few months—his courage.

"Bob had a hearty laugh that you recognized right away," she recalled recently. "It's been almost 40 years...I can still hear it. Has anybody ever told you about his laugh?"

Bobby Warmack, the Sooners' quarterback during Kalsu's career, won't ever forget it, either.

"Bob had an infectious laugh," Warmack said. "I loved his laugh."

*   *   *

It was October 8, 1966, as the Oklahoma Sooners' team airplane taxied on the airport runway, arriving home after an 18–9 victory over the rival Texas Longhorns earlier that day in Dallas.

The Sooners were off to a 3–0 start, and Oklahoma fans were in a frenzy.

Jan Darrow, a student at Central State College, was driving around town with a girlfriend "just to go out and get a Coke" as news of the team's pending arrival came over the car radio.

"Y'all want to come cheer the team as it arrives home," the voice on the radio said.

It was as if the voice was talking to the two girls. The Cokes could wait. They drove to the airport, scurried to the tarmac, and, suddenly, happy Sooners were hurrying down the stairs of the plane. It was then that Jan spotted Ron Winfrey, a lineman with whom she attended high school, walking down the steps.

"Ron!" Jan shouted, "I didn't know you played for OU."

As the two caught up on old times, Jan told him, "Golly, there are some cute guys on this football team."

"I will fix you up with one if you want me to," Winfrey replied.

"That would be great."

A few weeks went by before Winfrey called.

"Want to go on a double-date with me and my roommate?" he asked.

"What's his name?" Jan asked him.

Jan was taken aback at his answer.

"'Kalsu?' That sounded Oriental to me," she said. "I am 5'9" and I didn't want anyone shorter than me. But Ron assured me that he was tall enough for me."

That night, at a team party, and on their next date, in which Bob Kalsu devoured a chicken dinner as Jan nibbled at her cheesecake, the two fell madly in love.

"I never saw someone eat that gregariously," she recalled. "He would put a chicken leg in his mouth, and it would come out clean, except for the bone. I hadn't even started on my cheesecake when he was finished. Then he started on *my* cheesecake…"

Jan went home that night and told one of her younger sisters, "I think I met the man I am going to marry."

Bob was an only child and adored his parents and his grandparents, who had immigrated from Czechoslovakia. He was a natural athlete, starring in football and baseball at nearby Del City High. He always loved the Oklahoma Sooners. Off the field, he had great manners, earned good grades, and became one of the most popular players among his teammates. He was an All-American boy, born and raised in America's heartland.

"He had such respect for his parents and grandparents," Jan said. "He was an only child, but he was anything but spoiled. He had such high morals and self-discipline. He was Catholic. I was Catholic. He laughed loudly, and we had great fun no matter what we did. We just clicked right away. Everything in my heart told me this was the man of my dreams."

What Jan loved most besides his laugh and outgoing personality was his naïveté and gentleness for such a big man who played such a rough and violent sport.

"I could tease him and play jokes on him because he was so gullible," she recalled. "It was a form of pure innocence. And yet, he was more mature than most boys his age. He just seemed to be a natural-born leader."

In Jan's family—she had eight brothers and sisters—Bob found the siblings he never had.

"He had so much fun with my little brothers," Jan said. "He once told me, 'I finally have some brothers.'"

As a senior in 1967, as the Sooners finished 10–1—their best season since Bud Wilkinson's dynasty of the 1950s—Kalsu dominated on the offensive line, blowing away blockers on an offensive line that opened holes for a up-and-coming sophomore fullback named Steve Owens. He was named an All-American.

"Bob was our best offensive lineman, probably the best athlete we had," said then–offensive coordinator Barry Switzer. "He wasn't only a great player, he was a great leader."

"I have to say that he was larger than life," OU tight end Steve Zabel said of Kalsu.

"I know one thing—Bob loved Oklahoma and loved being a Sooner," Jan said.

Twenty-six days after the Sooners held on to beat Tennessee 26–24 in the 1968 Orange Bowl in Miami, Jan and Bob were married. Jill was born the following November. Also in January he was selected in the eighth round by the AFL's Buffalo Bills and became a starting guard during the '68 season. He was named the team's rookie of the year.

Following his rookie season, to satisfy his ROTC obligation, Kalsu entered the U.S. Army as a First Lieutenant, was made a member of C Battery, 2nd Battalion, 11th Field Artillery, 101st Airborne Division, and shipped out to Vietnam in November of 1969.

At the same time, a Bills rookie running back by the name of O.J. Simpson was struggling behind a rebuilt offensive line. He would have had Kalsu blocking in front of him that season, and likely for seasons to come, but Kalsu was not the type of man who wanted any preferential treatment simply because he was a pro football player.

"I made a commitment to my country," he said then. "Just because I play football shouldn't make any difference."

It was then that his wife made a deal with the Lord.

"When Bob went to Vietnam, I soon found out I was pregnant," Jan said. "I said this prayer: 'Lord Jesus, bring him home safely someday…but if you need Bob more than I do, then please give me a son to carry on the Kalsu name.'"

*   *   *

By the summer of 1970, two months following Kalsu's week of R&R with his wife and daughter in Hawaii, the Vietnam War was waging full-throttle ahead.

The 101st Airborne Division had secured Fire Support Base Ripcord, crucial to supporting a helicopter lifeline to move supplies in and personnel out of the front lines. The division also was in the midst of planning an offensive to destroy North Vietnamese Army supply bases in the mountains overlooking nearby A Shau Valley.

What the Americans didn't know was that North Vietnamese scouts had the base under surveillance for weeks.

On July 1, the North Vietnamese Army began to attack it.

For the next 22 days, the 101st waged a fierce battle to maintain the base despite being outnumbered roughly 10 to one. For almost three weeks, Kalsu was proven a hero over and over again, saving many of his men.

A few messages on the Vietnam Virtual Wall by men who were there relate as much:

> I am proud to say that I served under Lt. James Kalsu at Firebase Arsenal in 1970. We had a ground attack by

enemy sappers one night, and the whole hill was lit up with everyone running pell-mell to their posts. Lt. Kalsu made his rounds during the night, seeing to everyone's security, and was very much in control of the situation. He never barked out orders that I can remember, but carried a voice of authority that was matched by his character and genuineness as "one of the men." –Dr. Larry Taylor (former SP4 Taylor, Asst Gunner, 155mm Vietnam 1969–1971)

Another read:

I am proud to have served with Lt. Kalsu in Vietnam in June and July of 1970 on Firebase Ripcord. I was new to the unit, and the first person I met when I got off the chopper was a lieutenant with a big smile and a strong handshake. Even though all hell was about to break loose, he made us a little bit more comfortable. He was great with all of the guys in the unit and he gave us all respect. He was one of the few officers I have met that would hump ammo and he could carry three 155 rounds at a time.—Lt. John Beadle (A Btry, 2nd/11th Arty, 101st Abn [Ambl], Abington, Mass.)

The three-week battle took a heavy toll, however, as 250 U.S. soldiers were killed.

On the 20th day of the battle, on the top of a hill, an NVA mortar hit the base's ammunition supply. Kalsu and one of his men died on the top of that hill.

However, before the battle would be lost, the 101st destroyed eight of the enemy's nine battalions, which delayed the Eastern offensive of the North Vietnamese Army by a year.

Two days later, on July 23, the bloody battle ended as Jan rested in the maternity ward back in Oklahoma. She had given birth to a boy slightly after midnight and was filling out the paperwork to have their newborn son named Robert Todd Kalsu. All she could think about was getting word to her husband on the other side of the planet that he was a father of a son.

"We had it typed up, and it was about to be official," she recalled.

At that moment, Leah and Frank Kalsu, Bob's parents, walked through the door of her hospital room. Leah carried flowers and candy, purchased with money their only son had sent her for the pending birth.

Leah's eyes were filled with tears.

"Why are you crying, Leah?" her daughter-in-law asked. "Leah, are you worried about Bob?"

Leah said nothing, but her husband informed Jan that they had read that morning that Ripcord had undergone heaving shelling in the previous days. She had no news about Bob.

"Don't worry," Jan told his parents. "Bob told me he would be all right and he will come home someday. Don't cry. Bob will come home to us! I just know it."

With that, Leah and Frank Kalsu drove to Jan's parents house to pick up Jill for a day at the zoo.

The image of death then knocked on the front door, in the form of two soldiers in full-dress uniforms. They didn't have to say a word. Everyone inside the house broke down and cried hysterically. The soldiers were required to tell spouses the horrible news first, even though the Kalsus and Jan's parents begged the soldiers to give them the horrible news, so they could deliver it to Jan delicately.

The soldiers, however, were under strict orders and headed to the hospital to find Jan's room. Before they could arrive, Jan's doctor entered the room and pulled his chair close to her bed, took her hand in his, and said, "Some soldiers want to come talk to you." He then wrapped his arm around her and held her.

She began to sob, knowing that the only man she ever loved was gone.

A few moments later, the soldiers entered the room. One stood at the foot of her bed at rigid attention. He began to utter the words: "I regret to inform you that First Lieutenant James Robert Kalsu was—"

Jan Kalsu doesn't remember the rest of his words. She does remember the tears streaming down the soldier's cheeks as he stood there during the single worst moment of her life. She does remember telling her doctor, "I want to go home! I want to go home!" and ordering him to "get the statistician back in here right now."

When he obeyed, she instructed the hospital statistician, "I want to change my baby's name to James Robert Kalsu Jr."

She then was driven home, cradled Jill in her arms, and whispered, "Daddy's gone. Jill, Daddy's gone," until she fell asleep.

Bob Kalsu was one of 58,235 American soldiers to die or to be declared missing in action in Vietnam. He was the only professional athlete to lose his life there.

Before the funeral, Jan declined to see her husband's body for one final time.

"I just couldn't," she said. "He was the man I loved with all my heart."

Bob's uncle, Milt, identified his body in the casket. Bob's head was still bandaged, and his fingernails were dirty, facts that still anger Jan.

"You think they would have bathed my husband's body," she said.

Today, more than 38 years following that fateful day at FSB Ripcord, James Robert Kalsu Sr.'s legacy is secure as a true American hero.

There is a forward operating base in Babil, Iraq, named after him. The replacement company at Fort Campbell, Kentucky, is named the "1LT J. Robert Kalsu Replacement Company." Oklahoma coach Bob Stoops initiated the "Bob Kalsu Award" in 2001 to honor the Sooner who displays "uncommon dedication and fortitude."

Furthermore, the Buffalo Bills dedicated an area in the lobby of their administrative offices to Kalsu and placed his name on their Wall of Fame at Rich Stadium in Orchard Park, New York, in 2000. The Pro Football Hall of Fame in Canton, Ohio, includes a framed jersey that Kalsu wore with the Bills and bears a plaque in his honor. It reads: "No one will ever know how great a football player Bob might have been, but we do know how great a man he was to give up his life for his country."

Also, the football stadium at Del City High near Oklahoma City is named after him.

Those are the proper names, titles, honors and plaques. His flesh-and-blood legacy lives on through his widow, his children, and his grandchildren who cherish his surname, memories, and mementos.

"I thank God we started having kids right away after we got married," Jan said recently. "We have our legacy in them and in our grandkids.

"Someday, we will all be together again…someday, all of us will hear that big laugh again. I always told my kids that is the purpose of our journey. I told them a long time ago to live good lives, so we can get to heaven and all be together again."

*   *   *

If Bob Kalsu is the hero of this story, Jan Kalsu is the saint.

She made sure her children would have wonderful lives and grow into responsible and productive adults, even if it meant her social life would be limited to helping them with their homework or a movie now and then.

She raised them on her own and constantly reminded them of their father through all the stories of family, football, and war. He had dozens of friends, he saved lives, and he did it all with honor, honesty, and a personality that made him beloved.

"She always talked about my dad, so we could feel as if we knew him ourselves," Bob Jr. said.

Through the years, Jan purposely did not get married until each of her children were raised.

"Heck, my heart was still broken over Bob, but I waited to get married again until they were grown because I wanted to give them all of my attention," she said. "I thought I owed them that."

In the spring of 2007, after 19 years of marriage, Jan was divorced from her second husband and retook the Kalsu name. It felt like the perfect thing to do, she said.

"I had to," she said. "He was the love of my life."

Daughter Jill Horning admits she is "in awe" of what her mother sacrificed.

"She did everything for us," she said. "She is a very selfless person. She went through the nitty-gritty every day of her life, raising two kids by herself. She passed on her faith to us. She never went out. She never did things for herself. Really, she is no less a hero than my dad was."

True to their mother's intentions, Bob Jr. and Jill have lived very good lives, held together by their Catholic faith and their belief their father gave his life for a noble and just cause. For that, they are not bitter and never have been.

"My dad stood for something important," Jill said.

Today, she lives in Longmont, Colorado, with her husband and five children. "I was a school teacher by trade and a momma by choice," she said, laughing.

She admits her heart still aches for the father she misses. It always will, she suspects. She also realizes he would have been the best possible father to her and Bob Jr., and now, grandfather.

"I know he was a good person through all the stories I have heard," she said. "I know I have my father's personality from what everybody tells me. He was so down to earth, had that infectious laugh, and enjoyed every moment of life to the fullest.

"I really missed having him in my life. I missed having a dad. I missed having a grandpa in my kids' lives. Not a day goes by that I don't say a prayer for him or talk to him. At times, part of me gets feeling sorry for myself or angry at the way he died.

"But I know deep down that what he did was right."

Lt. Col. Kennan Horn, professor of military science at the University of Oklahoma, knew it, too, even though he never met Kalsu. He admitted he was surprised nothing had been done to honor him before Horn arrived at the school in 2005. Horn and fellow ROTC members decided to take on a project, starting by contacting the OU Letterman's Football Association.

"When people heard about this, they lined up," Horn said.

Steve Owens, the 1969 Heisman Trophy winner who knew Kalsu well because he was one of his lead blockers during

Owens's sophomore season, and Charlie Newton, the OU Lettermen's Association president, wrote letters to association members asking for donations.

Almost immediately, Owens said, "The checks came flowing in. He was a hero…I think a hero in every sense of the word. His country called, he went and served, and gave his life for his country. That's what they call a hero."

The result was a commissioned painting of Kalsu that was unveiled at the ROTC building during a ceremony in October 2007. Jan, Bob Jr., and Jill were honored guests that night, and as an NFL Films documentary of Bob's life was being shown, Jill glanced over at her five children.

"All five of them were sobbing," she said.

The Kalsus are very appreciative every time Bob's memory has been honored. They have made several appearances at ceremonies held by the Bills and have been guests in owner Ralph Wilson's suite. Not a Christmas has passed since 1970 in which Wilson did not send a card, a gift, or call Jan.

"The Buffalo Bills have been so good to us, from day one," Jan said. "Their owner, Mr. Wilson, is just a wonderful man who has done so many things for us. I can't thank him enough for all he has done."

"It's just nice to know that our father hasn't been forgotten," Jill said. "We are honored every time Dad is honored."

Today, Bob Jr. is a successful attorney and lives in Oklahoma City with his wife and three children (when this book was being published, his wife was pregnant with their fourth child). He talks to his sister every day on the telephone.

On his office wall hangs the Bills' No. 51 jersey and Sooners' No. 77 jersey his father once wore. Framed next to those is the 2001 *Sports Illustrated* issue that featured his father's picture on the cover and his heroic story inside. People tell him often that he looks just like his father. And when strangers in Oklahoma hear or see his name, they ask, "Aren't you the son of…"

"I hear it more often in certain places, such as at an OU event or a game," he said. "It happens frequently."

It wasn't always that way. Jan Kalsu will never forget the day Bob Jr. was denied an important scholarship because his father was not a member of the Knights of Columbus. It made her angry, but she refrained from telling those involved with the scholarship exactly why Bob Kalsu Sr. could not possibly be a member.

"It seems for years nobody knew what happened to my husband," she said. "Not many people knew our story for some reason."

The NFL Films documentary and the subsequent cover story by *Sports Illustrated* changed all that a few years ago.

When Bob Jr. once visited the Vietnam Wall in Washington, he asked a volunteer for help, simply because the massive wall does not list the names etched in granite alphabetically, and locating a particular name can be time-consuming and tedious.

"I want to find James Robert Kalsu," he told the man.

"I can help you with that," the volunteer said, "because it's the most-requested name I have to find every day."

The volunteer then asked why he wanted to see that particular name.

"He's my father," Bob Jr. said.

The skeptical volunteer made him pull out his Oklahoma drivers license to prove it.

These days, thousands of Americans, not just Oklahomans, know Bob Kalsu's name and his heroic story.

"I have always hoped that a little bit of Bob's story would rub off on Americans," Jan explained. "We wouldn't be a free country without our soldiers. Wouldn't it be great if they were recognized and admired and respected the way they deserve?"

At the same time, Jan has fretted that Pat Tillman, who gave up his NFL career to join the U.S. Army Rangers, may have done so after reading about her husband. Tillman, who by all accounts was motivated to join the military by the events of September 11, 2001, was killed by friendly fire in Afghanistan in 2004.

"I have prayed that he didn't leave the NFL after reading Bob's story," she said. "I know what the Tillman family is going through. I know their pain and I know there is nothing anyone can say to make it go away. They will miss Pat always, just as we will miss Bob always."

Nearly 40 years have passed since the events on that hilltop at Ripcord took the love of Jan's life. There was Watergate, Elvis' death, the Iran hostage crisis, the Berlin Wall has come down, 9/11, four more Sooners national championships, and two wars in Iraq.

It is a long time to live with a broken heart.

"There is no pain like it…I miss Bob so much to this day," Jan said, sobbing. "Not a day goes by when I don't talk to him. I can still picture that day in Hawaii when I held his hand for the final time and the tram jerked it out of my hand. I can still see his face, hear his voice…

"And I can still hear his laugh."

chapter 9

The 1970s: From Chuck to Barry, Good Times Ahead

Chuck Fairbanks welcomes Nebraska head coach Bob Devaney to Norman on November 24, 1971, prior to their monumental game on Thanksgiving Day.

Once again, transition was about to challenge the program, and this time the Sooners would respond, again rising to the national-championship level.

Heisman Trophy winner Steve Owens was now a workhorse in the NFL, and two more key contributors—tight end Steve Zabel and linebacker Jim Files—also had been selected in the first round.

Chuck Fairbanks was entering his fourth season as head coach, but his teams were coming off two consecutive four-loss seasons, and not many fans remembered his 10–1 start in 1967.

The good news was that Jack Mildren was back as the starting quarterback, and there was plenty of talent in the OU locker room.

That spring, the coaches decided to scrap the I formation—which had featured Owens left, Owens up the middle, and Owens right—and had implemented the Houston veer.

"We used split backs and were going to throw it more," Mildren recalled. "It sounded good to me, and I was excited about it. We moved up and down the field during the spring."

As Mildren and the coaches had hoped, the offense looked fine during the first two games of the 1970 season, working out the usual kinks while scoring 28 points against SMU and 21 against Wisconsin in relatively easy wins.

Then came a 23–14 shocking upset to unheralded Oregon State at Memorial Stadium, and all hell broke loose.

"We were called to a meeting the next day and told we were switching offenses to the wishbone," Mildren said. "It takes a lot of courage to switch offenses in the middle of the season."

With two weeks to go before meeting rival Texas, Fairbanks and offensive coordinator Barry Switzer, who had studied the offense and talked the head coach into the move, figured now was as good a time as any. With a week off and the veer going nowhere, Switzer recalled, it was now or never. At the time, Texas was winning big with the wishbone. The Longhorns were 23–1–1 in their previous 25 games, heading into the 1970 game against the Sooners.

"I had watched people trying to stop Darrell [Royal]'s wishbone, and nobody could do it," Switzer recalled. "It seemed to me that we should be running the wishbone, too."

Switzer had immersed himself in film, studying every facet of the offense before teaching it to his offensive players. He labeled Mildren as a quarterback "born to run the wishbone." Plus, they may just catch the Longhorns by surprise, the coaches figured.

No matter how you slice it, the switch was a great risk, something coaches rarely, if ever tried, during the modern era of college football. From an outsider's perspective, it reeked of desperation.

"I think about it now, and the coaches' jobs were on the line," Mildren explained recently.

That may have been true. Fairbanks and his staff had a 25–10 record at this point, but were only 15–9 in the previous 24 games following the humiliating loss at home to the Beavers.

"Oklahoma fans took this as a major embarrassment," Switzer wrote in his autobiography. "You could almost hear our Oilys howling to load the entire coaching staff on the first boxcar heading to Yukon."

The Sooners' wishbone wasn't quite the finished product that Texas's was, of course, and the Longhorns won easily, 41–9.

Suddenly, the "Chuck Chuck" bumper stickers were a common sight in the state of Oklahoma, and now there was some severe pressure on the coaching staff. Starting 2–2 and losing by 32 points to your rival is one thing, but doing it after switching offenses in midstream is another.

What the new offense needed was time, and the coaches realized that but weren't sure they would receive it if they didn't start winning quickly.

They were right.

The Sooners, feeling more comfortable with each passing week in the wishbone, finished the regular season by winning four of their final games and routed Oklahoma State 66–6.

"We could have scored 100 that day if we wanted," Mildren said. "Maybe that was the first time the light came on for all of us."

They then tied Alabama 24–24 on New Year's Eve in the Astro-Bluebonnet Bowl to finish 7–4–1 as Fairbanks and his talented staff survived to see another season.

The Game of the Century

The 1971 season showed just how far Oklahoma's new offense had progressed. It was simply, without question, college football's most explosive offense, ranking No. 1 in almost every category.

Consider these startling numbers: OU averaged 7.6 yards per play—a full yard better than any team in school history; 556.8 yards per game—almost 50 yards better than any team in school history; 469.6 yards rushing per game—31 yards better than any other team in school history; and 44.5 points per game—surpassed only by Bud Wilkinson's national championship team of 1956, which averaged 46.6 points per game.

"I heard coach Switzer once say that [the rushing yards per game] record will never be broken," center Tom Brahaney said.

"It won't," Switzer said. "I still feel that way."

That season the Sooners defeated Kansas State 75–28 and gained 785 yards. In that game, Greg Pruitt rushed for 294 yards—still the OU single-game rushing record.

"We scored on 11 of 12 possessions that day," Mildren said.

They also rolled up 696 yards on Oklahoma State, 679 on Iowa State, and 670 on Colorado—four of the top-10 yardage outputs in the 103-year history of OU football. They scored 50 or more on three other opponents and 40 or more in eight of their 12 games.

They scored 33 in a win at USC, in which Pruitt had gained more than 200 yards, and Mildren did not pass for a single yard.

"We hadn't thrown a pass all day because Pruitt was averaging about 10 yards per carry, and near the end of the game, Mildren came to the sideline and said, 'Could we just throw one?'" Switzer recalled.

Switzer relented before Mildren's only attempt of the day fell incomplete. When he reached the sideline, Switzer joked, "See!"

Yes, you could say the wishbone, in less than two full seasons of existence, had taken root and flourished like King Kong on steroids.

"I would put that offense up against anybody's offense [in the history of college football]," stated Mildren, who rushed for 1,289 yards that season—the best rushing season ever for an OU quarterback. It is why today Mildren still is known around Oklahoma as the "Father of the Wishbone."

Five offensive players—Brahaney, Pruitt, guard Ken Jones, tight end Albert Chandler, and Mildren—were named All–Big 8, while Pruitt, Brahaney, and Mildren were named All-Americans.

However, no matter how prolific the Sooners were offensively, none of it would result in a national championship unless they defeated Nebraska in the monumental showdown on Thanksgiving Day in Norman.

The Cornhuskers, which had the nation's top-ranked defense and had surrendered 10 points or more only twice all season, entered the game 10–0 and ranked No. 1. OU was 9–0 and ranked No. 2. Being the only game on television that day, and nearly two weeks of pregame excitement catapulted the meeting into the "Game of the Century" moniker.

"Games like the 'Game of the Century' are why we all come to Oklahoma," Mildren explained.

Surprisingly, the quality of the game matched the hype.

The Sooners held a 17–14 halftime lead, thanks to two Mildren-to–Jon Harrison touchdown passes. But Nebraska, behind workhorse running back Jeff Kinney, fought back, and the game seesawed into the fourth quarter. OU led 31–28 late in the game before Kinney carried Nebraska's offense on his back for 74 yards and scored the winning touchdown on a two-yard run with only 1:38 remaining.

Many Sooners feel they would have answered that score and won the game, if only they had more time.

"Once they went ahead, time became a problem, and we ran out of it at the end of the game," said Mildren, who has always thought about his overthrown pass to Harrison late in the game.

"Life has its ups and downs," he said recently. "I just don't want to be defined by [the score]. I have never been embarrassed that we lost to Nebraska that day. That game has a life of its own now, and it has stood the test of time. It's ironic that at a school that has so many big victories, so much time has been spent talking about a game we didn't win."

The hype of the game and the result itself have grown legendary as the years have passed. In fact, not a year passes in which you won't see a replay of the punt return by Johnny Rodgers that staked Nebraska to a 7–0 lead. And several books have been written about the game.

As the Cornhuskers went on to win the national title, the Sooners manhandled Oklahoma State 58–14 and then beat Auburn 40–22 in the Sugar Bowl to finish ranked No. 2. Colorado finished No. 3, giving the Big 8 an amazing 1–2–3 finish in the nation in the Associated Press Poll. (OU was voted No. 3 in the UPI poll, behind Alabama).

The numbers show that both the 1971 Nebraska and Oklahoma teams were so dominating that each could have gone down as two of the best teams ever to play college football—but they had to play each other, and one of them had to lose.

And unfortunately for those Sooners, who don't have national championship rings on their fingers today, it had to be them.

The Year of the Forfeits

On the field, the Sooners were explosive again in 1972, rolling to an 11–1 record, including a 14–0 win over Penn State in the Sugar Bowl.

The only blemish was a 20–14 stunner at Colorado in the first game of the Big 8 season, but OU rebounded to win its final seven games, including a 17–14 win in the rematch at Nebraska. That win secured the Big 8 title.

However, when it was revealed much later that two players from Galveston (Texas) Ball High School, quarterback Kerry Jackson and freshman center Mike Phillips, needed doctored transcripts to be accepted at Oklahoma, the Sooners were forced to forfeit eight victories in which Jackson played.

The two players, however, had nothing to do with the fake transcripts and also had no knowledge of it.

Assistant Bill Michael, the offensive line coach who, according to the university, "admitted knowing about the tampering," resigned in the wake of the scandal.

It certainly marred the final season in Norman for Fairbanks, who announced the following January that he was leaving to coach the NFL's New England Patriots, even though he denied any knowledge of the false transcripts.

"I would not hesitate to offer Bill Michael a job," Fairbanks said at the time.

Jackson, the first black quarterback at Oklahoma, broke down and cried when informed of the doctored transcripts.

As a sidelight to the scandal, Dan Ruster will never forget the telephone call he received from Oregon quarterback Dan Fouts a few months later. The Sooners walloped Fouts's Ducks 68–3 in the second game of the season, and then Ruster and his roommate, All-American center Tom Brahaney, had befriended Fouts when Brahaney played in the Hula Bowl following the season.

"They became friends, and when Tom and I moved out of the dorm and into an apartment, I became friends with Fouts over the phone," Ruster explained. "Anyway, in April when the NCAA cited OU with the recruiting violations and we had to forfeit the eight games in which Kerry Jackson played, one of the games was the win over Oregon.

"Fouts then called the apartment that very day the news came out, and I answered. He said, 'I knew we beat you guys...it just 'took seven months!"

Following the season, when Fairbanks resigned, he recommended Switzer as his replacement.

Switzer, who already had turned down Iowa State once because he figured it was a dead-end job, figured to become a head coach someplace sometime soon, was announced as Oklahoma's new head coach on January 29, 1973.

He was only 35 years old.

His appointment continued a pattern for the University of Oklahoma. When they were named head coaches of OU, Bennie Owen was 30 and Bud Wilkinson was 31—and you could say that their careers in Norman turned out just fine.

No Tube-Time, No Bowls, No Problem

During Switzer's first three seasons as head coach, 1973, '74, and '75, the Sooners' image was somewhat sullied nationally due to NCAA probation. For the first two seasons, they would not be eligible to play in a bowl. For the latter two, they would not play on national television.

Before his first season as the boss began, Switzer gathered his team around him and used the penalties to motivate his players.

"Listen, you don't like this and I don't like this," he told them. "They tell us we can't play on TV and they tell us we can't play in a bowl, but they didn't tell us we can't win. The greatest reward in football is winning. That's why they have scoreboards. When they put us on probation, they made one mistake. They didn't tell us we couldn't win the Big 8 Conference, and nobody said we couldn't win the national championship. Men, that is our challenge."

Aside from a 7–7 tie at Southern Cal in the second game, the Sooners met the challenge—playing almost perfectly on their way to a 10–0–1 season and another Big 8 Championship. They finished ranked No. 3, behind national champions Alabama (UPI) and Notre Dame (AP).

Before the 1974 season, in what many saw as a specific slap at Oklahoma, the UPI board of coaches voted to no longer include schools on probation in their weekly college football poll. That would prove extremely relevant to the Sooners as the '74 season progressed.

Offensively, they were almost as unstoppable as the '71 team, leading the nation in almost every offensive category. And it was

OU's wishbone, not Texas's or Alabama's, that was now the prototype that other schools studied.

That season, they averaged 507.7 total yards, 438.8 rushing yards, and 43 points per game. They were so good that *Sports Illustrated* described the Sooners as "The Best Team You'll Never See."

"That 1974 team was by far the best team during my time at Oklahoma," said Tinker Owens, a wide receiver from 1972 to 1975. "We had only one close game that year, a 16–13 win over Texas."

Switzer and Joe Washington even believed that the TV ban cost the running back the Heisman Trophy that season.

"Not being on TV and not going to bowls for those two years because of the probation probably affected me a great deal, at least it did in 1974 as far as the Heisman is concerned," Washington said in recent years. "At the time, you really don't think about those things much. But you would have loved to be introduced by Chris Schenkel on TV or have Keith Jackson call your name."

For the record, Washington rushed for 1,321 yards and scored 12 touchdowns in 1974—the ninth-best single season among OU running backs. Heisman Trophy winner Archie Griffin of Ohio State rushed for 1,695 yards that season.

Steve Davis: Simply a Winner

Remarkably, quarterback Steve Davis received the final scholarship OU offered in 1971 only because their original offer was rejected by another recruit. He had grown up as a huge Sooners fan, idolizing Bobby Warmack.

"That is soon after they went to the red helmet and the double chinstrap," Davis recalled of the late 1960s. "Bobby wore the eyeblack and a towel in the front of his pants. I did everything he did and tried to look like him."

It appeared, however, that he would never make it to Norman to follow in his idol's footsteps.

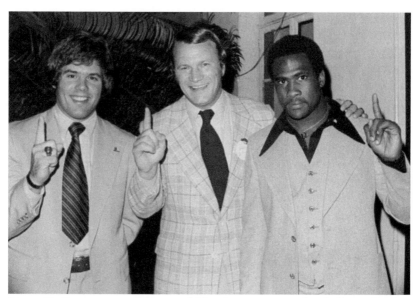

Barry Switzer poses with two of his players, quarterback Steve Davis, left, and running back Joe Washington, as they give the No. 1 sign in Miami Beach on January 2, 1976, after the AP named the Sooners national champs for the second year in a row.

"They really weren't recruiting me, but [assistant coach] Leon Cross was my biggest supporter. He called one day and said, "So-and-so is going to Colorado, we got one for you...do you want it?" Davis recalled.

"I said, 'Hell, yes, I want it!' I got the last scholarship."

Once he got to Norman, Davis was so far down on the depth chart that he needed a ladder to see the scout team, but he credits assistant coach Ron Fletcher with preparing him mentally.

"Ron Fletcher made a statement that has lived with me forever. He looked at all the wide-eyed freshmen and said, 'Guys, prepare for your opportunity. Someday you'll get it,'" Davis said.

"I had dreamed about being an Oklahoma football player forever, and when I got there, I was the eighth quarterback on an eight-man depth chart. All of them were trying to replace Jack Mildren, who had graduated. At one point, I had gotten overweight and frustrated and wanted to leave, and my father told me, 'Son, you haven't even tried to play yet. Why don't you go get your ass in shape and make something happen!'"

Following a redshirt season, Davis climbed the depth chart to the top to start 34 games, from 1973 to 1975, orchestrating Oklahoma's 32–1–1 record. No quarterback has ever won more games for the Sooners.

"Steve Davis needs to be given more credit after all these years," said Jimbo Elrod, a defensive end on those teams. "A lot of people don't realize how good he was at running that wishbone."

Davis rushed for 34 touchdowns and had 11 100-yard games during his career.

"It all worked out," Davis said recently.

A Weighty Matter

Even as recently as the mid-1970s, many major-college football teams were not practicing weight-training on an organized basis. Some players lifted weights but did so on their own. In fact, the Sooners' weight room consisted of a small storage room beneath Memorial Stadium.

"They didn't even have enough weights back then for the Selmon brothers to lift," wide receiver Tinker Owens said.

Nebraska became one of the first to institute a formal weight-lifting program, and the Sooners, like most other major-college programs, followed by the time the 1980s rolled around.

Not coincidentally, that is the period in which the average weight of offensive linemen climbed from 230 pounds to around 270.

The Selmons: Men Among Boys

When Lucious Selmon took a recruiting trip to Oklahoma in 1969, everyone noticed his two large companions as they chowed down in the cafeteria.

"They were piling food a foot high on their cafeteria trays," Switzer said.

He pointed and asked another assistant, "Who's that?"

Told they were Lucious's "little" brothers, Dewey and Lee Roy, Switzer couldn't believe it, especially when he discovered they were sophomore running backs at Eufaula High School.

It would mark the beginning of a long-lasting love affair between the Sooners and the Selmon family.

At different times from 1972 through 1975, at least two Selmons were starting and dominating on the Oklahoma defensive line. Lucious, 1971 to 1973, was named an All-American for one season, while Dewey and Lee Roy would be named twice. Lee Roy, widely regarded as OU's finest player ever at any position, won the Outland Trophy and Lombardi Award during his senior season of 1975.

"All the Selmons were good, but Lee Roy was the special one," said a man who should know, OU offensive tackle Mike Vaughan (1974–1976). "He was so smart and he was as quick as a cat— that's why we called him 'Big Cat'—and he was enormously strong. Lee Roy had the most perfect set of arms and shoulders of any guy I saw in football."

What many fans didn't know, however, was the severity of Lee Roy's illness before his sophomore season in 1973.

"I had some discomfort in my chest and didn't know what it was," Lee Roy recalled.

Following some tests in his hometown, he was admitted to a hospital in Norman and diagnosed with pericarditis—an inflammation of the lining surrounding the heart. He was hospitalized for two weeks and then placed on bed rest for two more. His football career was in serious jeopardy.

"I don't think the doctors ever let me know how serious it was," Lee Roy said recently. "I found out much later once I did some research on my own that it was something pretty serious."

The missed time upset Lee Roy because he knew it was his only season in which to play on the line next to Lucious, then a senior.

The first game Lee Roy started that season was the fourth game, against Texas. Over the next eight games, all three Selmons started and gave opposing offensive linemen fraternal nightmares. Not coincidentally, the Sooners won all eight easily.

Joe's Famed Silver Shoes

This is something quarterback Dan Ruster (1969–1972) will never forget. He only had wished he had been as ingenious as Joe Washington.

"In high school I wore football shoes made of kangaroo skin," Ruster explained. "They were very light, but they would not fit snug on my feet, so even before Joe Namath and his white shoes, I would tape them to my feet with white tape. As a freshman at OU, our first game was against Tulsa in 1969, I was the starting quarterback on the freshman team. Interestingly enough, Drew Pearson was the starting quarterback for Tulsa that day.

"When we went out for warm-ups, I was wearing my same high school shoes and taped them like I had always done. When we came in before we went out for the kickoff, our head coach, [Don] Jimerson, came up to me and told me very directly, 'We have no showboats on this team, now take some black eye-gloss and cover those white shoes!'

"The funny thing is, two years later the whole team was in white shoes. Anyway, three years later, in 1972, we were playing at Colorado. We took two freshmen on the trip that day—Little Joe Washington and Tinker Owens. After we went out to warm up and came back in before kickoff, I had to use the bathroom and went into the stall. All of a sudden, I heard this hissing and I smelled paint from the stall next to me. So I stood up on the toilet seat and looked into the next stall, and there was Joe, sitting on the pot spraying his shoes with silver paint.

"I asked him, 'What in the world are you doing?'

"'If I had sprayed them before we went out to warm up, the coaches would've told me to change them,'" he answered, "'but now before kickoff, they won't have time to make me change them'

"The rest is history," Ruster concluded.

"Actually, the first time I did it was at Kansas," Washington said. "Jack Baer, our equipment manager, smelled that paint.

"'What do I smell?' I could hear him asking everyone. 'Is that paint?'

"I had a pretty good game. I ran well and made some blocks, but nobody said a thing about my shoes. So we were sitting in the film room after the game, and Barry was clicking the film back and forth.

"All of a sudden, he asked, 'Little Joe! What are those goddamn things on your feet?'

"'Those are my silver shoes, Coach,'" I told him.

"'Oh, okay,' he said.

"That was the only thing he ever said about it," Washington recalled recently. "I knew then that I would always get along with him. A couple of years later, people were giving him a hard time about players being undisciplined and for letting me wear silver shoes and all that crap.

"It was before the Colorado game, and we were on the field when he told me how people gave him crap about my shoes. I asked, 'What do you want me to do, Coach?'

"He told me, 'Just put a couple of hundred on them today, will you?'"

Washington rushed for 211 yards that day, and critics complained a little less about his silver shoes.

Joe admitted that his brother came up with the idea first when both Washingtons wore white shoes for a high school homecoming game.

"When I decided to wear silver at Oklahoma, my brother told me to put red shoestrings in them because silver and red go together," he recalled. "We tried it, and they looked fantastic, and I knew that summer that's what I would do. But I waited about half the season before I broke them out. I never practiced in them, either."

From 1972 to 1975, Washington gained 4,071 yards and scored 43 touchdowns—and most of that production happened with his feet covered in silver.

Switzer has since admitted he knew all along that Washington would wear silver shoes, while the rest of the team wore white, and he had no problem with it. Contrastingly, most teams in the 1970s wore black shoes.

"When we recruited Little Joe out of Port Arthur, Texas, I had heard he wanted to wear silver shoes in college," Switzer admitted. "I also heard [Texas coach] Darrell [Royal] say, 'He is going to wear what we wear as a team,' and I heard the coaches at Colorado say the same thing. I hadn't even seen tape of the guy yet.

"Once I saw that, I said, 'I don't care if the s.o.b. plays barefoot. I didn't care what he played in. Just give him the ball!'"

Where Did "Tinker" Come From?

Every Sooners fan knows there is only one Tinker, the brother of Steve Owens, who made a name for himself as a big-play wide receiver from 1972 to 1975.

So just how did Charles Wayne Owens become "Tinker?"

"When I was four or five years old, I loved watching the TV show *Pinky Lee*, Owens recalled recently. "I couldn't say it, they tell me, but I could say 'Tinky,' so my sisters started calling me 'Tinky' and that involved into 'Tinker.' It stuck. Hey, I thought Tinker was definitely better than 'Pinky' or 'Tinky.' I like it better than Charles."

And for the record, Steve Owens isn't Steve Owens. His given name is Loren Everett Owens, "but one of our sisters started calling him 'Little Steve' when he was a kid and it stuck," Tinker said.

Combined, the Owens boys accounted for more than 5,700 yards of offense and 68 touchdowns for Oklahoma.

Nice to Meet You, Joe!

Washington said he was always petrified to approach Bud Wilkinson when the former OU coach occasionally stopped by a

Sooners practice during the 1970s. He never officially met him or shook hands with him until he played in the NFL.

And it had to be one of the most unconventional meetings ever.

"Well, when I was at Oklahoma, I was just scared to introduce myself or speak to him. He was larger than life," Washington recalled. "Then when I was with Baltimore, he is now with St. Louis [as head coach from 1978 to 1979]. And he was still larger than life to me.

"[Before] one game against us, he is walking across the field, and I want to say something to him, but I don't. Finally, during the game, I catch a pitchout and I get run out of bounds on the St. Louis sideline near him. Then I tried to introduce myself to him during the game, so I said something to him.

"He said, 'Look, Joe, I know who you are. It is nice meeting you, now get back to the huddle!'"

Who Was That Iowa Defensive Back?

In 1979 Oklahoma opened the season at home against the Big Ten's Iowa Hawkeyes.

That day Memorial Stadium and the game-day atmosphere in Norman made quite an impression on a young, redshirt freshman defensive back for the Hawkeyes.

"I had heard so much about Norman and what it was like on game days," Bob Stoops said. "I can remember pulling into town and thinking what a neat place this was."

The Sooners defeated Iowa 21–6 that day to begin an 11–1 season, but that experience would someday help bring that particular ex-Hawkeye to Norman when he was needed the most. A great picture endures from that game—Stoops tackling OU's Steve Rhodes as Billy Sims watches in the background.

All these years later, now that the one-time Iowa defensive back has returned Oklahoma to national prominence, who would have thunk it?

chapter 10

The 1980s: From J.C. to Jamelle, Another Title for Barry's Boys

Quarterback J.C. Watts scrambles for yards during action in the Orange Bowl on January 1, 1981. OU defeated Florida State 18–17, and Watts was named the game's MVP.

In 1973 the tiny town of Eufaula, Oklahoma, threw a parade for one of their own, Sooners defensive lineman Lucious Selmon. The oldest of the Selmon boys rode atop a red flat-bed trailer with his head coach, Barry Switzer, directly behind him, as the parade slowly proceeded down Main Street.

Suddenly, Selmon turned to Switzer, pointed, and yelled, "Hey, Coach, see that kid standing over there? That's going to be your quarterback some day. His name is J.C. Watts."

Julius Caesar Watts, just a sophomore in high school, had been killing time outside the town's pool hall. He looked up at Selmon and Switzer, who smiled and waved.

"The thing I remember is that we made eye contact, and he had asked about me in front of all my friends," Watts recalled. "I am telling you, I don't know if life gets any better than that for a 15-year-old kid."

Selmon was correct, because three years later, Watts became a Sooner. After a frustrating start to his career, in which he almost quit the team, he led Oklahoma to a 22–3 record in 25 starts and was Most Valuable Player of the 1980 and '81 Orange Bowl victories over Florida State.

He recorded 3,605 total yards and accounted for 44 touchdowns during his career.

Watts later became a youth minister before serving the state of Oklahoma in the U.S. House of Representatives from 1994 to 2002. He is noted as the first black Republican elected to Congress from a southern state since the Reconstruction. He also wrote his autobiography, *What Color Is a Conservative?*

In other words, Watts came a long way from the Eufaula pool hall. Since retiring from Congress, he has worked as a lobbyist and started his own company. Today, he credits the University of Oklahoma, Switzer, and his experience as a Sooner with helping him succeed.

"The tradition was intact when I went there, and that air of expectancy followed me into politics and into business," he said. "I expected to succeed."

Watts said he really had only one regret with his time at OU. Port Robertson advised him to major in business, but he chose journalism instead.

"He literally begged me to major in business," Watts recalled. "I would change that if I could, but not much else."

Elway's Big Day

The Sooners were coming off an impressive 11–1 season behind the leadership of Watts and Billy Sims heading into the 1980 season.

A 29–7 win over Kentucky at Memorial Stadium was a fine start to the season, and with nine starters back on offense and ranked No. 4 in the country, they were heavy favorites over Stanford in the season's second game.

The field was slick amid a dreary, rainy day September 27 in Norman. That is the day most of the country first learned of a young, blond quarterback named John Elway. Only a sophomore, Elway, working mostly out of the shotgun before the shotgun was as common as it is today, passed for 237 yards and three touchdowns, and ran for 95 and one more touchdown as Stanford shocked the Sooners 31–14.

"I never saw a guy like John Elway before," said Sooners guard Terry Crouch, who watched the Stanford offense from the OU sideline that day. "He would run one way and throw it across the field 50 yards for a touchdown. And he was laughing as he did it."

Oklahoma rebounded to finish 10–2 (the other loss was to Texas, 20–13) and beat Florida State in the Orange Bowl for the second consecutive year, but Elway's big day was what many Sooners remembered from the season.

"It was raining when I attempted to sack their somewhat unknown quarterback," linebacker Sherdeill Breathett recalled recently. "He was an elusive and talented player. Prior to the game, our focus was primarily on stopping their scat back, Darrin Nelson, but he did not play due to an ankle sprain. When John saw me coming at him, he acted as though he would throw the ball, so I jumped into the air to block the pass. That's when he ducked under me and ran, but while I was in the air I kicked him as hard as I could in the face mask—I know I got him good—hoping to bring him down, but it did not phase him, and he rain for a few extra yards before being tackled.

"I must confess that he was one of the toughest if not the toughest quarterbacks I had ever come across. I knew at that moment that he was something special."

Barry Calls Off the Dogs

A few other interesting stories came from the 1980 season.

For example, the Sooners met up with a familiar face when they traveled to Colorado in the game following Elway's national splash. The Buffaloes were coached by former OU head coach Chuck Fairbanks, who had left Norman seven years earlier to coach the NFL's New England Patriots.

This day, the Sooners were putting an 82–42 pounding on a beat-up Colorado team when Fairbanks called in a favor.

"Chuck had lost all his cornerbacks," Switzer recalled. "[Offensive coordinator] Galen [Hall] called down [over the headset] and said, 'You're not going to believe this, but Chuck sent one of his graduate assistants down. He knocked on our door and said that Chuck said, 'Don't run any more options. We're out of cornerbacks and we can't stop you. Hand the ball to the fullback.'

"I said, 'Okay, Coach, let's do it,' and that's what we did. We fixed the fourth quarter!"

L.T.'s Forgettable Appearance in Norman

Before the seventh game of the season, an improving North Carolina team was headed to Norman. The Tar Heels, led by a rising defensive star in Lawrence Taylor and running back "Famous" Amos Lawrence, were talking a good game. They as much as predicted a Tar Heel victory.

"They were a hell of a football team," Switzer recalled. "But I knew what was going to happen to 'em. They played East Carolina the week before, and I talked to [a reporter], and he had talked to the North Carolina people.

"'North Carolina says they're ready to play you, because they just played East Carolina and they run the same wishbone. Same plays, same everything,' the reporter told me.

"I said, 'It's not the same wishbone.' We never ran the option that day toward Lawrence Taylor, and he never made a tackle that day."

"That was a cocky team," OU linebacker Jackie Shipp said of the Tar Heels. "I remember them coming to Norman and talking smack to us before the game. I put a hit on Famous Amos Lawrence that knocked him out of the game."

The Sooners won easily, 41–7.

The Name's "Dick"

A funny story occurred before that game, as Switzer made idle chit-chat with the Tar Heels' head coach on the field during their walk-through practice on Friday at Memorial Stadium.

"I walked up to him and said, 'Hey, Denny, it's great to have you here,'" Switzer recalled. "When I said that, I noticed he just stared at me, didn't smile or anything."

Switzer went on to say "Denny" this and "Denny" that through what was basically a one-sided conversation.

The next day, during the customary coaches meeting at midfield during warmups, Switzer noticed Crum was quiet again but had no idea why. Maybe that was just his personality, Switzer figured.

Following the game, as the two shared a cold handshake, Crum said only, "The name's not Denny; it's Dick."

All this time, Switzer had been invoking the name of the longtime University of Louisville basketball coach Denny Crum.

For the record, Dick Crum, spent 17 seasons as a head coach (10 at North Carolina) and had 117 career victories, making a name for himself—even if OU's head coach didn't know what it was.

"Don't Touch Me, Doc"

Through the years, some Sooners believed in the so-called myth surrounding longtime team doctor Donald O'Donoghue. Legend had it that if he touched you before a game, you would become injured that day.

"They would say, 'Whatever you do, don't let him touch you before the game,'" Shipp said. "'Every guy he has touched before a game has blown out a knee.'

"So before the Missouri game [in 1981], I was sitting there when Doctor O'Donoghue walked by and touched my knee and said, 'Have a good game.'"

Shipp entered the game a nervous wreck. He finished it with Oklahoma's single-game record of 23 tackles. And he completed the game in good health.

Marcus's Huge Day, Wasted Talent

The raw talent of freshman running back Marcus Dupree was on full display in the 1983 Fiesta Bowl. The Mississippi native ran through, around, and over Arizona State's defense, rushing for 239 yards on only 17 carries. But the Sun Devils scored two late touchdowns to rally for a 32–21 win.

Still, Switzer was angry that Dupree, who did not score a touchdown that day, broke several runs into the open field only to be caught from behind.

"Marcus should have had more than 400 yards that day," Switzer wrote in his autobiography. "He said he had a sore hamstring. It looked to me as if Marcus was too heavy and out of shape.

"I lost my head and criticized Marcus in front of the sportswriters afterward. I should not have done that. The teacher should never criticize the student in public."

Dupree started with 138 yards against Stanford in the opening game the next season and then struggled, trying to play overweight. After being held to 50 yards in a 28–16 loss to Texas, he left the team and returned home to Mississippi.

His career amounted to 17 regular season games and 1,274 regular-season yards gained in a Sooners uniform, and he is listed only once in the current OU media guide—under letter winners for the 1982 season. In other words, he is a forgotten man when he possessed the talent to become a legend.

"He might have become the best ever, but we'll never know," Switzer said. "It's really a shame."

"Marcus was an incredible athlete," said OU defensive end Rick Bryan (1980–1983). "He could do it all. The only thing was that Marcus didn't really want to be there. He would have been one of the greatest Sooners in history."

Dupree transferred to Southern Mississippi but never played due to a knee injury. He then had several stints with USFL and NFL teams, but never lived up to his All-Pro potential. As of early 2008, he lives in Tallahassee, Florida. He owns a building company and has two adult sons.

Keith Jackson, the Tight End

From 1984 to 1987, there likely wasn't a better tight end in college football than the Sooners' Keith Jackson.

Did his statistics prove it? No, but when the game was on the line, or just about anytime Jackson touched the football, he made something great happen. Jackson is one Sooner whose career is not defined by his numbers. It's just that the Sooners' wishbone offense wasn't fit perfectly for his talents.

"Really, I don't know why Keith Jackson would come to Oklahoma," Switzer said. "But I am sure glad he did."

There were plenty of times, however, Jackson figured he made a mistake in choosing the Sooners because of OU's wishbone. He caught 15 passes as a freshman, 22 as a sophomore, 15 as a junior, and 16 as a senior.

"He came in my office one day," Switzer recalled, "and he said, 'I need the ball in my hands. You don't throw the ball around here enough for me.'

"I walked him down to the offensive coordinator's office and said, 'I don't care how you do it, but we got a great football player here, let's get the damn ball in his hands.'"

That week, before the 1985 Nebraska game, the Sooners installed a tight-end reverse.

"It was the first third-down of the game, and we were 88 yards from the goal line," Switzer said. "So we called it. Keith runs 88 yards for a touchdown. I said, 'Keith, why didn't you come to me sooner?'"

Aikman Once Was a Sooner

Another future NFL star, Troy Aikman, began his collegiate career in Norman. The Henrietta, Oklahoma, native was a high school superstar and quite a catch for Switzer's recruiting machine, even though he was a drop-back passer and the Sooners ran the wishbone at the time.

Aikman was a superb talent, but he seemed to be a square peg for OU's round hole of an offense.

After Oklahoma started 3–0 in 1985, but scored only 13 points against Minnesota and 14 against Texas, the Sooners struggled mightily against a talented Miami team, losing 27–14 in Norman.

During the game, Miami's 300-pound defensive tackle Jerome Brown, who later would be killed in a car accident, fell on Aikman's leg, breaking it and ending his season. Redshirt freshman Jamelle Holieway sprinted into the huddle, as the offensive veterans suddenly found themselves raising their eyebrows at his confident demeanor.

"I was in the huddle when Jamelle came into the game," Spencer Tillman said. "I think he was 17 at the time. He is even shorter than I am. He didn't have any experience. And he comes in the huddle and says, 'Let's roll.'

"I looked at Lydell [Carr] and said, 'What's this fool talking about?' We lost that game, but we didn't lose another game that season."

Aikman then transferred to UCLA, where he became an All-American in the Bruins' pro-style offense. He was taken with the first pick of the NFL Draft by the Dallas Cowboys, leading them to three Super Bowl championships—the last coached by Switzer himself—and was later inducted into the Pro Football Hall of Fame.

Holieway ranks fourth on OU's total offense list, totaling 5,143 yards. He accounted for 54 touchdowns.

In other words, everything worked out best for all parties.

"In some respects, I am glad that injury happened to Troy," linebacker Brian Bosworth said recently. "He went on to have a fabulous career at UCLA and we got back to Oklahoma football."

The 1985 "Ice Bowl"

The Sooners and Oklahoma State gave in to ESPN's demand that their meeting in 1985 be moved from an afternoon kickoff to 7:00 that night, even though the game was to be played November 30.

It is anybody's guess what kind of weather a late November day, or night in this case, would bring in the state of Oklahoma.

If the game had been played during that day, it would have been played during a typical cold November day. But an ice storm moved through Stillwater that night, turning the playing field into a slippery rink more conducive to a hockey game.

"It was just like an ice rink," Switzer recalled. "We were worried about getting people hurt and freezing at the same time. In all my years of coaching, those were the worst conditions I ever saw."

Oklahoma State managed only 131 yards, and the Sooners recorded a 13–0 shutout.

National Champions Once Again

Thanks largely to Holieway's surprising performance over those final eight games, that '85 team never lost after meeting Miami and, in reality, did not play another close game.

The Sooners had whipped rival Nebraska 27–7 in the previous game, before taking care of SMU 35–13 in the final regular-season game, setting up a meeting with Penn State in the Orange Bowl.

And again, as they had been 10 years earlier, they were the benefactors of the No. 1 team stubbing its toe. The first time it was Ohio State being shocked in the Rose Bowl, allowing Switzer to win his second national title.

This time, it was the Hurricanes themselves and Switzer's old pal Jimmy Johnson, whose top-ranked team was clobbered by huge underdog Tennessee, 35–7, in the Sugar Bowl, opening the door for Oklahoma.

And the Sooners kicked it in, winning Switzer's third and final national championship.

"Just before the game, I heard somebody say, 'Hey, man, Miami just got beat in the Sugar Bowl,'" Bosworth recalled.

"All of a sudden, we were all looking at each other and thinking, '"This is it. We are now playing for all the marbles,'" guard Anthony Phillips recalled.

Oklahoma had a relatively easy time with Penn State, beating the Nittany Lions 25–10, but the game was not as close as the score indicates.

"That was pretty easy, because they weren't very good," Bosworth said.

"Walking off the field that night, knowing we were the best team in the nation," guard Mark Hutson recalled, "it was the best feeling I ever had in any form of athletics."

chapter 11

Two Sides of "The Boz"

Love him or hate him, Brian Bosworth is a memorable figure in Sooners lore.

There undoubtedly has not been a player or a figure in the rich history of Oklahoma football as polarizing as Brian Bosworth.

On the field, he could be dominating and imposing, an All-American linebacker in the truest sense of the definition. In the classroom, he worked to become an honor student and had the brains of an Ivy Leaguer. In front of a microphone or a camera, he often could appear as a first-class jerk or an immature brat sporting an unconventional haircut that was painted different colors at different times.

Some OU fans loved him. Some may have despised him. Some loved him *and* despised him simultaneously, while most just wished they could have the good Bosworth the player without hearing from "The Boz" caricature he had created.

And by the time he had left Norman, a junior who had gained the NCAA's wrath and had declared himself eligible for the NFL Draft, almost everybody affiliated with the Sooners—fans, teammates, coaches, and administrators—were ready for him to go.

"I made mistakes, but I learned from them," Bosworth said recently. "I have three kids now, and time does go by pretty quickly, but that program and school still are important to me. I still watch their games, and it is important to me that Oklahoma does well. It hurts me when they lose.

"The funny thing is, I still dream about my time there. I dream a few times every month about being in the locker room, hearing one of Switzer's speeches, or I dream something like being stuck in traffic while the game is starting without me."

Bosworth grew up in Irving, Texas, the son of a hard-nosed veteran who pushed his son to be the best football player he could be. He drilled Brian to be tough and strong as he taught him the fundamentals of the game.

"He worked me so hard when I was young because I think he wanted me to achieve," Bosworth said of his father, Austin Bosworth. "That's a big reason why I worked so hard—so I wouldn't disappoint him. He started me playing football in the Pop Warner League, and I loved it from the beginning."

Bosworth also credits his grandfather, who lived in Oklahoma and was a big Sooners fan, with planting the seed that he could play the game and someday become a Sooner.

"He told me once, 'If you ever make it big, buy me a pink Cadillac,'" Bosworth recalled.

By the time Brian reached MacArthur High in Dallas, he played quarterback and defensive end and already was a college prospect. Following his senior year, he had committed first to Southern Methodist and then to Texas A&M before Barry Switzer visited his school.

"I was sitting in the cafeteria telling my buddies, 'I am going to A&M,'" he recalled. "And I look up and see this huge mink coat standing at the entrance to the cafeteria. Nobody in Texas wears a mink coat. Then I heard this booming voice coming from the mink coat, 'Where's Bosworth? Where's Bosworth? I know he wants one of these.'"

"Somebody at our table said, 'That's Barry Switzer!'"

"He was showing his national championship ring," Bosworth recalled.

Once Bosworth visited Norman, he put SMU and A&M in his rearview mirror.

"As I walked around, I just knew, 'This is where I am supposed to be.'"

When it came time to assign numbers, Bosworth had to stick up for himself to get Switzer to stick to a promise.

"He gave me 44, and I think Lydell Carr was a big recruit who also wanted 44," Bosworth recalled. "He came to me and said, 'Boz, we want to give your number to Lydell Carr.'

"I said, 'Coach, you made a promise—you ain't giving my number away.'"

After a redshirt season, he was instantly growing into one of the Sooners leaders, which Switzer had appointed him to be, leading up to the 1984 game against Texas. Earlier that week, his girlfriend broke up with him and told him she was dating a Texas student. Then she asked for tickets to the Red River Shootout.

So as he was being interviewed before that game, Bosworth gave the local reporters a notebook full.

"I f*cking hate Texas," he said. "I hate their colors. I hate the city of Austin. I don't like [Texas coach] Fred Akers. That's why I didn't go to Texas! I am so mad, I can't wait to play them Saturday!"

Some 20 years later, Bosworth recalled, "That's when 'The Boz' was born. I wasn't even thinking at the time, but that quote was going from my mouth to this guy's pen to a newspaper to the bulletin board at Texas.

"Coach Switzer called me in and said, 'What are you, Bulletin Board Bosworth?'"

That game ended in a 15–15 tie, and as Bosworth proudly says, "I never lost to them or Nebraska or Oklahoma State. A loss to Texas really would have haunted me all these years."

By the end of his junior season, Bosworth had captured the first two Butkus Awards, recorded 413 tackles (sixth on OU's career list), was a three-time All–Big 8 player, two-time All-American, and an Academic All-American to boot.

But as the Sooners prepared for the Orange Bowl game against Arkansas, Bosworth tested positive for steroids, and the NCAA suspended him from the game. During the game, he appeared on the OU sideline wearing a T-shirt that read: "The NCAA: National Communists Against Athletes."

University administrators understandably were upset and wanted Bosworth disciplined.

"I didn't say much until I looked at the tape of the game to see for myself," Switzer wrote in his autobiography. "Then I phoned [athletics director] Donnie Duncan and said, 'Bosworth is through here. He will not play his senior year.'"

That forced the linebacker's hand; he had no choice but to declare himself eligible for the NFL Draft.

As the years have passed, Bosworth knew he had crossed the line.

"I have always regretted wearing that T-shirt," Bosworth admitted. "I never regretted the message, but it was the way I put that message out there that was wrong. I made a statement on a stage in which my team was the main cast member, and I shouldn't have done it. And I certainly shouldn't have done it with that T-shirt.

"I made a poor choice in Miami and, after that, it kind of forced Switzer's hand that it was time for The Boz to move on. So leaving after my junior season was the right thing to do, according to the people around me. In my heart, it really wasn't."

In fact, Bosworth apologized publicly to many of the Sooners greats during the filming of an OU Legends Reunion in 2003.

He broke down and cried as he told them, "I think I shamed the program in a lot of ways and I want to apologize to each and every one of you guys. I took my shirt off [in Miami] and I think that is when I shamed the program. At that point, I was out of control and I thought I was bigger than the program, when it fact, the program was responsible for making me a man."

He also penned an autobiography, titled—what else?—*The Boz.*

It is a tag that even Switzer came to abhor.

"I loved Brian," he said.

"The Boz was an asshole who strutted around Norman like he owned the place, stiffing and intimidating people," Switzer wrote in his autobiography. "Bosworth's worst enemy was his mouth. At the sight of a TV camera, he would break into an outrageous song and dance."

To this day, however, Bosworth and Switzer remain good friends.

"He has been a very good friend to me," Bosworth said. "He told me when he recruited me that I would be part of that family, and you never turn your back on your family. A lot of people turned their backs on me, but he wasn't one of them. He believed in Brian. I wasn't The Boz to him."

Serious shoulder injuries limited Bosworth's NFL career to a mere 24 games with the Seattle Seahawks.

He maintained recently that, "Had I not been hurt I would have been the best frickin' linebacker to play the game, no question. But every athlete has to think and play like that, and accept what happens. And I do."

Today, Bosworth lives in Malibu, California, and works in several business ventures, including real estate and acting. He has appeared in 10 movies.

"Life is good," he said. "And I am happy."

chapter 12

Port Robertson: If You Needed Discipline, He "Loaned" You Some

Port Robertson, shown here in 1953, was one of the greatest wrestlers and later wrestling coaches in NCAA history. But he will never be forgotten by Sooners football players because of his longtime job as academic guidance counselor. Robertson was considered the disciplinarian who complimented Bud Wilkinson's mild-mannered management perfectly. Photo courtesy of University of Oklahoma.

Through the decades of Oklahoma's football greatness, there may have been one man the Sooners players of the 1940s, '50s, and '60s respected and, finally, grew to love as much as Bud Wilkinson.

There was one man that the players later feared even more than Chuck Fairbanks and, even more recently, wanted to please more than Barry Switzer.

He didn't play football, but he was a teacher, coach, and a leader at Oklahoma in various capacities over four decades. He inspired them to achieve academically and socially, and drove them physically to limits they never thought they could reach.

He oozed discipline as if it flowed from his sweat glands.

And even though he made his official mark on the athletic world in wrestling, and as an assistant football coach for OU for 19 years, he was beloved by most Sooners football players for his role as the athletic guidance counselor from 1954 to 1986.

When you envision the degree of courage and the type of man it required to rush those German machine guns that fateful June day of the Normandy invasion in 1944, you picture a man like him, his barrel chest and meaty arms just a symbol for the inner strength he possessed.

Yes, Port Glen Robertson was a man's man.

When Tom Brokaw wrote the book *The Greatest Generation*, he had people of Port's character and integrity in mind.

Port was the John Wayne and the Abe Lincoln of Oklahoma, if you will. He was as tough as he was honest. He also was a Sooner's Sooner, bleeding Crimson and Cream.

"Everybody has a Port Robertson story," said Jack Mildren, OU's quarterback from 1969 to 1971. "He is a legend around Oklahoma."

If Wilkinson, Fairbanks, and Switzer were the faces of Sooners football, Robertson was the backbone. If those head coaches were the brains of the program, Robertson was the soul.

Robbie Robertson, in his mid-eighties these days while living on a quiet dead-end street in Norman, still follows the Sooners and loves Oklahoma. And when the subject of his oldest brother comes up, he gets misty-eyed.

"Let me tell you what an exceptional person he was," Robbie said recently of Port, who was 10 years older. "When he was working on his master's degree in Michigan, he worked at a rug-cleaning outfit. Port was a very frugal person and didn't spend much, but he never once came home without finding my billfold to slide a little money into it when I was asleep."

Port Robertson was born in 1914 in Harrah, Oklahoma, the second of five children, but was raised on a farm outside of Edmond. He starred in wrestling, track, and football at Edmond High, winning the state wrestling title at 155 pounds in 1933.

He wanted terribly to play football for the Sooners, but a knee injury during his freshman season steered him back to wrestling. There, he thrived. Under coach Paul Keen, Robertson won 20 of 24 matches and two Big 6 conference titles (1935 and '37). He graduated with a degree in history in 1937 and earned his master's in history from the University of Michigan four years later.

Port was married August 1, 1939. The Robertsons' first child, Jerry, was born on March 30, 1944. Their second child, Jane Ann, was born on October 19, 1945.

Before he ever saw his children, however, he was on his way to becoming a war hero.

After he quickly achieved the rank of captain, he was credited with saving many lives during the swim ashore of the Normandy invasion. A few weeks later, as a forward artillery observer, while sitting in a foxhole providing coordinates for artillery fire on German positions, he was narrowly missed by an incoming round. However, the explosion shattered his walkie-talkie into his left ear. Subsequently, he struggled with hearing loss his entire life and was scarred on the left side of his face. He earned the Bronze Star and Purple Heart for his heroics, although he proved he was a modest man with no pretense or braggadocio.

"He got the Silver Star for gallantry, and nobody knew it," Robbie Robertson said. "He never told anybody about it. We only knew it because somebody called the house about it. Can you imagine that?"

No Sooner, either, ever recalls Port mentioning Normandy or his heroics during the war.

"The scar was most visible on his left ear," said Leon Cross, an OU lineman who knew Port well. "Since he was a wrestler at OU, all of us thought the scar was a 'cauliflower ear,' which many of the wrestlers in his era sustained since they didn't wear protective head gear. He never told us he had been severely wounded during the Normandy invasion."

When the war ended, Robertson returned to Norman to coach the OU wrestling team for 15 years, producing three NCAA championship teams (1951, '52, and '57) and three national runners-up. His wrestlers captured 15 individual NCAA titles and five outstanding wrestler awards.

When it came to his coaching strategy, Port firmly believed that the goal of a wrestler is to win by a fall. Over a span of eight national tournaments, his Sooners pinned 39 opponents, 11 of them in their 1957 NCAA championship matches.

In 1960 he coached the U.S. Olympic team to three individual gold medals—the only such success between the Olympiads of 1932 and 1972—and a team silver medal, finishing behind the Soviets.

One of his favorite sayings to his wrestlers was, "A lean dog is lots hungrier than a fat one."

He once defined his approach to recruiting as a wrestling coach bluntly: "First of all, a boy has to want to come here to get an education. If he thinks wrestling is more important than that, he's not going to do well in either. Then he has to realize what it takes to be a good wrestler. It depends on how much of himself he wants to spend. He has to learn to know himself. Once he gets self-discipline in wrestling, he'll have it throughout his life."

OU wrestler John Eagleton once said, "If you are an average wrestler, Port will make you a good one. If you are a good wrestler, Port will make you a great wrestler."

Two-time NCAA champion Tommy Evans (1952 and '54), who later coached the Sooners to the 1960 and 1963 national championships, admitted once that he owed just about all his success to his mentor.

"I never would have made it without Port," said Evans, who died in March 2008, at the age of 77. "I really owe everything to him. He was like a father to me. In fact, it's a good bet that many, many OU wrestlers and football players wouldn't have graduated without Port's help."

Robertson's role in providing a model for educating thousands of Sooners is the role in which he is best known. In 1954 he was named athletic guidance counselor, succeeding Frank "Pop" Ivy. It was a position he held for the next three decades.

In other words, he was the away-from-home father of hundreds of Sooners, teaching them to study, to go to class, and subsequently, graduate. But more than that, he taught them the discipline required to live a successful life.

"He continued to be a force in my life long after I got off the mat," recalled Ed Corr, an OU wrestler along with twin brother Bert, in the mid-1950s. "He helped direct me through life."

Or, as Eddie Lancaster, a lineman in the 1960s, put it, "Port was an angel given to a bunch of boys to drive us to manhood—and we all loved him as our own father."

President Teddy Roosevelt always joked about speaking softly and carrying a big stick. It was no joke to Port—he spoke sternly and actually carried a big stick. It was back in the day when he could use it, too, without fear of litigation, termination, or an athlete's mommy complaining to the OU president.

If a football player missed a class, ran afoul of dorm rules, or even failed to keep his room tidy, he was summoned to Port's office.

"For Dad, I think it was 'the good-cop, bad-cop' situation," Jay Wilkinson said recently. "He didn't have to resort to any negative type of control over his players because Port was the enforcer."

"Port was the disciplinarian," Bob "Hog" Harrison, the OU center from 1956 to 1958, said. "You had to keep your room clean and he made you into a gentleman, whether you wanted to be one or not."

To deliver his message, Robertson utilized unique sayings and his own terminology, known as "Portisms," which became a campus-wide language for student-athletes at Oklahoma. For instance, when referring to grades, he called A's "Alphas," B's "Bravos," C's "Charley's," D's "Dogs," and F's "Flags." If you received any Flags, you were certain to be spending extra time with Port.

His pupils were known as "little dogs" or more often, "pea heads."

"I loved his colorful terms for grades," said Bart Conner, the gold-medal-winning Olympic gymnast who attended OU. "I always loved Port's meeting at the start of every semester. He would scare the heck out of all of us. First, he would warn us about keeping our grades up. Then, of course, he would lecture us about not having TVs in our rooms or about making sure our girlfriends were out of the dorm by a certain hour of the night.

"Sometimes, I wondered what kind of man was behind that tough exterior."

Port was a stickler for personal discipline and wanted his pupils to realize that even the smallest details spoke volumes about themselves. For example, one time he had summoned Danny Mullen (1970–1972) to his office while his roommate, Bill Orendorff, happened to tag along.

"In the middle of my ass-chewing, Port looked at Oren and said, "'Mr. Orendorff, did you shave this morning?'"

"Bill stammered for an answer, but before he could finish, Port asked, 'How long has it been since you had a haircut?'

"Then as he stood to leave, Port noticed his shirt-tail was out. Port then stopped him in his tracks as only he could do and had Bill go over to the wall, standing only inches away. He had to hit his head on the wall 'so we could hear it.'

"As Bill slammed his head on the wall, Port resumed his ass-chewing on me as if nothing out of the ordinary was happening. It was classic."

Another time, Mullen once told Port that he wanted to be like "the average students."

So Port grabbed him by the ear, walked him over to the window of the study hall, and pointed out a few students walking by who happened to have long hair and appeared as if they needed a bath and a shave.

"That is what *average* looks like," Port told him. "If you want to be average, you don't belong at Oklahoma."

A religious man, Robertson held 5:30 AM prayer meetings at the football stadium for the student-athletes who wanted to attend.

One of the best stories that details Port's faith is this one from Wade Walker, the Sooners' All-American lineman in the 1940s who later became the OU athletics director. He once asked Port how and why he never uttered a curse word.

"Well, I made a deal with the Lord at Normandy," Port told him, in one of his very rare references to his World War II experience, "and I have tried to live up to that promise."

An extraordinary thought from an extraordinary man.

Each day, when his prayer meetings concluded, Port supervised the running of the stadium steps—the main conditioning tactic that led to the Sooners being in better shape than most of their opponents during Wilkinson's championship seasons.

The scariest sight for any OU football player was to see a small yellow piece of paper that read: "See me, PGR" taped to his dormitory door.

Normally, it meant there was some type of transgression that ultimately required the running of the stadium steps—72 rows up and 72 rows down. Over and over again. It didn't matter if you were a walk-on freshman or a senior All-American. Port treated you the same, and you ran those 72 rows until you threw up whatever meal preceded the punishment. Furthermore, the transgressors could not jog up the steps—they had to reach the top in 15 seconds—or they had to be run again. And again.

It is a fact that most Sooners football players from the 1950s through the 1980s memorized each and every one of those 72 steps. And Robertson had little patience or sympathy for those who couldn't handle it.

"Needless to say, there are a bunch of athletes who tossed their cookies while attempting to meet Port's demands," Leon Cross said. "Ronnie Payne, a football player from Breckenridge, Texas, got very sick one day on about his 12th trip up and down the steps.

"He was lying on his back throwing up into the morning air. Port approached him and said, 'Mr. Payne, please roll over on your side. You are a disgusting sight!'"

Cross said that Payne never missed another class while at Oklahoma.

"At first, you could hit every other step," Bob Flanagan said of his stadium-step strategy. "But about halfway up, the steps got steeper, so you had to hit every one. If you didn't make the time, yours didn't count, and I wanted all of mine to count."

One of the saddest days for Port was when the university added backs to the seats of the stadium benches, taking away one of the greatest forms of discipline. He adjusted, having them run the narrow isle stairs or washing dishes.

Of Port's many sayings and monikers, none is more famous than the "pea head" tag.

It is likely that every Sooner from the late 1940s through 1986 was at least once labeled a "pea head." And there were different levels of "pea head"—some affectionate, some derogatory, and some in jest.

One time, Port, who was a stickler for requiring his charges to dress appropriately for study hall, noticed a hippy-looking young man wearing cut-off shorts, a dirty T-shirt, and flip-flops. Port proceeded to berate the transgressor as he thumped him on the forehead with his keys. Meanwhile, the rest of the room broke into hearty laughter.

"What are you pea-heads laughing at?" Port asked them.

"Coach," one of them answered, "that's the tutor you hired for us."

"This is my favorite Port story," Lancaster said. "My freshman year, we were all having lunch when across the table from me was David 'Hog' Hammond. Hog was squeezing the ketchup from [one of] those squirt bottles, and it splashed all over my white shirt. I called him a dirty name and picked up the mustard bottle, and he ran. I chased him to the door and I shot a stream of mustard from his feet to his head.

"As the door opened, there was none other than Port Robertson entering the dining hall. I was caught red-handed.

"Port looked at me and said, 'Eddie J. Lancaster, and by the way, I don't like that…'

"He was referring to the fact I have no middle name, just a middle initial. But he continued, 'Pea head! Be in my office at 1:00 PM and bring your room key!' I almost passed out. I had an hour to worry. Once there, he asked me, 'How many freshmen do we have on scholarship on our football team?'

"I answered, 'Coach, I think it's 95.'

"Port looked at me and said, 'Well, you may not be as dumb as you look.' Then he said, 'If you're not number 95, you're number 94! Guys like you do not screw up, or we'll drop you like a bag of dirt.'

"I thought he was going to ask for my room key and I was being sent home. He hesitated for what seemed like an hour and said, 'Meet me at the stadium tomorrow morning at 6:30 and don't let the doorknob hit you in the butt on the way out of here!'"

The next day, Lancaster ran stadium steps with all the other "pea heads" who either skipped a class or did something to gain Port's ire.

"Seventy-two rows, and I counted every one," Lancaster recalled. "I don't remember how many we ran, but everyone but me ended up throwing up. Anyway, he sent everyone who puked to the dorm and told me to stay. Then he made me roll from one end zone to the other as he walked beside me. After I finished the first 100 yards, I looked up at him and asked, 'Coach, you're trying to make me puke, aren't you?'

"'You are not as dumb as you look!' he said as he gave me the slightest of grins.

"As I started rolling back to the other end zone, I forced my finger down my throat, which is no easy task as you're rolling—and I forced myself to throw up. He then sent me back to the dorm and said he would 'break my plate' if I pulled any other stunts, meaning I wouldn't get to eat in the dining hall.

"I was never in trouble with Port again."

The discipline didn't begin and end with academics and athletics, however. Making sure his pea heads kept their dorms in order, Port's dorm inspections would make a Marine drill sergeant envious.

"Port would come over to the dorm during class hours every now and then and do a room check," Flanagan remembered. "Beds needed to be made the military way so he could bounce a coin off the top of them. Everything needed to be in its place. And he would inspect with the infamous 'finger swipe.' Any dust picked up on that finger from anywhere was reason enough for the stadium steps."

Another weapon Port used was memorizing every student's middle name. Then he used it to get their attention.

"Port always memorized the middle names of the freshmen, so he would call them 'John Henry' or 'James Patrick,'" his brother Robbie recalled. "Once, I asked him, 'Why do you do that?'

"'So they knew I have gone to the trouble of finding it out,' he told me. 'Then they wonder just how much more I know about them.'"

Just because he was disciplined and old-school, don't for a minute think that Port didn't have a great sense of humor, either. It was just as dry as the old Oklahoma Plains during the Dust Bowl.

Once, he and Gomer Jones were riding in a car in Miami during the week of an Orange Bowl. Suddenly, some birds hit the windshield.

"Were those birds?" Jones asked Robertson.

"Well," Port said, "they had feathers, beaks, and wings, and they were flying when they hit the car..."

Another time, Wilkinson asked Port how Wahoo McDaniel, not one of the Sooners' better students in the 1950s, was progressing in class.

"I guess I'll have to enroll him in Sand Piles 1," Port answered. "I had him enrolled in Sand Piles 2, but he got covered up!"

Another time, Port told the story of a freshman who had been raised on a farm and wasn't too worldly. Once on campus, he had trouble grasping his surroundings or the hectic balance between class, studying, and the responsibilities of football.

Port, who also was a farmer, walked him over to the armory and pointed to the huge clock on the union building.

"When the big hand is on 12 and the little hand is on three, Coach Wilkinson would like you to report to practice," he told the player.

Later, Port cracked, "The darned kid got the hands mixed up and showed up for practice at 12:15."

Here are a few more memories of Port:

Bob Warmack, OU quarterback (1966–1968): "One summer Port needed help hauling hay at his farm, so he got about four of us to help him. We thought we would work Port into the ground, but guess what? He never broke stride. He worked us into the ground. I never drank so much Kool-Aid at lunch in my life. I made $19 that day, and it was the hardest $19 I ever made."

Charles Bowman, OU lineman (1957): "In the spring of 1956 Port advised Bud Wilkinson to take an interest in a new organization called the Fellowship of Christian Athletes. A former team manager for Hank Iba at Oklahoma A&M had founded FCA in the late 1940s. Coach Wilkinson listened to Port and agreed to have FCA representatives speak to the football team. Following a spring practice one day, Doak Walker, Otto Graham, and Pepper Martin spoke to the team and coaches in the football dormitory. I believe that meeting gave that team a vision of what they should be and could be beyond football. Port was never given the credit for the championships in football, but no one ever doubted how important he was to the entire university."

Dick Gwinn, OU wrestler and lineman (1955–1959): "After my senior year of football, I spent some time rolling around the wrestling room. I had gone home to Tulsa one weekend when Stan Abel called to tell me that Dale Lewis, our heavyweight, had gotten sick, and the team wanted me to go on a wrestling trip to Colorado and Wyoming. We had won matches at Fort Collins and Greeley, Colorado, and were on our way to Laramie, Wyoming. The team was traveling in two cars, one driven by Tommy Evans and the other by Coach Robertson. He was driving a little over the speed limit, and we hit some black ice. The car spun around in circles a number of times, completely out of control. We slid off the road backwards onto the I-70 median.

"Coach Robertson calmly shifted to second gear and drove back onto the interstate. It was silent for a couple of minutes, until he said, 'Anybody have a weight problem?'

"Stan answered, 'Let me shake out my pants and then I'll tell you.'"

"I will never forget those times," Gwinn added. "Port was a father figure to a majority of us. He taught us responsibility and kept us morally straight, and if you had any kind of problem, he was the first one you went to for advice and help. I never recall him swearing or doing anything out of character. He was a tough, consistent, caring man. I miss him every day, and I believe the young people of today have no idea what they have missed by not having a man like Port in their lives."

Shortly before he died in 2004, Prentice Gautt wrote this in an email: "Port was the consummate father figure for us. He was there for support and structure in our lives. And while he cajoled us with his endearing term 'pea head,' we all had joy in our hearts when branded with that label, for we knew he truly cared. His intentional, circumstantial, and ultimate behavioral requirements—with a spiritual priority—have served as a model and remain with us through the years. Many have passed them on."

Flanagan credits Robertson with changing the direction of his life. During his senior year, he had gotten drunk and had gotten into an altercation with a man he thought was a student.

"I almost punched him," Flanagan recalled. "I was always mean and a jerk when I was drunk. The man I had almost beat up was a professor and he wanted my scalp. Word got back to Port somehow. The professor wanted me kicked out of school. Then Port did something I will always remember."

Robertson sent Greg Ruth, an Olympic wrestler, to talk to the professor, trying to persuade him to accept an apology from Flanagan. It worked, Flanagan was spared, and he earned a 3.4 GPA during his senior year before graduating.

"Without a degree, I would have been headed to Vietnam and I would not have come back," he said. "I am too tall and too blind. I certainly did not deserve the help Port gave me, but I think he did something that saved my life.

"Something happened in that last year to turn things around and put priorities in perspective. That something was Port Robertson. I am now in my sixties, and I wake up each day and put my O Club ring on my finger. I remember what it is to be a Sooner and I am proud that I was. But above all else in my life, I remember the man with the barrel chest who taught me the beginnings of being responsible for my actions."

To his ultimate credit, Robertson never stopped caring for his pupils once they moved on, either. His heart, those close to him said, was as big as the state of Oklahoma.

"It was the spring of 1966, and I had left OU and was coaching at Kansas State," Jerry Thompson recalled. "I was out of town on a recruiting trip (remember, there were no cell phones back then), so when I returned the next day, I discovered that my house had burned. It was half-gone, and my wife and two boys had moved to a motel.

"The first person to call [at the motel] was Port. He was known as being direct, so he said something like, 'Give it to me straight and don't beat around the bush—how much money do you need to get by? Tell me now and I'll wire it to you today.'"

Bud Belz, an OU wrestler, details Port's generosity with this story.

"In 1963 OU won the NCAA wrestling championship, but I was injured and unable to make the trip to the nationals," Belz recalled. "Tommy Evans was mad at Bill Carter, the defending national champion, for not going to the nationals. Carter, on advice from his doctor, was told not to wrestle to avoid further injury. I think Evans did not feel Carter's doctor was credible.

"Anyway, after the team won the championship, all members were presented a ceremonial watch. To avoid presenting one to Carter, Evans also did not give a watch to me since I did not wrestle, either. When Port found out about this, he gave me his watch. I will never forget his generosity. And that watch has always meant a lot to me."

In 1977, in recognition of his achievements and leadership as a coach—and his lasting influence on the lives of young men—Port

G. Robertson was honored as a Distinguished Member of the National Wrestling Hall of Fame.

In 1984 Oklahoma held a roast for Port, who was near retirement. Hundreds of his former pupils showed up and spent a night telling stories and jokes, but ended the evening by telling Port how much he meant to all of them.

Then he stood in front of the podium and told them:

> I have thought about this many times, and I am sure most of you have wondered why I have stayed here so long. But I want to tell you this, generally speaking, I had a captive audience. I am very sincere about this, but I have had the best job at the University of Oklahoma. I generally try to say things that I mean and I try to mean things that I say. I have been through three presidents, two interim presidents, and five head football coaches. All of us have been helped along the way at one time or another, and I think it behooves us to remember that. We try to help other people along through life. Not many people get to stand up and see as many friends as I have here tonight. In fact, in life, you can about count your friends on one hand, maybe two. I really want to express to you how I feel about you. I think all of us would agree that the ultimate lesson in athletics is to have self-discipline. Now, I think all of you would agree that when you were freshmen and sophomores and even one or two juniors, you didn't have all of the self-discipline you needed, so I tried to loan you a little now and then. I do want to stand up here and tell you I love every one of you. When you left my office [after being disciplined], I never told you this, but I may have been feeling as bad as you were, maybe worse.
>
> It's been meaningful to me. It's been a meaningful life. Finally, I want to tell you that you are not looking at the handsomest guy on the block. I am sure that you know I am not the smartest guy on the block. But I do want you to know, I am the most *grateful* guy on the block.

With that, he sat down to a standing ovation that lasted several minutes.

In 1986 he retired from Oklahoma. Today, the school's wrestling building is named the "Port Robertson Wrestling Facility."

"The thing that is accurate is to say that all he did for all the people at Oklahoma all those years made him happy," Robbie Robertson said. "It made him very happy inside."

"I will say this about Port Robertson," Switzer said. "There is no individual in the University of Oklahoma athletic history that had more positive influence on people—in every sport, not just football.

"All of the athletes that passed through OU have great stories about Port...and most of them have to do with disciplinary issues. But nobody was more respected."

When hundreds of former wrestlers, football players, and OU administrators held a surprise 83rd birthday party for Port, Phil Waller, who served as "Little Red" for years, noticed the respect everyone had for their mentor when he walked slowly through the door of the restaurant.

While the crowd sang "Happy Birthday," the men at Max Boydston's (1951–1954) table "suddenly hit him for smoking," Waller noted.

"That's the kind of respect we have for you, Port," Waller said, pointing to Robertson. "Here we are, all of us in our fifties and sixties, and we don't want you to see any of us doing something wrong."

Before he blew out the candles that day, Port addressed the crowd: "Looking out over the crowd here and seeing the fellas I see, I knew them when they were freshmen. I watched them over the years, and I see some of them with gray hair now. When you work with young people, no matter how hard you work, no matter how long you work, it is rewarding.

"I saw them as something beside being athletes. I want you to know I never had a birthday like this one. I never thought I would get a chance to thank you like this. All in all, I am very grateful to you."

Flanagan said he last saw Port before an OU game in 2000.

"He looked frail, but he had a big smile on his face," Flanagan recalled. "I caught his eye and, before I could speak, I heard, 'Well, my gosh, Bob Flanagan, how are you doing?'"

He introduced Port to his wife, Karin, whom he met in Lake Tahoe in 1966 through a summer job that Robertson had arranged (the couple now has three children and two grandchildren), as he said, "This is the man who had a great impact on my life, more than he'll ever know."

"Thank you, Bob," Port replied.

Flanagan then whispered into his ear, "Thank you, Coach, for all that you did for me," and he kissed him on his cheek.

"I keep a picture of Port on my work desk now," Flanagan said. "It's of him, sitting behind his desk, an 'OU' on his blazer, eyes straight ahead, with a very slight smile on his face. You can almost make out his barrel chest.

"That picture reminds me to work hard, to have courage, and to ask for help if you need it and to do the right thing. I don't think Port is gone. He's a part of me and a part of a lot of other people out there. He is the one who helped me become a good man."

In his final months as illness took over, many of his former students, wrestlers, and football players visited Port, who died June 10, 2003.

"I know one thing," his brother Robbie said recently. "They just don't make 'em like Port anymore."

chapter 13

Barry Switzer: From Crossett to the Hall of Fame

Barry Switzer holds a banner and indicates his Sooners are No. 1 after beating Michigan in the Orange Bowl on January 1, 1976.

"I guarantee you that I am a fighter, I am a winner, and I am a competitor—and you will be, too!"

"That's the first thing I heard Barry Switzer say," recalled Jimbo Elrod, an Oklahoma defensive end from 1973 to 1975.

It was spring practice, 1973. Sooners head coach Chuck Fairbanks had just accepted a job with the New England Patriots, and the University of Oklahoma decided to promote his young offensive coordinator to replace him.

That day, he gathered his team around him, and in his first speech as the head coach, delivered those words.

Overnight there was a new king of the OU football throne, and over the next 16 seasons he certainly proved to the college football world that he was a fighter, a winner, and a competitor—and he made his Sooners all those things, adding three more national championship trophies and 12 Big 8 titles to the school's trophy case.

More than 35 years later, those trophies are located in the Barry Switzer Center, a sprawling complex on the south end of Memorial Stadium.

For Switzer, who turned 70 on October 5, 2007, having a building named for him finalized a long, winding road from Crossett, Arkansas, to Norman, Oklahoma, to Dallas and back to Norman and on to the College Football Hall of Fame.

"When I see the [Barry Switzer Center] and I think about the Hall of Fame, I think of the hundreds of kids, coaches, and other people who made it all possible," Switzer said recently. "That's really how I look at it. It didn't happen just because of me."

Switzer has transformed from a tough, overachieving player to a workaholic assistant coach, to a swashbuckling, shoot-from-the-lip head coach who won championships and took few prisoners, to an embarrassed ex-coach who was forced to resign or be fired from the only job he ever loved, to a Super Bowl champion, to a retired grandfather of eight, gracefully living the good life.

And along the way, he shaped his own unique legend.

When he first arrived in Norman as an assistant coach for Jim Mackenzie in 1966, he knew exactly who and where he was. He was an Arkansas native, first a Razorbacks linebacker from 1956 to 1959 and then an assistant coach under Frank Broyles. And he realized he was stepping into a place where a college football dynasty once thrived, and where it possibly could exist again.

"I knew all about Oklahoma's winning tradition before I arrived," he said. "I knew all about Bud Wilkinson's great teams and the 47-game winning streak and all that. For starters, Bud Wilkinson was a giant—he cast a huge shadow. The way he carried himself...he really could have been a college professor. He was a very intelligent guy. He kind of had that Billy Graham look about him."

One more thing Switzer knew: he could never become Wilkinson. He was a country boy who liked to throw around an expletive now and then and throw down a stiff drink once in a while.

An assistant for the first six years at Oklahoma, Switzer worked hard at developing offenses for five of those years for Fairbanks, who became head coach when Mackenzie suddenly died of a heart attack. Just 29 years old, he immersed himself into the nuts and bolts of the game as OU's offensive coordinator, convincing Fairbanks to switch to the wishbone offense in 1970.

"I threw myself into the job because I was an unbridled young assistant coach full of enthusiasm—and I knew we were going to win big," he said.

The wishbone almost immediately became Oklahoma's identity. Once that happened, in addition to an aggressive recruiting strategy to raid the state of Texas as consistently as possible, the Sooners soon reached the pinnacle of the sport—again.

Then, when Fairbanks had decided to leave for the NFL, Switzer took his last step up the coaching ladder.

Despite not having head-coaching experience at the age of 35, he won big immediately, starting his career with a 29–0–1 record over the first 30 games and never looking back. He was on his way to becoming the school's winningest coach with a 157–29–4 record—an .837 winning percentage that was higher than even Wilkinson's.

"I had a fun ride as the Oklahoma Sooners won a lot of games, three national championships, 12 Big 8 Championships," he said. "Let me tell you—it went by pretty fast."

A Coach Who Loved His Players

Aside from winning, obviously, what made Switzer popular among his players was that he was real and genuine to them. He connected with them and told them how he felt most of the time, a far cry from football coaches of the 1950s and '60s who worked players into the ground while their main form of communication was grumbling and growling. Switzer cried in front of his players, laughed with them, wrapped his arms around them, and helped them through the difficult times off the field.

When football coaches say they love a certain player, you don't really know if they love that player's ability to win games for them, or they love that player's attitude and work ethic. But when Switzer said it, he meant he loved his players, as people, almost as if they were an extended member of a huge family.

Running back Spencer Tillman grew close to Switzer during his career at OU during the early 1980s. In fact, he baby-sat for the coach's three kids, Doug, Greg, and Kathy, just as Joe Washington had done before him. One time just moments before a game against Nebraska, Switzer walked up to Tillman and threw his arm around the running back.

"He jutted that jaw out as he always did and he said, 'Spencer, I just want to tell you that I love you.'

"Now that was right as we came out of the tunnel there and ready to take the field. I knew he meant it, too, and it meant so much to me."

Recently, Tillman said, "Let me say that I love Coach Switzer. He is the most loyal individual in terms of player relations."

Those words have been echoed by dozens of Sooners over the years.

Switzer said that was just his way, and it was the only way for him. Caring for his players and his ex-players wasn't a prerequisite for winning, but it came naturally for Switzer the man.

"Coaching is about relationships and being able to make a difference in a young man's life, it's not so impersonal as it is in pro football," he said. "In college coaching, you take young men into your program for four or five years, you have them 365/24/7 and you develop relationships from the time you recruit them. You have that for life!

"You know where they are today and you never lose contact with them. They are yours and you raise them. I realized that 99.9 percent of them never go to pro ball anyway, so they are your family and extension of your family, and that's what college coaching is all about."

As a Recruiter

In the old days, nobody recruited better than coaches such as Bud Wilkinson, Paul "Bear" Bryant, and Woody Hayes. Bobby Bowden built a career as the game's winningest coach ever through his warm, down-home recruiting style. In recent years, Texas' Mack Brown and USC's Pete Carroll have won national championships mainly because they could stockpile talent.

But nobody, and I mean nobody, turned recruiting into an art form like Switzer. They say he could charm the parka off a freezing man's back. It probably isn't a stretch to say that Switzer was more at home in a recruit's living room, talking to his parents, than he was on the sideline of a football field.

His approach was simple. He basically walked in as if he had been there a million times before, kicked off his shoes, and started talking about anything. Sometimes, the subject of football even came up. The thing is, he was as genuine and as down-to-earth as the day is long. There was no orchestrated presentation.

He was just being Barry Switzer.

"What I remember is that Coach Switzer was the most relaxed coach ever to visit my house," said linebacker Jackie Shipp

(1980–1983). "He had a different aura about him. Recruiting wasn't a business trip to him. It was like visiting family. Some coaches sat in my den with a suit and tie. Coach Switzer took off his shoes and moved around the house like he had been there a thousand times. You couldn't help but like his personality."

The ultimate compliment was what Shipp said to his parents when Switzer left his house.

"I didn't know you already knew Coach Switzer," he told them.

"We didn't," they answered.

It only seemed that way.

Keith Jackson, the All-American tight end, concurred. A Little Rock, Arkansas, native, Jackson was set to go to Switzer's alma mater, until he met the Oklahoma head coach.

"There couldn't have been a better recruiter anywhere in the country as Coach Switzer," Jackson said. "He comes into our house, sits down on the couch with his little loafers on, and then he kicks them off. My mother looks at him kind of funny, and I know she is thinking, 'What's this white man doing taking his shoes off in my house?'

"Then he says to her, 'Let me ask you a question. Now...do you just cook regular cornbread or do you make hot-water corn-bread?' Then he goes from that to collard greens to beans. They are both from Arkansas. They talked for two hours about food, and he did not say a thing about football. He walks out the door and tells her, 'If he if comes to Oklahoma, I will take care of him.'

"Now, my mom was a 100 percent Razorbacks fan, and she said to me, 'If you are not going to Arkansas, [Oklahoma] is your only other choice.'"

Mark Hutson, an All-American guard (1984–1987), said Switzer never kicked his loafers off in his house during his recruiting visit.

"He showed up in blue jeans and cowboy boots," Hutson recalled. "But I think the thing that really won me over was the way he got along with my younger brother, Mike, who was mentally and physically handicapped. Barry took the time to visit with Mike and talk to him, unlike some of the other recruiters."

That story may illustrate the essence of Switzer's communication skills and how he views others. Whether you were black or white, from the country or city, rich or poor, an adult or a child, Barry Switzer would talk to you. He could reach you. And he would listen to you. He's still that way.

Furthermore, it must be said that Switzer was not recruiting for Rice or Baylor. He had a rich tradition to sell, and he was employed by a university that cared deeply about winning and played in front of fans who supported the program. There was no need for insecurity or to beg a recruit to come to Norman.

"When I went in to a recruit's house to sell my program," he said, "I was able to sell it because of what Bud and his players were able to accomplish over the years—and then because of all those players and coaches that came after them. Oklahoma is a great place to go to school and to play football."

A Huge Heart

Once they got there, they realized that Switzer would do just about anything for them. Switzer not only took care of his players, he often extended a helping hand to ordinary Joes, too.

For all his critics and his mistakes, he surely trumped those with his good deeds. He didn't publicize all of them, but there are hundreds of stories of his helping those less fortunate, whether it was visiting a terminally ill Sooners fan in the hospital or paying for an airplane ticket so a student could fly home to be with family during a holiday break from school.

Once, when a family of Sooners fans lost their money to a pickpocket in Miami before an Orange Bowl, the coach heard of it and provided them with tickets to the game and arranged for them to be fed during the game.

And, like Wilkinson, he enjoyed signing autographs and getting his picture taken with fans. That, along with his gregarious, fun-loving personality, won over Oklahoma fans for decades as his team won championships.

His Motivational Speeches

As good as he was at recruiting, he may have been even better at motivating his players, whether they needed a pep-talk or not.

To be fair, there surely have been better X-and-O coaches in college football. There probably have been harder workers and smarter coaches, too. But Switzer had a Ph.D. in motivation.

Every Sooner who played for Switzer can tell you a story about his speeches. His words, they say, could light a fire under an Eskimo's behind. His pregame talks were legendary, especially before the big games against rivals Texas, Nebraska, Oklahoma State, and bowl games.

Before the 1982 meeting with Oklahoma State, for instance, Switzer had been building up the Cowboys' running back Earnest Anderson, who led the nation in rushing at the time. In most of his interviews during the week leading up to the game, he couldn't say enough good things about Anderson.

"I wish we had him on our team," he said over and over again. "I don't know how we're going to stop him."

As he gathered his Sooners around him in the locker room before the game, his tone changed 180 degrees. Switzer told them, "Now you remember that bullshit I have been saying about Anderson? To hell with that! I didn't even recruit the little s.o.b. Now go out and stop him!"

The Sooners did just that, winning 27–9.

"On the first play of the game, he caught a screen pass and out of the 11 guys on our defense, nine of us ended up on top of Anderson," Shipp recalled. "That's how well Coach Switzer could motivate you."

The ploy of using the media was all by design, and Switzer often utilized it over the years. He also often used humor during his motivational talks, sometimes he used fear, and other times he simply tried to anger his players so they would take it out on the opponent. Many speeches were of the fire-and-brimstone variety straight out of Knute Rockne's handbook.

"I will tell you that I cannot imagine anyone better than Barry Switzer at giving those pregame speeches," J.C. Watts said. "He would stand there and talk about having a patent on winning at the University of Oklahoma. He would recite statistics, data, circumstances, and analogies. He used everything to fire you up."

He Had His Share of Critics

As much as his players loved him, perhaps no collegiate head coach has had as many critics over the years. For starters, he wasn't stately and soft-spoken like Wilkinson or Nebraska's Tom Osborne. He threw around swear words like a sailor on shore leave. He admitted bending some of what he deemed were the frivolous NCAA rules.

There are those who believed he broke the major rules, too, or at least bent them, depending on whom you believe. Some regarded him as a cocky, arrogant renegade. Others believed he made negative recruiting a staple and even played the race card, in the wake of his consistent success in luring black players to Norman.

You could count Texas legend Darrell Royal in all those categories. Royal, an OU alumnus, and Switzer, feuded openly. Their issues were many, including one time when Royal accused Switzer of orchestrating a spy campaign on the Longhorns' practices.

In the end, one of the things that made Switzer so successful and popular among his players—treating them as men and giving them freedom to make their own choices—came back to haunt him and ended his Oklahoma career prematurely.

In January 1989, less than two weeks after the Sooners finished off a 9–3 season with two consecutive losses, one player shot another in Bud Wilkinson House, where many players lived. The victim, defensive lineman Zarek Peters, fortunately, lived to tell about it. There was a rape in the dorm involving a few more football players a week later. That was followed with starting quarterback Charles Thompson, who was coming off a fine sophomore season, getting nabbed for selling cocaine.

Suddenly, the media was not writing about wins and losses, but a series of off-the-field events that cast the program in a terrible light. This didn't sit well with OU president David Swank, who essentially blamed Switzer for it all. As the year wore on, some prominent alumni and even a few former OU players joined him in the avalanche of calls for Switzer's job.

Finally, as the pressure intensified that summer, Switzer was forced to resign on June 19, 1989—23 years, six months, and two weeks after he first arrived in Norman.

"Throughout my head-coaching career, I have worn the black hat," he admitted in his autobiography. "I have been accused of cheating, maintaining slush funds, of spying, of ticket-scalping, and even of purposely losing the Orange Bowl and the national championship in a big upset to Arkansas—maybe the most painful night of my career.

"This is the sort of heat that comes with a long string of 11–1 records. You draw attention. You make enemies. You become a wooden duck in a shooting gallery."

Once the fall of 1989 had arrived, and his assistant and friend Gary Gibbs had been promoted to head coach, Switzer was forced to find new waters in which to swim. He admitted he was bitter for the first few years following his resignation.

"When I got out, I was tired. I was burned out. I was in a defensive, negative mode," he said.

To his credit, he had become a polarizing figure and he recognized it. He was always honest, always calling it as he saw it, no matter the topic. And at times, he may have said too much, but that was just Barry's way.

"I think one of the things that makes people of Oklahoma love Barry so much is that he is going to tell you how he feels," said Merv Johnson, an OU assistant under Switzer (1979–1988). "Most of us are careful and guarded in what we say, but he says what he thinks."

It was a sad ending not only for Switzer, but for hundreds of players who adored him.

"The shooting on campus and Charles Thompson getting busted happened after the season, and suddenly, it was somewhat like the perfect storm," said guard Anthony Phillips (1985–1988). "All of these events happened in a short time, and it was tough to end a career that way. You watched your fellow teammates suffer. You watched your coaches suffer.

"I can say this about it: when you get 100 kids together like that from all different backgrounds, there will be issues. Switzer had the philosophy of being hands-off and letting kids be themselves. When you have the right people, that works really well. When you have some bad people, it doesn't. The sad thing is that the media back then labeled us all bad people."

Which, of course, couldn't have been further from the truth. Most of Oklahoma's players, as those at most schools, are good people who go to class regularly, love their parents, help an old lady across the street now and then, and treat their teammates with respect.

The perception, however, magnified through the media coverage of college football today, is not always reality. The fact remained that three major incidents during one month was too much for a coach to endure, even a coach who had won three national championships.

When he looked back on that period, Switzer acknowledged recently that he would have probably stayed at Oklahoma "well into the '90s."

"I don't know exactly how long," he admitted. "It would have depended on how much I enjoyed it. But I will say this, all of those great [high-school] players wouldn't have got out of the state in the '90s if I was there, and the program wouldn't have had that rut."

Who is to doubt him? Perhaps the best testament to Switzer's recruiting and coaching ability, if not his three championships and unmatched winning percentage, is the fact that the Sooners slid to a 61–50–3 record during the 10 years following his resignation.

The NFL Calls Him

A redemption of sorts for Barry is that the 16–7 win over Missouri on November 12, 1988, his final OU victory, would not be the final time he tasted success on the sidelines.

When Dallas Cowboys owner Jerry Jones, a member of the 1964 Arkansas national championship team for which Switzer was an assistant coach, called him to replace Jimmy Johnson in 1994, most NFL observers laughed out loud, at least metaphorically. They figured Jones had lost his mind, or at least wanted a puppet regime of which he could prove his own worth as a football mind.

In his second of four seasons in Dallas, Switzer proved the critics wrong as the Cowboys won the Super Bowl. Still, there would be doubters who would contend, however, that Dallas was so talented that Mickey Mouse could have coached them to a title. Although real football people know better, the Cowboys' title resulted from an abundance of Hall-of-Fame talent, such as Troy Aikman, Emmitt Smith, and Michael Irvin, which Switzer held together and motivated.

"Do you think there's any mystery why I won and guys like [Steve] Spurrier didn't?" he once asked. "Spurrier didn't have the players in Washington. Neither does Gibbs the second time around, and neither did [Bill] Parcells in Dallas. Not like Jimmy and I did."

Even though he joined Johnson as the only other coach to win a national championship and an NFL title, there is no doubt to which brand of football Switzer preferred.

"College coaching is so different than pro football," he said. "Pro football is about winning, and that's all it's about. In college, you recruit 'em and you have 'em for life. I had 53 kids on that squad with the Dallas Cowboys that won the Super Bowl, and the next year, 15 of them were gone through free agency or draft choices replacing them or whatever. Now, guess how many of those 53 have contacted me over the years?

"The answer—three or four."

He wouldn't dare guess how many times he hears from one of his Oklahoma players. Several times each week they call or stop by.

"I said—you got 'em for life," he said. "They are like family. I'll do anything for them."

Even today, most fans have forgiven him for what happened in January 1989, and he is very popular in Norman, where he resides with his second wife, Becky, the former OU gymnastics coach, while his children and grandchildren live nearby. They live in a house not far from Memorial Stadium, and when he's in town, the Switzers often host a pre- and postgame party every Saturday.

And thanks to Bob Stoops and father time, Switzer is close to the Oklahoma program again, having spoken to the team several times in recent years—and he has often attended practices, the Texas game, or a bowl game.

"I still celebrate the Sooners' success and bleed for them when they lose," he said a few years ago. "As Bud Wilkinson did for me, I'm trying to be as supportive as I can of Bob Stoops, who has made Oklahoma dominant again. It's Bob Stoops's monster to feed now, and it's a whole lot of fun to watch."

As far as work, Switzer devotes his time to various business interests, and he keeps his nose in college football, hosting an XM radio show and doing commentary for Fox Sports.

Loyal to the End

Perhaps Switzer's biggest attribute has been his loyalty, mainly to his former players, even though they long ago stopped winning games for him.

For example, on New Year's Eve 2002, Tinker Owens was doing business at a bank in downtown Norman when Switzer called him on his cell phone.

"Stay right there," the former coach instructed. "I'll be right down."

When he arrived, he presented Owens with a glass case that included an unused 1972 Sugar Bowl game ticket, on which were printed the date, price, and the team names.

"Thirty years ago today," Switzer told Tinker, "you were the MVP of the Sugar Bowl. I want you to have this."

"Somebody had given him two, and he saved one for me," Owens said. "That is the kind of relationship he has with his players. It didn't end after we were done playing and he was done coaching. He would help me with anything, and I would do the same for him."

When Lee Roy Selmon was inducted into the GTE Academic Hall of Fame in 1994, he sent out several invitations, some just as a courtesy, since he realized travel would be hard on some people.

"I sent one to Barry, but the ceremony was in Washington, D.C., just a few weeks after he had been named head coach of the Dallas Cowboys," he said.

He should have known Switzer better.

"I couldn't believe it," he said. "He had to be busy with his new job, but he took the time to fly up there for me. That's the Barry Switzer I know."

Like Wilkinson's, Switzer's legacy in the state of Oklahoma will live on long after he is gone: he is one of only two coaches ever to win a collegiate national championship and a Super Bowl, he is a member of the College Football Hall of Fame (Class of 2001), and he has a building on the OU campus named after him. Those are the bricks and mortar, the trophies, and the plaques.

To his players, however, his legacy always will be as their coach, mentor, friend, and family member. Because, like Barry Switzer always said, when you recruit 'em to be in the family, you got 'em for life.

Barry Switzer by the Numbers

Born: October 5, 1937, Crossett, Arkansas
Married: Kay McCollum, 1963–1981 (divorced); Becky Buwick, 2000–present
Education: Bachelor's degree, University of Arkansas, 1960
Assistant Coach: Arkansas, 1961–1965; University of Oklahoma, 1966–1972
Head Coach: University of Oklahoma, 1973–1988; Dallas Cowboys, 1994–1997

Record: 157–29–4 (.837 winning percentage) at Oklahoma; 45–26 at Dallas (won Super Bowl XXX)
Against Texas: 9–5–2
Against Nebraska: 12–5
Bowl Record: 8–5
National Championships: Three (1974, '75, and '85)

chapter 14
1989–1998:
The Dreadful Years

John Blake ponders a question from the media during the Big 12 Conference media day in July 1997.

The end of the Barry Switzer era was both sad and bittersweet across the great state of Oklahoma.

Problem was, the state seemed to be divided on the issue.

Many fans loved Switzer because of the fact his teams won games and championships and he had a fun-loving, gregarious personality. The fact is that Barry was always fun to be around. Some fans probably didn't care what his players did off the field, as long as they didn't kill anybody or burn down villages. However, in January of 1989, three major incidents—a shooting among two players, a gang rape by three others, and drug-dealing by the starting quarterback—were serious crimes.

A large percentage of fans who once loved Switzer for winning had grown tired of the off-the-field troubles and blamed him for his players' lack of control. According to interviews, even Dr. George Lynn Cross, OU's long-time president, now retired, fell into this category.

Then there were those who wanted the entire program cleaned with Clorox from top to bottom, to repair what they saw was a sullied image.

One thing was for sure, following "the King" as head football coach of the Machine wouldn't be an easy task for Vince Lombardi or even Knute Rockne, if they were alive and inclined to take the job.

Accordingly, the next three men who tried failed miserably.

Mister Gary Gibbs

Gary Gibbs, who was Switzer's defensive coordinator and an OU linebacker from 1972 to 1974 who was highly regarded by those who knew the game, was named the new head coach on June 20, 1989—just a day after Switzer had resigned. Switzer himself recommended Gibbs as his successor.

Gibbs had things stacked against him from the beginning, given that the Sooners served NCAA probation for his first two seasons, which included a one-year ban on televised games and a two-year ban on bowl appearances. He was hampered more by scholarship reductions and the ensuing negative publicity.

And it seemed he could never decide on what style of offense he favored, switching offensive coordinators three times.

Still, he started his OU career with 7–4, 8–3, and 9–3 seasons. It was respectable, but of those 10 losses, eight came against rivals Texas, Colorado, and Nebraska, which means his teams couldn't beat the teams he needed to beat in order to survive.

One of the few bright spots was a 48–14 thrashing of Virginia in the 1991 Gator Bowl, in which the Sooners rolled up 618 yards and 36 first downs, both Gator Bowl records. Things were looking up suddenly, but the euphoria would not carry over to 1992.

For one reason, Gibbs was not popular among his players, either. Following the 15–15 tie against Oklahoma State, which dropped OU to 5–3–2, his team formed a near-mutiny. They boycotted a practice leading up the season-ending game against Nebraska.

They were unhappy that certain players had been benched and that Gibbs seemed to show favoritism to others. The team also was divided on the quarterback issue, some wanting Cale Gundy to start while others wanted Steve Collins.

The Cornhuskers then crushed OU 33–9 for a 5–4–2 record—the school's worst season since 1965.

Heading into the 1994 season, with 16 starters returning, Gibbs declared it the best OU team in years. It didn't show on the field, however.

The end came after a season-ending 13–3 loss to Nebraska to cap a 6–5 regular season. OU allowed Gibbs to coach his team in one final game, a 31–6 embarrassing loss to BYU in the Copper Bowl.

Gibbs finished his six seasons 44–23–2, but was a miserable 2–15–1 against Texas, Colorado, and Nebraska.

"Now, Gary Gibbs is a hell of a football coach, but more than that goes into whether you win or lose," Switzer said. "I think there were a lot of factors. At the end of the Gibbs regime, of the top 25 teams that year, there were 17 starters on those teams from

Oklahoma. They just got away and went elsewhere. The blue-chip recruit was leaving the state."

The 11 Months of Schnellenberger

When he was hired to replace Gibbs, Howard Schnellenberger bragged that movies would be made and books written about his impending tenure as the Sooners' boss. It would last for years and championships would fill the OU trophy cases, he stated.

"I thought it was time I jumped on the elevator halfway up the mountain," Schnellenberger quipped when taking the OU job, referring to how much of his time spent at Miami and Louisville was spent raising money to improve facilities.

In the past, his teams were always highly regarded and well-prepared for the most part, while Schnellenberger favored a wide-open, yet balanced offense. On paper, it may have appeared to be a coup for the Sooners, despite Schnellenberger's age.

But the coach was 60 years old, and that's late in the coaching business to be starting a tenure at a football power like Oklahoma. Furthermore, he had never coached west of the Mississippi River.

Schnellenberger never was hesitant about boasting. He was a charter member of the Braggadocio Hall of Fame.

He had coached the Baltimore Colts in the NFL and then the Miami Hurricanes to their first national title. He had spent the previous 10 years building Louisville from a loser into a contender. His collegiate head-coaching record was 96–71–2. And he never was shy about reciting these highlights of his résumé.

What he wasn't was a conveyor of Sooners history. In fact, he resented it. And that, in the end, was his downfall.

From the beginning, he and OU president David Boren clashed. His relationship with the players also was troubled, with several of them telling recruits not to come to OU.

He was a Bear Bryant disciple who hadn't quite evolved enough to adapt to a tradition-rich program that he didn't make the effort to fit into. He alienated his players, limiting water breaks during practice and running them like boot camps. Two players became dehydrated and seriously ill during a practice, having to be hospitalized.

The Sooners returned 19 starters and were ranked 15th to start the season, moving up to No. 10 before a prime-time, nationally televised meeting with Colorado at Memorial Stadium. That would be the end of Schnellenberger's honeymoon as the Buffs whipped OU 38–17.

Not much went right from then on. As the season progressed, there were rumors about rampant drinking by the head coach. The nightmare ended with three consecutive losses to Kansas State, Oklahoma State, and Nebraska to conclude a 5–5–1 season. All these ingredients mixed into a recipe for disaster in the Schnellenberger-OU marriage. It ended in divorce in a little less than 12 months.

He termed it a resignation, but most Sooners know better.

"My decision has nothing to do with the inaccurate reports or hurtful rumors that often accompany head coaches and top programs," Schnellenberger said in a statement. With that, he left town and headed back East, leaving another coach to pick up the pieces.

John Blake's Miserable Three Years

That would be John Blake, an OU graduate who had coached the defensive line for four seasons under Gibbs and had been serving in the same capacity under Switzer for the Dallas Cowboys in 1995.

He seemed to be a perfect fit for the Sooners' head-coaching chair, given he was a member of the family and a great recruiter.

Like the others, Blake, too, proclaimed it was a new era and that whatever the outcome, his team would never quit. They would play hard for 60 minutes and, "If we fall back, it won't be for a lack of effort or excitement from those players. There is no way we are going to let you down. We are here for a new era, and this is truly special."

Actually, it was worse.

Blake's first team lost its first four games before shocking Texas 30–27 in overtime. The 1996 Sooners finished 3–8 and were not much improved over the next two seasons. His first two teams endured four-game losing streaks, and his third team suffered through a five-game losing streak.

Blake even attempted to revive the wishbone, but that failed. He shuffled quarterbacks like a deck of cards, and his teams were always heavily penalized.

Even though OU won his final two games in 1998, it wasn't enough to save Blake's job.

"John Blake did a good job recruiting at Oklahoma," Switzer said recently. "He didn't have a strong offensive staff around him, but he did have some talent. I don't care how good of a coach you are, if you don't have good players, you're not going to win. That's why my attitude was always, I'm going to be a great recruiter because I don't want to test my coaching abilities.

"The fact is that his offenses were terrible, and he had no quarterback."

Even though the cupboard was stocked somewhat, as the next coach would prove, the program had hit bottom during the Blake era. The Sooners' 12–22 record under Blake stands as the worst three-year period in school history. It was noted for inconsistency on offense, blocked kicks and punts, too-many-men-and-not-enough-men-on-the-field penalties, and general mismanagement.

Among the lowest points were the successive 73–21 and 69–7 losses to Nebraska in 1996 and '97, respectively.

Switzer, busy coaching the Cowboys, couldn't help but notice.

"I was shocked," he said recently. "When I saw Nebraska hung half a hundred on them, I couldn't believe this was the Oklahoma I coached."

In fact, it was a different Oklahoma, which was poorly coached, undermotivated, and generally out of shape.

"John Blake could recruit, no matter what his record was," safety Roy Williams said. "He was pretty laid back, but he could recruit. Some people had taken advantage of the fact that Blake was laid back, not taking him seriously enough. I don't want to say that we had no discipline; maybe just not enough.

"We were over there chilling together when we should have been training."

The thing that Gibbs, Schnellenberger, and Blake had in common were problems on offense. And they weren't exactly open to hearing about Oklahoma's glorious past under Wilkinson and Switzer, even though Gibbs and Blake were OU graduates. Perhaps the reminders of the Sooners' success made them insecure or uncomfortable, or both, but they surely didn't embrace it.

"In the '90s, we had some leadership which did not do that [embrace OU's history]," said Merv Johnson. "And we suffered."

To recap, Oklahoma had a 61–50–3 record in the 10 seasons following Barry Switzer's departure. They had played in three minor bowls but didn't come close to winning a conference championship. There had been dissension in the ranks and a near-mutiny by the players.

In short, the program was a mess, and Sooner Magic was as real as a fairy tale.

"This program is headed in the right direction," Blake said while fighting back tears during his final press conference. "We came here for a purpose, to get the foundation established to be a winner."

He was right about the direction of the program. The decade of misery was about to end.

New athletics director Joe Castiglione had his eye on a young defensive coordinator at the University of Florida. In Oklahoma, it wasn't as if he was relatively unknown.

He was unknown.

But he was about to make a huge name for himself among all Sooners faithful.

chapter 15

Bob Stoops:
The Sooners' Savior

In his first game as OU's head coach, Bob Stoops gestures to the defense on September 11, 1999, against Indiana State. OU won the game 49–0.

In a detached way, Bob Stoops remembers being disgusted. It were as if he was watching a Monet painting being defaced by a graffiti artist or witnessing a classic Rolls Royce being keyed by an angry girlfriend.

It was August 23, 1997.

Stoops had just walked off the football field at the University of Florida campus in Gainesville where the Gators had finished a scrimmage. As defensive coordinator, Stoops had spent the day preparing his younger players for the season opener a week later against Southern Mississippi.

While in the coaches' locker room, he looked up at the television and didn't like what he was seeing. The Oklahoma Sooners, a football program with a proud history and as rich a tradition as most any in the land, were performing so poorly that they would have had trouble hanging with a Pop Warner team from Ada.

The Sooners were committing 10 penalties, four turnovers, and generally stinking up Chicago's Soldier Field on their way to a lackluster 24–0 loss to Northwestern in the season opener, the Pigskin Classic. It would be their 13th loss in their last 18 games.

And it made Stoops want to turn the channel.

An Ohio native, Iowa graduate, and now a Florida assistant coach, it's not that he was a huge Sooners fan or had any ties to the state of Oklahoma at that point, but he always had regarded the OU program as a pillar of the college game.

"As I watched a few plays from that game, I had mentioned to some of our other coaches that it was a shame that the Oklahoma program was not living up to its potential," he recalled, noting that many of those assistants scoffed.

"At the time, I called Oklahoma 'a sleeping giant.'"

John Blake's Sooners would go on stumble to a 4–8 record that season, followed by another losing record, 5–6, the following year. Stoops, meanwhile had shaped a Gators defense highly responsible for the '96 national title and then successive 10–2 records in '97 and '98.

When Blake resigned, it was time for Oklahoma athletics director Joe Castiglione to search for Oklahoma's 21st head football coach. He believed that he knew a man perfect for the job, even though Oklahomans had never heard of him.

"I had followed Bob Stoops's career from the beginning," Castiglione said. "I figured he might be the right man for the job."

Castiglione had calculated that this was the man to awaken the sleeping giant.

The day he was hired in December 1998, Stoops proclaimed he would not run from nor be intimidated by Oklahoma's tradition of success and the high expectations from the win-starved fans.

He would embrace it and use it to rebuild the Sooners into contenders each and every season. After all, they had experienced standing atop the college football world in the 1950s, '60s, '70s, and '80s, and that is where he wanted to lead them once again.

"There should be great expectations here," he said. "It's a program with the championships that should expect championships. I know we'll operate with no excuses. There are no excuses. You succeed or you don't."

He did. Immediately.

No new coach has ever won faster in big games. Stoops won 11 of his first 12 games against top-10 opponents and compiled a remarkable 17–2 record against ranked opponents through the middle of the 2003 season.

And it is the way his Sooners have played the game that helped captivate OU fans again. They have attacked the opponent on both sides of the ball, through a wide-open offense that can be as balanced as a ballerina, as well as employing an aggressive defense as tenacious as a starving piranha.

The similarities between Stoops's immediate success and that of Bud Wilkinson and Barry Switzer are stunning. Each won national championships during their second seasons.

Even though his first team finished 7–5 with an Independence Bowl loss to Mississippi, Stoops and his staff used the year to get their message across. Things would be done the right way, thoroughly and completely. Players would work hard, report to preseason camp in top physical condition, and there would be no monkey business off the field.

"You could see right away this guy has what it takes," Switzer said. "He had it all: personality, smarts, and toughness—it was part of his package from the start. He was clearly a young man who didn't have to be shown things more than once."

When he was hired, Stoops set the highest goal: winning a national championship. It took only two seasons, as his 2000 team, which entered the season ranked No. 19, completed an improbable 13–0 season with a defense-dominated 13–2 win over defending champion and heavily favored Florida State in the BCS Championship Game in the Orange Bowl.

The Seminoles' top-ranked offense struggled to get back to the line of scrimmage throughout the game.

"We simply could not get anything going offensively," Seminoles coach Bobby Bowden said. "[Stoops] did a great job of confusing us. I'd say he made all the right moves."

Along the way, the Sooners had accumulated wins over then–No. 1 Nebraska, 31–14, No. 3 Kansas State, 41–31, and in the game that earned everyone's attention, they delivered a 63–14 shellacking of rival Texas.

"As much as anything, I remember our kids not being in awe against Texas," Stoops said. "We told them, 'You are one of the elite teams. You are Oklahoma! We've won a lot of big games at Oklahoma. We fully expect to win this game and win a lot more.'"

By now, it was already safe to say that Robert Anthony Stoops was *the* man for the job. That is his given name, but by the end of the 2000 season, some fans and sportswriters had labeled him "Big Game Bob."

Following his first nine years in Norman, he has guided the Sooners to a 97–22 record (an .815 winning percentage) and their seventh national championship as well as five more conference championships.

He has directed them to a bowl game each season, including all the majors: Rose, Orange (twice), Sugar, Cotton, and Fiesta (twice).

But through all that, he has single-handedly transformed a downtrodden program, and its once-discouraged fans, giving them back their happiness again. He has made Oklahoma proud again, just as Bud Wilkinson had from 1947 to 1963 and Switzer had from 1973 to 1988, through winning and championships.

Switzer himself is at the top of the list among those happy that not only has Stoops built a perennial title contender again, but that he has wrapped his arms around Oklahoma's glorious past. He has invited many Sooners greats to address his teams over the past eight seasons.

"Bob has embraced that," Switzer said. "It was the right thing to do. He is a smart guy. He has embraced all the family and tradition. He made everybody proud to be an Oklahoma Sooners football player. Every program has its ups and downs, and you fight through them, but those tough times are behind us now.

"He has reached out to Oklahoma. Embraced it. Made us feel comfortable in our own home. I wasn't around the place for 10 years because I was not invited. Now I like to tell him that he has made us comfortable in our own home."

As he accepted Oklahoma's past, the players Blake had left behind had accepted him in turn. After all, they had little choice. They either could leave to find another school or stay and trust what the new coach told them—if they stayed, they would be champions.

Several Sooners transferred or quit the team in Stoops's first year. Those who stayed became tougher—mentally and physically.

"The ones who were defiant, he ran them out right away," All-American safety Roy Williams recalled. "A few? No, I think he ran almost the whole defense off, about 11 of those guys were from the defense. Most of them quit or transferred. I guess some of them just didn't like being told what to do."

The transformation of attitude began immediately, as Stoops and his assistants ran an off-season conditioning program and a preseason camp as Marine drill sergeants run boot camps. It was rough, physical, and at times very painful to those who were not in excellent physical shape.

Stoops had convinced Castiglione to hire Jerry Schmidt as the new strength and conditioning coach. Schmidt had been at Florida, too.

"I had thought I was in pretty good shape, but I guess I wasn't," said Jason White, who would win the Heisman Trophy in 2003. "I was amazed at how hard it was. Coach Schmidt about killed me that summer."

The intensity of the conditioning drills was a shock to the younger players as well as a sudden change for the upperclassmen, used to the laid-back ways of Blake's regime. One of the first things Stoops noticed after taking the job was that the Sooners were not in excellent physical condition by any means. It was proven quickly by how many of them up-chucked during the first conditioning drills.

In fact, several younger players wanted to cut and run.

"I admit there were times that some of us freshmen sat around the dorm and wanted to quit," linebacker Teddy Lehman said. "We had to talk Dan Cody into staying, and look how his career turned out [Cody was a first-team All-American in 2004]. It was by far the hardest camp I had ever been through.

"Coach Stoops's first year had been the year before, and all the upperclassmen had talked about were those conditioning sessions when he got there. I worked out real hard that summer, but even then it was unbelievably tough. That system of strength training and conditioning they have at Oklahoma under Coach Schmidt is one reason I was successful, because I am naturally a lazy person. Everything was detailed and disciplined at Oklahoma. Every moment was used. For example, if one player failed to touch the line during the drills, Coach Schmidt would make everyone start the workout over. We did things until they became second nature. That is why OU wins."

Most Sooners players could tell that even though he had never been a head coach previously, Stoops knew what it took to win big on a consistent basis.

"We embraced him from the beginning, but we did not know a thing about him," Williams said. "He put his foot down right away. He gave the program a face-lift, and that is what we needed. It was for the best.

"We knew this man was for real. He was all business. There was no more playing around anymore. We were going to do great things and we had to buy into what he was telling us. I was saying, 'Let's give this guy the benefit of the doubt and do what he asks of us.'"

White, too, believed the new head coach's intensity would wear off on his players.

"When I met Coach Stoops, I could tell he had a fire lit under him from the get-go," he said. "Whatever he said, I believed it. He was so intense. I could tell that he really wanted to get something done at Oklahoma."

Nearing the end of his first decade at Oklahoma, nobody questions his ways and means these days.

The only real question is, how long will Bob Stoops remain a Sooner? Will he coach OU 15 to 20 years, as Wilkinson and Switzer had, or perhaps even longer since he will turn only 48 years old September 9, 2008, or will he go to the NFL someday, seeking another challenge as Chuck Fairbanks did following two successive 11–1 seasons?

It seems that following every season, Stoops has to deal with rumors that he is headed to an NFL team. The Cleveland Browns, New York Giants, and Kansas City Chiefs have been a few of the teams mentioned in which he is a potential candidate.

Has any of it been true? Not according to the source himself.

"You know, I don't know where all that comes from," he said following the 2006 season, when rumors circulated that he would become head coach of the Chiefs. "I don't sit around and monitor what the pulse of my well-being is or what everybody thinks I'm doing.

"No, that's not something I'm looking to do. I love what I'm doing here. I feel our future's incredibly bright. We still have more to do here. And again, I'm excited too much about what I'm doing. I don't know where people…somebody called and told me I had already interviewed for a job. You don't have a job like I have and go interviewing. That's what I don't think people get. I'm not going to be going interviewing for anything."

The closest Stoops ever came to leaving Oklahoma was to return to Florida when Steve Spurrier left for the NFL following the 2001 season. In the end, he turned down the Gators to remain a Sooner.

Furthermore, if he has any interest in the NFL, he hasn't shown it yet. Bear in mind that he also remains close friends with Spurrier, whose advice concerning what it takes to win in the NFL has to sour him on the idea. Spurrier coached for two years with the Washington Redskins and abruptly resigned with three years remaining on his contract.

"It's a different world in the NFL, and I know that," Stoops admitted. "I do know a lot of these people around the league that I am friends with and know pretty well that if I speak with them those are private conversations, and I'm not going to divulge whether I have or haven't spoke to anybody. But I'm not going to interview anywhere and be one of five candidates trying to get a job. That doesn't make sense in the position we're in here and what our future looks like here."

In other words, for an NFL team to lure him from Norman, they would need to flat-out offer the job, along with complete control of personnel and a fat salary that easily surpasses what he earns at OU. And it would need to be a franchise and ownership structure conducive to winning a Super Bowl.

For starters, the Oklahoma head coach is well-compensated among his peers. As of 2007, he earned more than $3.4 million per year and had been the top-paid collegiate head coach in the country until Alabama gave Nick Saban an eight-year, $32 million contract. Stoops also will collect a 10-year anniversary bonus of $3 million following the 2008 season.

"Bob Stoops is worth every penny he gets," Castiglione told *USA Today* recently.

Essentially, winning in Division I football today translates to financial success in the entire athletics department, just as extended losing means athletics departments operating in the red. Thus, Stoops's teams' success has provided for a healthy OU athletics department.

The school's athletics revenue jumped from $26.1 million in 1998–1999, the year before his arrival, to $64.6 million in 2005–2006, putting the program, which sponsors 20 men's and women's intercollegiate teams, in the black. Furthermore, every one of the 58 games at Memorial Stadium—where his teams own an amazing 54–2 record—have been sold out since he became head coach.

However, as long as he continues to win, rumors will continue to exist every January that another school or another NFL franchise wants him as their head coach.

"You appreciate that they feel your body of work or what you stand for is what they're looking for," he admitted. "But outside of that, I don't look at it as a pain because I'm not sitting around monitoring it. Anyhow, it really doesn't bother me, either. I just don't pay much attention to it.

"You just don't know in this business whether you'll be wanted to be around, how the climate in this world changes is always different. Again, I feel great and fortunate to be in the position we're in here and what we've accomplished and what the future looks like. So, I hope to be here. I'm not looking to do anything else, but you've got to admit, from year to year, you don't always know what's in front of you or what you need to do and the changes that happen within your family.

"Again, hopefully everything continues as it is and that people are hoping I'm still here."

Switzer sees no reason for Stoops to leave, believing the Oklahoma tradition and current qualities of the program and school will be enough to keep him in Norman for years.

"Bud had a great run, I had a great run," he said, "and Stoops will have a great run."

To continue that run he started so greatly, however, Stoops is challenged with picking up the pieces after a second consecutive Fiesta Bowl loss to a huge underdog and a fourth loss in their previous five bowls. The Sooners took an 11–2 record to Arizona to conclude the 2007 season and were a touchdown favorite to beat a West Virginia team that had lost is head coach in the previous weeks.

Plus, that Oklahoma team was perceived to be extremely motivated after losing the 43–42 overtime classic to Boise State on the same field a year earlier.

However, the Sooners turned in one of the most disappointing performances of their 41 bowl appearances, as the Mountaineers rolled through the OU defense for 525 yards. Furthermore, Oklahoma appeared unfocused, committing 13 penalties for 113 yards.

"Embarrassing, absolutely embarrassing," Stoops said. "No discipline whatsoever. That has to be a reflection on me. I am obviously not doing a good enough job of getting our players to understand how to play smart. It is embarrassing and just...guys just making a lot of poor choices in what they're doing. Anyway, it was just poor.

"They don't need to get it out of their minds too soon. Our players...we need to have some discipline to us. You just can't play like that. Obviously, I need to do things differently as a head coach."

His words of admonition may have been spoken out of frustration, or they may possess a kernel of the truth. Whatever the case, the Sooners entered the 2008 season—Stoops' 10th at OU—with more experience and more motivation than ever before.

And if his 97 wins in nine seasons, five Big 12 Conference championships, one national championship, and six wins over rival Texas are any indication, the Oklahoma Sooners program rests in good hands—its future as bright as its glorious past, which attracted Bob Stoops to Norman in the first place.

Bob Stoops by the Numbers

Born: September 9, 1960, Youngstown, Ohio
Married: Carol
Children: Mackenzie, Isaac, Drake
Education: Bachelor's degree, Iowa, 1983
Assistant Coach: Iowa, 1983–1987; Kent State, 1988; Kansas State, 1989–1995; Florida, 1996–1998
Head Coach: University of Oklahoma, 1999–present
Record: 97–22 at Oklahoma (.815 winning percentage)

Against Texas: 6–3
Bowl Record: 4–5
National Championship: 2000

chapter **16**

Oklahoma Potpourri:
Was "Sooner Magic" Real?
Just Ask Nebraska

Billy Sims crashes through the Ohio State defense for a first
down in a memorable "Sooner Magic" win in Columbus on
September 24, 1977.

It can be defined as something mystical, something surreal, something that always allowed Oklahoma to find a way to victory—in the face of all mathematical odds against it.

Opponents would call it just pure luck.

Barry Switzer termed it "Sooner Magic."

And those same opponents, especially those such as Texas and Nebraska, came to hate it.

"It wasn't something you could predict," Switzer said. "It just happened, and when it did, it was something special."

Even though Switzer coined the phrase, it just may have existed as far back as Bud Wilkinson's days patrolling the OU sideline.

Wilkinson's teams pulled out a few games in which they were outplayed during the famed 47-game winning streak, especially the 1954, '56, and '57 games against Colorado.

"A few times we won when we probably shouldn't have," Wilkinson once said. "I guess some of our opponents would call that being lucky. I don't know…maybe they are right."

Being good and never giving up until the clock read :00 was another part of the Sooners mystique. But if being lucky just needed a name, then Switzer was glad to oblige. And it just seemed to crop its head when Nebraska was on the opposing side of the field.

"Eight times in really major games, sometimes when it didn't seem remotely possible, Oklahoma would come from behind to beat Nebraska in some magical way," Switzer wrote in his autobiography. "Our fans started calling it 'Sooner Magic.'"

In 1976 in Lincoln the Cornhuskers dominated the game, but led only 17–7 late in the game. The Sooners scored on a halfback pass, then a hook-and-lateral play set up the winning touchdown with only 30 seconds remaining for a 20–17 win.

In 1980, also in Lincoln, with OU trailing Nebraska 17–14 late in the game, Buster Rhymes broke off a 43-yard gain to set up the winning touchdown in the final minute. In the Orange Bowl to conclude that season, Florida State had the Sooners dead to rights, leading 17–10, having dominated the game. J.C. Watts then led OU to a final-drive touchdown with only 1:27 remaining and a remarkable two-point conversion pass to Forrest Valora for a stirring one-point victory.

In 1986, in Lincoln again, the Sooners trailed 17–10 with only 1:22 remaining and pulled out a 20–17 win. It was almost eerie how it was the same score as the game played 10 years earlier, almost to the day, on the same field.

"We trailed at halftime, but Coach Switzer gave us a speech about tapping into some 'Sooner Magic,'" guard Mark Hutson said. "Sure enough, Jamelle Holieway hit Derrick Shepard late in the game to pull us within 17–16. I can still remember Nebraska fans booing as we kicked the extra point to tie the game.

"The booing stopped with 18 seconds remaining when Jamelle passed to Keith to set up Tim Lashar's game-winning field goal. The ending to that game was filled with Sooner Magic!"

Perhaps no game featured "Sooner Magic" as much as the 29–28 miracle over Ohio State in Columbus in 1977.

The Sooners trailed 28–20 late in the game, scored a touchdown, but failed on the potential tying two-point conversion against Woody Hayes's Buckeyes. The ensuing onside kick went directly into an Ohio State player's hands, but then bounced free for Mike Babb to recover. Backup quarterback Dean Blevins then completed a pass over the middle, and kicker Uwe von Schamann drilled a 41-yard field goal to steal the game.

"I've always said, and this is no cliché, you just win games by having players making big plays at the right time," Switzer said. "That is 'Sooner Magic.' And I would rather have the players than the magic."

Famous Voices

Walter Cronkite and Curt Gowdy owned two of the voices that handled play-by-play duties on the Sooners radio network in the old days.

Cronkite, arguably the most famous broadcaster in TV/radio history, called OU football games in 1937 for WKY radio.

Ironically, it was less than two years after Cronkite had left the University of Texas to begin his journalism career.

His first broadcast was of a 19–7 loss at Tulsa in the season opener. For that game, Cronkite had worked off of an electronic board that helped him identify players.

"The spotters would punch up who was carrying the ball and who made tackle, and the light would flash," he told the *Daily Oklahoman* in 2002. "The spotters turned out to be impossible, and I was looking at the board and not the game."

It would be the only season with Cronkite at the microphone.

He became famous as the anchor of the *CBS Evening News* from 1962 to 1981, telling the nation about such events as John F. Kennedy's assassination in 1963. He became known for his final line each night, "And that's the way it is," and once was called the "most trusted man in America."

A Wyoming native, Gowdy was the voice of the Sooners on KOMA Radio from 1945 to 1949, just as Wilkinson was building the program from mediocrity into a dynasty.

He later moved on to become the voice of the Boston Red Sox and then the main play-by-play announcer for the Rose Bowl, the NFL, and Major League Baseball for more than two decades for NBC Sports.

Gowdy died in 2006.

The Notre Dame Jinx

There certainly has been no "Sooner Magic" sightings when it comes to the Fighting Irish, no matter the era.

Get this: Oklahoma is 1–8 all-time against the Golden Domers.

Notre Dame is one of only three schools (USC and Texas are the others) that hold a winning record against Oklahoma in series that have consisted of more than two meetings.

The Irish formed their own bookend on OU's famed 47-game winning streak, beating the Sooners 28–21 on September 26,

1953, and on November 16, 1957. In those five years in between, OU was perfect, with the exception of a 7–7 tie with Pittsburgh the week after the first defeat to Notre Dame.

Wilkinson's teams were only 1–5 against Notre Dame, with the lone win coming by a 40–0 score at South Bend on October 27, 1956—in the midst of Oklahoma's second consecutive national championship season.

Notre Dame is 4–0 in games played at Norman.

And the Irish have even beaten a Bob Stoops–coached team—34–30 in South Bend in 1999.

"We went to Notre Dame and we were ahead by 17 points in the third quarter," quarterback Josh Heupel recalled. "And then the wheels fell off. How did we let that slip away? I really don't know."

It also was Stoops's first loss as the Sooners' head coach after a 3–0 start.

Those Alumni Games Were Tough

Oklahoma was one of the few major programs that held an alumni game for years. Former Sooners, many of whom were on NFL rosters at the time, played a spring game against the current OU team in the 1950s, '60s, and '70s. It was fierce, competitive, and the alumni often won.

"The toughest game we ever played was against the alumni team," said Jay O'Neal (1954–1956). "We never lost in college, but we never beat the alumni team, either. It was damn tough."

Jakie Sandefer III said he'll never forget an alumni game for this reason: he heard "Boomer Sooner" played by the band but did not like it.

"I was a hotshot freshman, playing safety," he said. "Indian Jack Jacobs kicks a punt about four miles high, and the guy playing back with me says, 'Fair catch it!' so I blame this on him. I should have let it go into the end zone, but it hits me on the shoulder pad, goes into the end zone, and the alumni fall on it for a touchdown— and the band starts playing 'Boomer Sooner.' It was the only time

I did something to allow a touchdown to be scored by the other team and they played 'Boomer Sooner.' I was horrified."

Offensive tackle Mike Vaughan (1974–1976) will never forget his meeting with Derland Moore (1971–1972), who was then playing for the New Orleans Saints.

"I was on the second team and in my first alumni game, I was coming off an ankle sprain," he recalled. "Derland Moore lined up across from me. He beat me inside, he beat me outside, and he beat me every which way that day. He was the MVP of the game, and I was responsible for it."

A year later, the two lined up across from each other once again.

"I was healthy and had a year's experience," Vaughan said. "I did pretty well against him, and he told me he would get me the next year."

Of course, like many all-star games have been, OU's alumni game was discontinued for fear of injuries.

Merv Johnson Makes a Home in Norman

Speaking of Notre Dame, Switzer called South Bend, Indiana, following the 1978 season when he needed a replacement for Gene Hochevar as offensive line coach.

"He said he was looking for one of the best offensive line coaches he could find and wanted to know if I had a recommendation," Merv Johnson recalled. "I said 'Yes, me!'"

Sure enough, Switzer hired Johnson, who arrived in time for the 1979 Orange Bowl and has been a Sooner since. He coached the offensive line and tight ends through Switzer's tenure and that of Gary Gibbs, Howard Schnellenberger, and John Blake, before moving into the OU athletics department as director of football operations in 1998.

"It's been a great run," said Johnson, a 1958 Missouri graduate.

Most offensive linemen who played for Johnson loved him.

"Merv Johnson was a coach of high integrity, and he instilled a great sense of pride, character, and work ethic in his players," said guard Anthony Phillips (1985–1988). "He treated us like men and expected us to act like men, and we did."

OU Family Rallies to Help Katrina Victim Oubre

Louis Oubre grew up in the Lower Ninth Ward of New Orleans, and while playing saxophone in the Saint Augustine High band, he heard the question that would change the direction of his life.

"Why don't you come out for football?" students and coaches would ask. "You're too big to play in the band."

Oubre traded in his sax for shoulder pads in the 10th grade, made the team, became a pretty good offensive lineman by his senior season, and played on an undefeated state championship team. He wasn't the bluest chip in the recruiting basket, but he was good enough to be offered scholarships by Oklahoma State; Grambling; his hometown school, Tulane; and nearby LSU.

Following his second consecutive national championship at Oklahoma, Switzer had been recruiting a defensive lineman named Terry Williams, who played at a rival school in New Orleans. When the Sooners coach watched film of Williams, he saw the all-state blue-chipper being blocked consistently by a smaller player, a fireplug of a lineman by the name of Oubre.

"He was about 6'5" and 265 pounds, with a little, bitty waist," Oubre recalled. "I was much smaller, about 6'2", 235, but I was all fired up because of the all the publicity he was receiving."

Switzer then offered Oubre a visit to Norman and, subsequently, a scholarship, telling him as he told all his recruits that, if he came to Oklahoma, he would join the Sooners family for life.

Oubre gladly accepted.

"It was a first-class place, and I knew then that was where I wanted to go," he recalled.

He never regretted his decision, falling in love with Norman and the Oklahoma program on his way to a career that was highlighted by being named an All-American during his senior season in 1980. He also was twice named All–Big 8, was a fifth-round pick of his hometown Saints, and spent four years in the NFL.

Recently, more than 30 years after that decision, the fact that he chose to be a Sooner greatly affected his life again.

It was August 26, 2005, a Friday night in New Orleans as Oubre drove home from his job as assistant football coach at McDonogh 35 High School. He was in a great mood, especially since his offensive line had dominated play during a jamboree scrimmage across town.

Nothing could buoy Oubre's spirits like seeing how far his protégés had progressed over the summer. He could tell they would be an effective blocking machine from tackle to tackle for the upcoming season.

"Those guys were like my kids, my babies," he said. "They were rated the number-one offensive line in Louisiana. We had a great jamboree on Friday. They knocked them all over the field that day."

By that night, Oubre had heard people mentioning some hurricane out in the Gulf of Mexico but didn't give it too much thought. On Saturday, his fiancée, Dana Rouzan, had sent her two boys to Houston with her mother. By Sunday morning, he and Dana awakened at 10:00 o'clock and promptly turned on the television. It is then that they learned a monster named Katrina was lurking.

"We turned on the news, and everyone was leaving [New Orleans]," he said. "I wasn't afraid. We had stayed through Hurricane Betsy, and that was a bad one. So this one couldn't be any worse, could it?"

By 1:00 o'clock that afternoon, Oubre and Dana had decided to leave, too, so they hopped in the car and tried to head west on I-10 toward Baton Rouge. They didn't get far.

"It was bumper-to-bumper," he said. "It took us 30 minutes to go a block. I said, 'Forget this, we are going back home!'"

They returned home, turned on the television again, and Dana grabbed a jar of peanuts. The folks on the TV now used phrases such as "185 mile-per-hour winds" and "mandatory evacuation." Now they had no choice.

"We looked at each other and said, 'We had better try again,'" Oubre recalled.

This time, they tried to head north across the causeway over Lake Pontchartrain. They could see angry clouds brewing to the east as they crept slowly with the traffic. They did not cross the lake until 5:00 o'clock. From there, they headed west and searched for a hotel room.

"We stopped at 30 hotels and couldn't find a room," Oubre recalled.

They continued driving, heading west and then north, and by 5:30 AM Monday found themselves in Mesquite, Texas, on the outskirts of Dallas.

"We found a room, went to bed, and woke up at 9:00 that night," Oubre said. "We turned on the TV and found out that New Orleans was flooded."

New Orleans, the town Louis and Dana and her two boys had loved, now was in their rear-view mirror and under water.

"It was the lowest point of our lives," Dana said. "It was awful, seeing our hometown like that."

It was then that being a part of the Oklahoma family would rescue Oubre's immediate future.

Former roommate and guard Terry Crouch, Oubre's best friend from his years at OU, had been calling Oubre since the previous Friday but could not get through since cellular phone service was spotty because of the massive storm.

On Monday, Oubre called Crouch, who happened to live in Dallas.

"Where the hell are you?" Crouch asked him.

"I am in some place called Mesquite," he answered.

"What could you bring?" Crouch asked.

"All I have is what is on my back," Oubre answered. "We didn't pack anything. We figured we would be back home the next day."

"Okay, partner," Crouch told him. "We'll take care of you."

Once the scope of the flood in New Orleans became clear to everyone, Crouch went to work, sending mass emails and making several calls to summon Sooners from near and far, including

Switzer. While a relief agency helped get Oubre and Dana out of the small, fleabag motel they had found into a larger and nicer apartment, Crouch organized for them to acquire the necessary belongings.

Then Switzer, who also put the word out via his radio show in Oklahoma, soon arrived with a truckload of furniture. Giftcards to Wal-Mart and cash poured in, all to provide Oubre and his wife and her two sons with clothes or whatever they needed.

"That's how Coach Switzer is," Oubre said. "He is like our second daddy. He told me when he recruited me that he signed me for life. Man, I did the right thing by going to Oklahoma. I knew that back then, but now..."

He was getting choked up, just as he did when he saw Switzer arrive with the furnishings and when Crouch helped out.

"It was the first time I saw Louis cry," Crouch said. "And I knew the man very well. He broke down and said, 'I didn't realize how many people cared about me.'"

Today, Louis and Dana are married and happily living in DeSoto, Texas, a suburb south of Dallas. (Switzer and former OU assistants Gene Hochevar and Jerry Pettibone attended their wedding.) They own a house. Louis teaches grade school in Cedar Hill and soon hopes to coach football again, while Dana teaches school in Dallas proper. Dana's boys have done very well adjusting to a new town, a new state, and new schools, while Oubre's daughter from a previous marriage is a student at OU.

"We have started a whole new life from scratch," Dana explained. "We owe Terry a lot. He helped us get situated here. He was just tremendous. We still miss that New Orleans flavor, and maybe someday we will go back, but right now the kids need stability."

Crouch said this story is typical of the Sooners family.

"I just wanted to help my tackle, the brother that played next to me and was my roommate all those years ago," he said. "This goes back to the relationship we had in school. We were like family. He didn't ask for help, but you know we were going to give it to him. That does make me feel good. That what it is all about, helping friends in need."

Oubre admits today that Katrina and the devastating aftermath was a terrible ordeal to endure, but it brought out the best in those he hadn't seen or talked to in several years. And it made him realize the goodness of others and just how important he is to them.

"And them to me," he said. "Man, it makes me feel wonderful."

Clayton, McGruder Are Heroes

Mark Clayton and Lynn McGruder will never forget the night of June 1, 2003.

Neither will Miss Oklahoma 2007.

Juniors-to-be Clayton and McGruder were returning to Norman from a visit to Texas on Interstate 35 in McClain County, Oklahoma, when all hell broke loose in front of them. All Clayton, who was driving, could see in front of him was smoke as he swerved to avoid what surely was a terrible crash.

By the time his car stopped spinning, he and his teammate saw a crushed red Ford Escort, with 19-year-old Alicia Layne dead inside and her sister critically injured. And five other people, all family members, were trapped inside a van that had been hit head-on by the Escort, which had crossed over the median.

The two Sooners responded instantly, kicking out the van's windows before pulling each family member to safety.

"You realize that your life is not about you," Clayton said recently. "The things you do, you impact other peoples' lives. No matter how you look at it, you're impacting somebody else in either a positive or negative way."

Clayton would go on to have a spectacular junior (83 receptions, 1,425 yards, 15 touchdowns) season, and by the time his career was finished, he was the Sooners' all-time leader in receptions (221), receiving yards (3,241), and touchdown receptions (31).

Remarkably, one of the women they rescued from the van went on to become famous in her own right. Makenna Smith, who was 19 at the time of the crash, was named Miss Oklahoma 2007, and was named Oklahoma's Seatbelt Ambassador. According to the Oklahoma Highway Patrol website, Smith worked tirelessly to present seatbelt safety information to schools across Oklahoma as she prepared for the 2008 Miss America pageant.

The Oregon Officiating Fiasco

Officials have made their share of glaring blunders over the years in college football. Remember Colorado's fifth-down game against Missouri in the early 1990s? Or the outcome of the 1979 Rose Bowl, determined when USC's Charles White was awarded a touchdown even though he fumbled at the 1-yard line—a call that cost Michigan a victory?

There have been countless others, many before the age of television and replay systems let viewers in on the gaffes.

Well, what happened in Eugene, Oregon, on September 16, 2006, has to rank right up there with the worst of them all.

The Sooners entered the game against the Oregon Ducks with a 2–0 record, having beaten UAB and Washington at home.

The game officials, as well as the video replay officials, made a series of errors in the final two minutes that allowed the Ducks to rally for a 34–33 win. It would have been labeled as a comedy of errors, except that none of it was funny to Oklahoma.

Leading 33–27 with 1:12 remaining in the game, the Sooners lined up to cover what surely would be an Oregon onside kick. Here's what ensued: Oregon's onside kick was touched by a Ducks player before it traveled 10 yards. Furthermore, an Oklahoma player recovered the ball, which was apparent from several angles on the video replays.

Not only did the officials not notice the illegal touching, but they awarded the ball to Oregon. It was one thing for the field officials to miss the calls, but furthermore, replay officials did not overturn the obvious on-field mistakes.

That was followed by a pass-interference call on Oklahoma, which should not have been made due to the fact the pass was tipped at the line of scrimmage, giving the Ducks excellent field position. They then scored to go ahead by one point before a final-play field-goal attempt by Oklahoma was blocked.

To put it bluntly, the Sooners got jobbed. And they got jobbed on the road by a Pac-10 officiating crew.

"I've made a million mistakes and I'll make a million more in each game, and in that game included, I wish there were things I could have done differently or changed," OU coach Bob Stoops said. "But unlike officials, players and coaches don't have that opportunity. They had an opportunity to get it right and they chose not to. So I find it still absolutely inexcusable and unacceptable."

A few days later, the Pac-10 suspended the officiating crew and the replay official, and issued an apology.

"Errors clearly were made and not corrected, and for that we apologize to the University of Oklahoma, Coach Bob Stoops, and his players. They played an outstanding college football game, as did Oregon, and it is regrettable that the outcome of the contest was affected by the officiating," Pac-10 Commissioner Tom Hansen stated.

"The fact that the errors on the onside kick altered the outcome of the game is most unfortunate and unsettling. We had a solid veteran crew assigned, and the instant-replay official had a fine career as a referee in the Pac-10. We believe in the ability and integrity of each individual involved. It should be noted that not all of the seven officials were directly involved in the play in question, but the entire crew bears responsibility for every play. Game officials and replay officials have positions of great responsibility and must be accountable for their actions."

It was no solace to Oklahoma President David Boren, Athletics Director Joe Castiglione, Stoops, or his players.

Boren sent a letter two days after the game to Big 12 Commissioner Kevin Weiberg, labeling the officiating and the outcome of the game "an outrageous injustice," as well as asking that the game be eliminated from the record books and having the officials involved in the game suspended for the remainder of the season.

Weiberg responded with a statement saying the result of the game would stand.

"There is no provision under NCAA or conference rules for a game result to be reversed or changed as a result of officiating errors, nor do I believe there should be," he said.

So the one-point loss went forever into the record books, even though OU surely would have won the game by six points had the officials not erred repeatedly. The Sooners would go on to lose 28–10 to Texas and 43–42 to Boise State in the Fiesta Bowl, as the season ended with a 11–3 record and another Big 12 title.

What's in a Name?

A huge issue, which nobody guessed would be a huge issue, arose when the Sooners played the 2006 season without names on the backs of their jerseys.

Due to an outcry among Sooners fans, the names were back on OU's jerseys in 2007.

"Bud Wilkinson's guys...they never had names on their jerseys," Stoops said before the 2007 season. "You knew them by their numbers. You knew who was No. 35—Billy Vessels.

"But we're putting them back on."

Still, Stoops told a crowd at the National Cowboy & Western Heritage Museum before the 2007 season that he didn't understand why it had become such a hot topic among fans.

"Why did they put numbers on the jerseys?" he asked. "So you could identify the players, right?"

chapter 17
Texas: The Team Oklahoma Loves to Hate

The games with Texas have always been spectacularly tough. Here, Greg Pruitt soars over the top of Texas defensive back Malcolm Minnick in the second quarter of the game in Dallas on October 9, 1971. Oklahoma won 48–27.

On October 10, 1900, the headline in the *Austin American-Statesman* warned local citizens: "The Red Football Warriors Arrive in This City to Play This Afternoon."

That day, the more experienced University of Texas Steers defeated the University of Oklahoma Rough Riders 28–2.

The next day, the same newspaper took a backhanded swipe at the Oklahoma team, which had played all of 10 football games in its brief history: "Practice Game Yesterday—Varsity Football Team Have a Stiff Practice Game with Oklahoma."

A practice game?

Talk about adding insult to injury, or defeat in this case. The OU team had traveled 500 miles in 17 hours on a cramped train to reach Austin, making 18 stops along the way. Then, after failing to score even one touchdown, the visitors had to endure it all over again to travel home, humbled and embarrassed while their ungracious hosts had rubbed their noses in the humiliating defeat.

About the only thing different today, in addition to the names, is the fact that neither team has to travel farther than the other for the game, which was moved in 1912 to Dallas as the main attraction at the Texas State Fair—an equal distance from Austin and Norman.

Today, more than a century and 102 meetings on the football field later, the Oklahoma Sooners and Texas Longhorns still don't like each other much. Oh, what the heck, let's be precise here—they generally *hate* each other, having accumulated more than a century of bad blood, feuds, and confrontations between the players, coaches, and their loyal fans.

"The Texas game is kind of a hate deal," Tinker Owens said. "It goes way beyond the football game. Oklahoma and Texas are forever battling over something. It starts in high school with the Oil Bowl."

Nowadays, the "Red River Shootout" or "Red River Rivalry," whichever you prefer, resembles a drawdown at high noon at the OK Corral, in front of more than 80,000 fans, half Sooners and half Longhorns, at the Cotton Bowl.

What makes a college football rivalry? Whatever the criteria, Oklahoma-Texas has all the ingredients.

Much of it has to do with how the participants perceive each other. Sooners regard Longhorns as cocky and arrogant, highbrow society types that raise a pinky when they knock back a glass of chardonnay. As the old axiom goes, they think that Bevo's excrement, and their own for that matter, doesn't reek.

Longhorns perceive Sooners as Okies or plain ol' country hicks, flossing their teeth with horse twine and chewing tobacco. As far as the men, well, they're even more unrefined.

You get the picture.

"Texas was always *the* game on the schedule for me," tackle Eddie Foster (1971–1973), explained. "I have never been to an Ohio State–Michigan, Auburn-Alabama, or Notre Dame–USC game, but I don't know how the atmosphere could be any better than Oklahoma-Texas."

Of course, the proximity of the two states, sharing the Red River and so forth, just adds to the disdain. The Cotton Bowl setting in Dallas also helps foster the rivalry, since its location allows Sooners and Longhorns fans to reach the game in equal numbers, even thousands who do not secure tickets arrive just for the party.

"When you go across that Red River and play in that Cotton Bowl setting," said OU linebacker Daryl Hunt (1975–1978), a native of Odessa, "it's something special."

It is as intense as it is special, the players say. In fact, it is the hardest-hitting, most intense game Oklahoma plays each season, no matter the records of each team, where they are ranked, or who is favored.

"I had heard about the Texas game and figured it was just another game," said Louis Oubre, a tackle from 1978 to 1980. "On the first play, I got hit on my left shoulder and it made my right shoulder hurt, so I soon realized the intensity of that game was like no other game I had ever played.

"It was even more intense than any game I ever played in the pros."

Oubre said the Longhorns would look for any opportunity to hit you, even away from the play.

"One time against Texas, I was running after a player who had intercepted a pass," he recalled. "They always said, 'Keep your head on a swivel,' but I didn't on that play. This Texas player ear-holed me, and I flipped over and broke my tail-bone."

Injuries, as well as extra time in the whirlpool, seem to mount the week following each Texas game.

"I remember the first Texas game I saw from the sideline when I was a redshirt freshman," Foster recalled. "Guys were coming off the field bleeding and needed stitches. It was so intense that you were halfway scared about playing in the game but couldn't wait for it."

These are two football powers, rich in tradition, proud of their history that is filled with championships, Heisman Trophy winners, and All-Americans. It is that combined quality, illustrated by the fact that in 31 meetings both teams entered ranked nationally, and since the end of World War II, at least one team has been ranked in 60 of the 62 meetings, that makes this rivalry one of college football's best.

"Beating Texas is hard to do," said Barry Switzer, who sported a 9–5–2 record against the Longhorns, "and for Texas, beating Oklahoma is hard to do."

Texas' 56–40–5 advantage in the series underscores the Longhorns' dominance during the early years. Consider that, from 1900 through 1947, which was Bud Wilkinson's first season as OU head coach, Texas had a 29–11–2 edge, accounting for the advantage in the overall series it holds today.

Since, it has been virtually dead even, even though the Sooners lost 12-of-13 meetings from 1958 through 1970 during Darrell Royal's heyday in Austin. Royal, the OU All-American from the 1940s, built the Longhorns' program into a power, only adding to the intensity of the rivalry.

It is absolutely no secret that Royal and Switzer never got along. In fact, they just plain didn't like each other. Before the 1976 meeting, Darrell claimed Switzer was part of an earlier spying incident on Texas's practices. He also has hinted that the OU coach may not have recruited strictly according to NCAA regulations. What likely also burned Royal had to be Oklahoma's recruiting success in the state of Texas, which obviously has produced more talented high-school players for generations because of the large population base.

The Sooners and Longhorns, as they do today, have competed for recruits on a head-to-head basis so commonly that the recruiting wars between the coaching staffs also bled into the mutual dislike between the two schools.

Another element that led to Oklahoma's success in attracting dozens of black players from Texas over the years, especially during the 1970s, was the perception that Texas did not want many blacks on its teams. Whether true or not, it was the perception among some blacks, and Switzer used it to his advantage.

"When I got to Norman [on a recruiting visit], there were a lot of recruits there from Texas, like Kenny King, Billy Sims, and Thomas Lott," George Cumby recalled. "Nobody wanted to go to the University of Texas at that time because they were saying that Texas didn't want black players."

All three ended up at OU, of course, and each became a star.

And most Texans who became Sooners, like Brian Bosworth and Thomas Lott, to name a couple, grew to *really* hate the Longhorns. Once they crossed the Red River to further their education and play football, they were often called "traitors."

"All of us Texans who played for Oklahoma had a grudge against Texas for one reason or another," Lott explained, adding that he was one of nine Texans starting for the Sooners in 1977. "We didn't like them too much, and they probably didn't like us."

When San Antonio native Lott told Royal during a recruiting trip that he would be visiting Oklahoma's campus, Royal stood up and shot back, "Oklahoma! What are you going to Oklahoma for?"

It was ironic, considering Royal was once a Sooners star himself.

Not much has changed today.

"I know this about the state of Texas. Most of those kids grow up wanting to be Longhorns or Aggies. That's how it is down there," said Bobby Jack Wright, a man who knows both sides of the rivalry. He was an assistant for 12 seasons at Texas and will enter his 10th year at OU in 2008.

"But Oklahoma's always been a place that's had a great attraction to those kids for years. Oklahoma's always been able to go down to the state of Texas to recruit against Texas and A&M and get the best players down there."

One thing is for sure—practices leading up to the game are taken a little more seriously. Coaches are more on edge, realizing the outcome of the game either leaves them with a year of satisfaction or a year of frustration before the next OU-Texas game.

"While I was playing, OU's preparations for the Texas game were extraordinary," J.C. Watts recalled. "Although we weren't competing with Texas for a conference championship, the pressure to win was intense. In order to prepare us for the noise of the Cotton Bowl, Coach Switzer would have 'The Eyes of Texas' played at ridiculous decibel levels over the loudspeakers during practice the week before the game."

Switzer said the desire to win is at its highest among OU alumni living in the Lone Star State.

"I don't think I've met anybody that's graduated [from the] University of Texas that has come North of the Red River to make a living," he said. "But we have got a lot of our graduates that have left and gone South of the Red River—in Dallas and Houston— around the state of Texas that make a living. And they're in social clubs and golf clubs and business and meetings. So it's very important to us."

Perhaps it's only natural for the states of Oklahoma and Texas not to care much for each other. They share a border and battle over the best high school football players in the Southwest. And they share a tunnel from their respective locker rooms before the game and back to them at halftime and after the game. It is in that tunnel that the stare-downs, the jawing, and the taunting occurs.

"Walking down that tunnel, you get such an adrenaline rush," Roy Williams said. "And I really do hate Texas. If you don't when you get to Oklahoma, you learn to hate Texas."

Williams said he will never forget Texas quarterback Major Applewhite talking trash as the two teams headed to the locker room at halftime of the 2000 game.

"I couldn't believe it," he said. "From that point on, I wanted to do something special every time we played Texas. We couldn't beat them by enough points to make me happy."

At times, thanks to Texas's live mascot, there have been obstacles to avoid before the play action on the field even begins.

"Greg Roberts always told me before we played Texas, 'Watch out when you walk down the ramp,'" guard Louis Oubre recalled.

"I would say, 'Watch out for what?'

"I found out. He was referring to Bevo, who would be shitting all the way down that ramp.

"Later, I told Greg, 'Now I see what you are talking about.'"

Before his first Texas game in 1972, Owens said he was petrified.

"We walked down that ramp, and Texas guys were to my left, jawing at us," he recalled. "I wasn't jawing back because this time I was scared to death of an opponent. Then they shot that big cannon, and I thought I lost it. It scared the you-know-what out of me. I looked over and saw that big steer, Bevo, standing there.

"It was an amazing sight, but once the first play of the game is over, you forget all that."

Before his first Texas game in 1980, linebacker Jackie Shipp asked guard Terry Crouch about the feeling a Sooner has when he walks down that ramp.

"That's all I keep hearing about," he said.

"You'll see," Crouch told him. "You'll see."

"So we walked down the ramp, and I saw all of those fans in the Cotton Bowl, and we ran the length of the field to go down and stretch before the game," Shipp recalled. "I bent down to touch my toes and started throwing up right there. I had puke all over my face mask, and Terry looked over at me and asked, 'Now you understand?'"

So you can just add vomit to the blood, sweat, and tears spent during the Oklahoma-Texas rivalries over the past century. Here's a quick look at some of the most memorable meetings.

1947: Was His Knee Down?

Late in the first half of a close game, Texas quarterback Bobby Layne picked up his own fumble and lateralled the ball to another Longhorn on a play that resulted in a touchdown. The problem was, all the Oklahoma players swore Layne's knee was on the ground as he picked up the fumble.

"He should have been ruled down," Buddy Burris said. "That play blew open a close game, and we lost 34–14."

But not before OU fans showed their displeasure. The game had to be halted to clear the bottles and cups from the playing field when the officials blew the call on Layne's lateral.

1974: A Hard-Hitting Slugfest

The Sooners entered the game riding a 12-game winning streak.

Defensive end Jimbo Elrod made the defensive play that saved the game. Tied 13–13, the Longhorns were driving late in the fourth quarter.

"We needed to make something happen," Elrod recalled. "Larry [Lacewell] was upstairs and he made the call for a stunt. I don't think [Texas quarterback] Marty Akins read it right, because he left the ball in Earl Campbell's hands."

Just then, Elrod collided with the star fullback, popping the football loose. Oklahoma recovered.

"I knew that when you took on Earl, you had to hit him in the mouth and not in the legs, because his legs were too big and too strong," Elrod said. "You would never win the battle with him if you went low. So I hit Earl right in the mouth, and the ball just came out."

Soon after, Tony DiRienzo kicked a field goal for a 16–13 win over the Longhorns. The Sooners would not lose, finishing 11–0 and winning a national title in Switzer's second season as head coach.

1976: "Are You Spying on Us?"

To this day, this is the most controversial game, simply because Royal believed (and still does) that the Sooners' coaches had spied on Texas's practices for years. He discovered this fact with evidence and announced his findings to the media two days prior to the game.

More than 30 years later, Royal is still bitter. Switzer has waffled on the subject, first writing in his autobiography that OU did spy on Texas, but has later denied it in recent interviews. Larry Lacewell has admitted in interviews it happened and asked Royal for forgiveness. The alleged spy, a man named Lonnie Williams, currently works for the Dallas Cowboys and won't talk about the issue.

Interestingly enough, before the game, President Gerald Ford handled the coin flip, as Switzer and Royal avoided each other during the midfield ceremony.

With Texas leading 6–0, Longhorns running back Ivy Suber, who had been hotly recruited by both teams, fumbled at his own 37 late in the game. OU, ranked third at the time, recovered and soon scored the game-tying touchdown.

All the Sooners needed was an Uwe von Schamann extra point—he was 149-of-150 in PATs for his career—but the snap was high, and he never received the chance to win the game.

When it was over, the scoreboard read 6–6, and neither team or coach was happy.

Royal stormed to the locker room, vomiting before he reached it. He called OU's coaches "sorry bastards." In his final season as Texas's head coach, he also would admit there is no game he ever wanted to win more throughout his playing and coaching career that spanned 30 years.

Switzer, too, believes his team should have won the game.

"We muffed the snap," Switzer said. "Should have won that game 7–6."

Recently, Lacewell told a Dallas newspaper of the alleged spy campaign, "We were young and ignorant and foolish. This is a great case of some overzealous young guys doing things they shouldn't have done. If I had to do it again today, I wouldn't do it, particularly against Coach Royal...I don't think any one of us would.

"Oklahoma-Texas is too great a rivalry to mess with."

1980: "Hold onto the Ball!"

No. 3–ranked Texas won 20–13 in by far the worst game of J.C. Watt's career. He lost three fumbles and threw four interceptions as the Sooners committed eight turnovers.

"I wished I'd had a pair of sunglasses and a Panama hat so I could have left the Cotton Bowl incognito," Watts said recently. "I had turned the ball over seven times...Coach Switzer once said the fastest man on a football field is the quarterback who just threw an interception. I was the fastest guy leaving the Cotton Bowl that day, for sure."

1984: Kiss Your Sister Again

This is the other game Switzer always believed should have been an Oklahoma victory.

Texas entered No. 1; OU was No. 3. During the game, Switzer wore a hat that read "Beat Texas."

On a rain-soaked field, Texas jumped to a 10–0 halftime lead, but OU rallied to lead 15–12 in the game's closing seconds. With 10 seconds remaining, Texas was driving and was within field-goal range, but decided to take one more shot at the end zone. The Sooners' Keith Stanberry appeared to make a clean interception in the end zone, but the officials ruled the pass incomplete. Texas's Jeff Ward subsequently kicked a field goal, and the game ended 15–15.

"In '84 we got screwed out of that one," Switzer said. "My record should have been the same against Texas as it was against

Nebraska. I went 9–5–2 against Texas. I should have been 11–5 against Texas."

1996: First Overtime Game

It didn't appear the Sooners would stand a chance, entering the game with an 0–4 record in John Blake's first season as head coach. OU had even been beaten by Tulsa 31–24 two weeks earlier for the first time since 1943. Texas, ranked No. 25, was a 22-point favorite.

Texas led 24–13 with 9:42 remaining, but the Sooners rallied with a touchdown, two-point conversion, and field goal to send the game into the first overtime in Big 12 Conference history. It was the first season in which the overtime format had been instituted by the NCAA.

After Texas kicked a field goal on its first possession of overtime, OU running back James Allen took control of the game three consecutive times, for 16 yards and then catching a screen pass to the 3-yard line. On the next play, he busted over the right side for the game-winning touchdown.

"I have heard of 'Sooner Magic,' and it was here today," said Sooners receiver Jarrail Jackson.

It would be one of only 12 victories for Blake in his three years as Oklahoma head coach, his only win over Texas, and his only victory over a ranked opponent.

2000-2004: Stoops Takes No Prisoners

Following a 38–28 loss in his first Texas game in 1999, Bob Stoops suddenly let the Longhorns know that there was a new sheriff in town and things would be different in this series from here on out.

He made his proclamation through a 63–14 crushing of the Longhorns in 2000.

It ended up as the most-lopsided OU-Texas score ever, but that record wouldn't last long. Sooners running back Quentin Griffin scored six touchdowns, also a record for the game. At one point, OU led 42–0 and held Texas to minus-7 yards rushing, an all-time regular-season low for the Longhorns.

OU went on to an undefeated season and first national championship in 15 years.

"Beating Texas is always special, but I really think that game was a turning point for the whole program," safety Roy Williams said.

The following year, OU used a stifling defense and a late interception of Texas quarterback Chris Simms to seal the deal 14–3.

Leading only 7–3, the Sooners executed a perfect pooch punt that nailed the Longhorns offense at its own 3-yard line. On first down, Williams blitzed and leaped over a would-be blocker to hit Simms as he threw a pass, which deflected into the air before linebacker Teddy Lehman caught it and trotted into the end zone for a game-clinching score.

Following a 35–24 win over Texas in 2002, the Sooners exploded to break the record margin of victory once again. This time the score was 65–13, another beat-down of the Longhorns of historic proportions.

Jason White threw four touchdown passes. Remarkably, it also was the first time in history that Oklahoma had scored 50 or more points in four consecutive games. The No. 1 Sooners entered the game having beaten Fresno State 52–28, UCLA 59–24, and Iowa State 53–7 in the preceding weeks.

Texas entered the 2004 game as the nation's leading rushing team, but managed only 154 yards against the Sooners, who recorded a 12–0 shutout.

It was Oklahoma's fifth-consecutive win in the series, and fans were wondering if Texas would ever beat the Sooners again, as long as Stoops and Mack Brown were on opposing sidelines.

Texas would win the next two meetings, 45–12 (in the Longhorns' first national title season since 1969) and 28–10 the following year, before the Sooners stopped the two-skid with a 28–21 win in 2007, thanks to redshirt freshman Sam Bradford's three touchdown passes.

It gave Stoops' teams a 6–3 advantage over Brown's Longhorns.

chapter 18

Sooners in the Bowls

Bud Wilkinson, left, and Paul Bryant of Kentucky, whose teams met in the Sugar Bowl on New Year's Day, jokingly dip their fingers in a sugar bowl at a luncheon in Oklahoma City on December 8, 1950.

Like national championships, Heisman Trophies, and a record number of victories that come with their rich college football tradition, the Oklahoma Sooners have been a prominent player during the bowl season, especially on the hallowed grounds of the Orange Bowl in Miami.

The Sooners have played in 41 bowls, winning 24 and tying one. Eighteen of those were Orange Bowls, 12 of which Oklahoma has won.

Currect coach Bob Stoops has the rare distinction of coaching all the big five bowls—the Rose, Sugar, Orange, Cotton, and Fiesta.

Here's a capsule look at other significant bowl appearances by Oklahoma.

Bud's First Bowl

The 1948 Sooners lost their opening game 20–17 to Santa Clara and then ripped off nine consecutive victories to earn a berth in the '49 Sugar Bowl against undefeated and third-ranked North Carolina, which was led by the famous Charlie "Choo Choo" Justice.

It was Bud Wilkinson's first bowl game as OU head coach and just the third bowl game in school history.

A huge crowd of 80,383 showed up in New Orleans on New Year's Day.

"Before that first Sugar Bowl, they wanted to get a picture of me and Choo Choo Justice," OU All-American lineman Paul "Buddy" Burris recalled. "But Choo Choo didn't want to pose for a picture with the enemy. It really pissed me off. It made me play a better ballgame. I got in a couple of good licks on Choo Choo that day, too."

Early in the game, OU struggled to gain any yards.

"We couldn't move the ball at all against North Carolina," OU quarterback Jack Mitchell said. "We came to the bench one time after the first quarter, and I heard this drunk guy behind the bench yelling something like, 'Jumper...toe ball on 'er line.'

"I couldn't make out what the heck he was saying because he was slurring his speech. He kept yelling at us. Nobody else knew what he was talking about, but finally I made it out. It was, 'Jump into the air and throw the ball over the line.'

"I thought, 'Shit, we got that play in the playbook, but we never use it. The next time I was in there, I faked the handoff and jumped up and threw it to Jimmy Owens, and we did that two or three times to set up one touchdown."

Linebacker Myrle Greathouse made the play of the game, snagging an interception of Justice and running 70 yards to set up Mitchell's one-yard touchdown run for another score. The Sooners won 14–6.

"They named me MVP of the game, but Myrle Greathouse should have gotten it," Mitchell admitted. "He had a great game. I didn't even have a good game."

Mitchell threw three passes and did not have a completion. Darrell Royal completed his only attempt. OU attempted only four passes that day.

The 10–1 Sooners finished ranked second to No. 1 Notre Dame, which did not play in a bowl.

"That 1948 team was a damn good team," Burris said.

For the record, the great double-threat Justice rushed for 84 yards and passed for 57 more.

"One time I knocked him down, and he looked up at me and said, 'I would rather be playing golf,'" OU All-American tackle Wade Walker recalled.

"New Orleans was so good to us that week. Gomer Jones said that Coach Wilkinson was worried about us getting into trouble that week, but I told him, 'Gomer, you don't have to worry about us. This bunch will be ready.' That was true. We were old enough to know not to get our noses bloodied on Bourbon Street. We knew why we were there. We knew how to train, and we knew how to knock the heck out of people. We knew how to study and we knew how to go to school. We were a mature group."

It would be the first of three consecutive Sugar Bowl appearances for Oklahoma.

The LSU Spying Scandal

Before the next season's Sugar Bowl, the Sooners practiced in Biloxi, Mississippi, the week before the game. It seems a former LSU player showed up to watch the practices, planning to send information to his former coaches to help the Tigers in the upcoming game.

"There was a big scandal about it," OU running back Leon Heath remembered. "That really made us mad, and we took it out on them."

It even angered Wilkinson, who rarely showed contempt for an opponent.

Heath rushed for 170 yards on only 15 carries and scored on runs of 86 and 34 yards. The Sooners pummeled LSU 35–0. It remains the largest margin of victory in a bowl for the Sooners.

The Bear Bites Back

Before the 1951 Sugar Bowl, the Sooners' third-consecutive New Year's Day spent in New Orleans, they were riding a 31-game winning streak. Yet, Kentucky coach Paul "Bear" Bryant brazenly predicted his team would beat Oklahoma.

"It was the third time we had been down there, and Bear Bryant knew Bud Wilkinson well," Heath said. "Bear said before the game that they would beat us. Sure enough, they did. We outplayed them statistically, but we got down to the 4-yard line and failed to score, and we had other turnovers."

In the 13–7 loss, OU out-gained Kentucky 227–189 and had 18 first downs to only seven for Kentucky, but lost five fumbles.

The game featured two legendary players. Kentucky's Babe Parilli, who completed 9-of-12 passes for 105 yards and one touchdown, went on to become a pro football legend. OU's Billy Vessels went on to win the Heisman Trophy the following season.

OU Befriends OB—The Orange Bowl, That Is

The Sooners and the Orange Bowl have a long-lasting and satisfying relationship, dating to the 1939 game.

Once the Big 7, which later became the Big 8, signed a deal to send its champion to the Miami-based bowl game beginning in 1954 on an annual basis, the relationship between the Sooners and the Orange Bowl became intimate.

Overall, Oklahoma has played in 18 Orange Bowls, winning 12.

Of those dozen victories, four resulted in national championships for the Sooners—the 1956 OB win over Maryland, the 1976 OB win over Michigan, the 1986 OB win over Penn State, and the 2001 OB win over Florida State.

Of course, there were a few Orange Bowl losses that possibly cost OU national titles.

JFK Attends Orange Bowl

President John F. Kennedy attended the 1963 Orange Bowl between Oklahoma and Alabama, which turned out to be Wilkinson's final bowl game.

And again, Bear Bryant's team got the better of Wilkinson's, as the Crimson Tide won 17–0.

"We got beat 17–0, but we played better than the score indicated," Leon Cross said. "We fumbled [twice] that day."

Kennedy visited both locker rooms and handled the coin toss from the stands. It was no secret that he was close with Wilkinson, who later entered politics.

"Here we are trying to get ready for the most important game we had ever played, and in walks the president of the United States," OU center-linebacker Wayne Lee recalled. "As everyone knew, he and Bud were good friends. The president came around to everyone and introduced himself, and some of us were standing there in a T-shirt and jock strap. It was an emotional experience, but at the same time, it was a huge distraction."

OU's loss to Namath and the Tide would not be the biggest story in the state that day. Legendary U.S. Senator Robert S. Kerr (D-Okla.) died of a heart attack, setting in motion a series of events that would include Wilkinson resigning his OU post to run for that seat in 1964.

Less than 11 months later, Kennedy was assassinated in Dallas.

The Vols Miss a Field Goal

The 1968 Orange Bowl was a fitting end to Chuck Fairbanks's first season as Sooners' head coach. And in the end, he was vindicated for an ill-fated decision to put the game away in the final minutes.

"It went down to the wire with us leading 26–24 and had a fourth-and-one at midfield," Owens recalled. "They called on me to get the yard, but Tennessee sent Jack 'Hacksaw' Reynolds on a blitz, and I never got back to the line of scrimmage."

The Volunteers then moved downfield to get in position for the potential game-winning field goal.

"I was on the sideline…feeling terrible about not getting that yard," Owens said. "As they lined up for the field goal, I couldn't even watch, so I just turned my back to the game and looked up at all of the Oklahoma fans to see their reaction. They went crazy after the kick, and that is how I knew we won the ballgame."

Tennessee's Karl Kremser was wide right on a 43-yard attempt with only seven seconds remaining.

OU would not return to the Orange Bowl for another eight years.

Two Sugar Bowls, One Year

The Sooners won two Sugar Bowls in one year. True story.

On New Year's Day, 1972, Oklahoma clobbered Auburn 40–22 to finish ranked No. 2 for the 1971 season.

Three hundred and sixty-five days later, on New Year's Eve 1972, they shut out Penn State 14–0 to win the Sugar Bowl again.

"We are the only team to win two Sugar Bowls in one year," tackle Eddie Foster said.

The Sooners prepared for the second Sugar Bowl in a unique way. The coaches found a teaching tape designed for coaches' clinics made by Joe Paterno, titled "How to Defend the Wishbone." Oklahoma watched it over and over again.

"I'll be darned if Penn State didn't do exactly what was on that tape," Foster recalled.

The Revenge Game

The 1987 Orange Bowl gave Switzer a chance to avenge his most embarrassing bowl loss.

The Sooners were to meet Arkansas, his alma mater, which had demolished OU on the same field nine years earlier.

"For nine years I had been telling the home folks back in Arkansas that someday I would get them another Orange Bowl bid to meet Oklahoma and [I] would wipe out that personal humiliating loss that cost Oklahoma a national title," Switzer wrote in his autobiography.

"This was my chance. I wanted to beat Arkansas really bad—this is the only game I ever asked any team to win for *me*."

The Sooners delivered, intercepting five Arkansas passes in a 42–8 rout that awarded the head coach his redemption on his alma mater.

Just Who Is the Underdog?

The 2001 Orange Bowl signaled the arrival of Bob Stoops as one of the game's greatest present-day coaches. Florida State, despite being ranked No. 2, entered as the game a heavy favorite over the top-ranked and 12–0 Sooners.

That in itself irked Stoops, who lectured the media about tradition and history.

"People are talking about us as if we just started playing football," he said. "Oklahoma has a long and proud tradition and if you check, I think we have more national championships [than Florida State]."

They would add one more that night, as well.

The Seminoles had Heisman Trophy–winning quarterback Chris Weinke and the nation's top-ranked offense, but Oklahoma's defensive staff put together an excellent game plan, limiting FSU to 27 rushing yards and no points as OU stunned the Seminoles 13–2. Florida State's only points came on a safety late in the game.

"We knew Weinke wasn't mobile, so we would pressure him," safety Roy Williams said. "All they had in running plays was toss-left and toss-right. Their game plan was so simple. We attacked them. We were relentless that night. I don't think they crossed the 50-yard line for a long time in that game."

Most of the Sooners felt moments before the game that it would be a night to fulfill their dreams.

"That was the most focused group of football players I had ever been around," linebacker Teddy Lehman said. "You could have heard a pin drop on that bus and in the locker room before the game that night.

"One big play I remember that night was when Torrance [Marshall] had an interception and was bringing it down the sideline when Dante Jones sprinted from behind and mashed one of their offensive lineman. Our team just went nuts—we were so hyped up.

"As the game wore on, I got the feeling that Florida State wouldn't score no matter how long the game lasted. At one point, I thought, 'Man, I can't believe it is only 6–0, it feels like we are beating them 50–0.'"

The Sooners all believed that Florida State entered the game overconfident.

"I knew heading into that Orange Bowl game that Florida State underestimated us," Williams said. "They thought we were a hillbilly school from the Big 12. We were walking down South Beach one day, and we always believed in good sportsmanship, but when we tried to speak to a few of their players, some of them were very cocky. They didn't even want to acknowledge us."

"I still can't put into words how that [win] feels, even today," quarterback Josh Heupel said. "It's as good a feeling as you can ever imagine. To be able to share that with 100 other individuals, from players to coaches to support staff...it is something special."

A Rose Is a Rose

Thanks to the Bowl Championship Series's new formula, the Sooners received an opportunity to play in the Rose Bowl to cap the 2002 season. The bowl had been strictly a Pac-10 versus Big Ten affair for more than 50 years, but with Big Ten champion Ohio State playing in the BCS title game that season, it left an opportunity for the Rose Bowl. The Sooners gladly accepted and proceeded to whip an outmanned Washington State team 34–14.

With it, OU became only the fourth school to win each of the Orange, Sugar, Fiesta, Cotton, and Rose Bowls. The others are Notre Dame, Ohio State, and Penn State.

The Sooners sacked Washington State quarterback Jason Gesser six times, forced three turnovers, and held the Cougars to 243 total yards.

"At the Rose Bowl, we were motivated to play a great game because everybody was talking about Washington State's offense," linebacker Teddy Lehman said. "We knew that we could shut them down because we were more talented, more physical, and more aggressive. They played a different kind of football in the Pac-10 than what we played. That was a great day to be a Sooner."

The Debacle Loss to USC

No Oklahoma team has been as manhandled as the 2004 squad was in the 2005 Orange Bowl.

The Sooners entered 12–0 and ranked No. 2, having played only two games they did not win by more than seven points. USC entered 12–0 and ranked No. 1. At the end, a 55–19 loss to USC was as shocking as it was embarrassing.

The Sooners committed five turnovers to none for USC. Three of those were interceptions thrown by Jason White in the final game of his career.

"We really wanted to establish the run against USC and throw the ball and do all the things we had done all year," White said. "But they played their best game of the season and, obviously, we did things we had never done before. Things took a turn for the worse early in the game and never got better.

"We turned the ball over, and that killed us. We had to play catch-up for the rest of the game. They played a great game and they were very well-coached. They were prepared to play. They had a great front four, and their team speed was extremely fast. That loss was very disappointing because I and all the other seniors worked so hard, and to not go out on top was tough on all of us."

An Amazing, Remarkable Game...But Still, a Loss

The 2007 Fiesta Bowl will be talked about for decades to come.

It was exhilarating, exciting, and will go down as one of the best games, let alone one of the best bowl games, in college football history.

Unfortunately for the Sooners, history will record them as the loser—43–42 in overtime to undefeated Boise State.

The Sooners had rallied from a 28–10 deficit to the underdog Broncos to take a 35–28 lead into the final minute. But a "hook-and-ladder" pass play by Boise State resulted in a game-tying touchdown on fourth-and-18 yards that sent the contest into overtime. After Oklahoma scored on Adrian Peterson's 25-yard run on the first play in overtime, the Broncos scored again on a fourth-down pass.

In a daring move, they then went for two points, converting with a Statue of Liberty running play around the left end to win the game by one point.

The game became what pop culture now calls "an instant classic," but it will always be remembered by Sooners fans, coaches, and players as a huge disappointment.

The subject grew old on Bob Stoops, since it continued to surface during the 2007 season, especially once OU earned another trip to the Fiesta Bowl a year later.

"It was a long time ago," Stoops said during OU's return trip to Arizona. "I loved that everybody wanted to write about that all spring and through the summer. It had absolutely no effect on us whatsoever."

"It was a classic game that everybody else loves to watch over and over," OU receiver Malcolm Kelly said. "But to us, it's still just a loss."

A year later, in the 2008 Fiesta, OU had yet another surprising loss, this time 48–28 to a West Virginia team that had lost its previous game and its head coach leading up to the game. Stoops's bowl record has taken a swing for the worse following a 3–1 start, which included wins in the Orange, Cotton, and Rose Bowls in successive seasons.

Two of Stoops's teams' bowl losses came on the final play—the 1999 Independence Bowl where Mississippi's Les Binkley kicked a 39-yard field goal to give the Rebels a 27–25 win over the Sooners, and the aforementioned Fiesta Bowl loss to Boise State.

chapter 19

Oklahoma and the Heisman Trophy

Billy Sims poses with the Heisman Trophy he received at the Downtown Athletic Club in New York City in December 1978.

Only three schools (Notre Dame, USC, and Ohio State, all of whom have produced seven winners each) have a more enduring relationship with the Heisman Trophy than the Oklahoma Sooners, who have claimed four winners since the prestigious award was created in 1935.

Billy Vessels (1952), Steve Owens (1969), Billy Sims (1978), and Jason White (2003) are the four who have been presented with the 13½-inch high, 25-pound, leather-helmeted, bronzed, stiff-arming trophy.

Here's a look at their careers, their words, their statistics, and their Heisman-winning facts.

Billy Vessels (1952)

The stats: Vessels rushed for 1,072 yards and 17 touchdowns during his Heisman-winning season, which are pretty good numbers for that era. He also passed for 209 yards and three touchdowns, but what is most impressive is that he averaged 6.4 yards per carry. It was a 195-yard, three-touchdown performance against Notre Dame that gained everyone's attention. He led the Sooners to a 26–4–1 record during his three seasons. Vessels scored 15 touchdowns during his sophomore season, in which OU won its first national championship. His junior season was marred by a broken leg, which forced him to miss six games.

The runner-up: Jack Scarbath, quarterback, Maryland

Margin of victory: 158 points

In his words: "I never even had heard of the Heisman Trophy. When I went to New York the next week [for the ceremony], I realized its full impact."

From his coach: "He was the first player that I had ever been around who was the fastest player on the field and also the toughest." —Bud Wilkinson

After Oklahoma: Vessels played for the Edmonton Eskimos of the Western Interprovincial Football Union (which became the

Canadian Football League) in 1953 before serving as an officer in the U.S. Army. He later played the 1956 season with the Baltimore Colts before a leg injury ended his career. He was inducted into the National Football Foundation and College Hall of Fame in 1974. Vessels, who lived most of his adult life in Coral Gables, Florida, worked in real estate and horse-breeding, as well as an officer on the Florida Pari-Mutuel Wagering Commission. He died November 17, 2001, of congestive heart failure at the age of 70. He was survived by his wife Susanne, and children Chase, Lance, and Jane.

The best story: Wilkinson and Vessels flew to New York together for the ceremony. On the way, the coach gave his star player the best advice he had ever heard: "You are going to have these writers talk to you and make this big production of you. Don't pay any attention to it. What really counts is what you are 25 years later."

Vessels said he never forgot that lesson. A native of Cleveland, Oklahoma, Vessels was known as "Curly." As a kid, he often cut off his naturally curly hair to get away from the nickname. Today, the high school football stadium in Cleveland is named Billy Vessels Memorial Stadium.

Steve Owens (1969)

The stats: One of college football's all-time great workhorses, Owens carried 358 times for 1,523 yards and 23 touchdowns during his Heisman-winning season. That followed up a junior season in which he rushed for 1,649 yards and 21 touchdowns. He holds five OU career records, including most carries in one game (55) and most carries in a career (958).

The runner-up: Mike Phipps, quarterback, Purdue

Margin of victory: 154 points

In his words: "The ceremony was on a Thursday night, and I remember meeting Tom Seaver of the Mets. They had just won the World Series that year. I just couldn't believe this was happening to me. On Friday, I appeared on *The Tonight Show with Johnny Carson*. As I sat in the green room waiting to go on the show, Muhammad Ali was in there with me. Someone stuck their head inside the door and said, 'Mr. Owens, you have a call from the president of the United States.'

"An aide to President Nixon was calling to see if I would ride with him aboard Air Force One down to the Arkansas-Texas game. So the next day, we flew down to Fayetteville aboard Air Force One, and I got to spend time on board with the president. He gave me some horseshoe cuff-links, which I still have, and I gave him a Heisman memento. The funny thing is, after the game, Barbara and I rode back to Norman with some friends in an old, beat-up Chevy. We arrived on Air Force One and departed in a clunker. We still laugh about that."

From his coach: "Steve is the greatest inside runner I've ever seen. He is remarkable at diagnosing defenses and finding holes. He has tremendous durability and strength." —Chuck Fairbanks.

After Oklahoma: A first-round draft pick of the Detroit Lions, Owens was a consensus All-Pro in 1971 and '72. He played five seasons with the Lions and finished with 2,451 career rushing yards and 22 touchdowns. He was inducted into the College Football Hall of Fame in 1991. He is CEO of Steve Owens & Associates and Steve Owens Insurance Group in Norman. Owens also is a founding member of both the Norman Public School Foundation and the Miami, Oklahoma, Public School Foundation. He has been a spokesman for the Ronald McDonald House and played a key role in raising funds to create the facility in Oklahoma City. He also has been involved with the Make-A-Wish Foundation, the Cystic Fibrosis Foundation, the Child Welfare Citizens Advisory Board, the Oklahoma Chapter of the National Football Foundation, and the Advisory Board for the Norman Family Y. He is on the board of directors for the Jim Thorpe Association, the Oklahoma Sports Hall of Fame, Roy Williams Safety Net Foundation, and Arvest Bank. He also runs the Steve Owens Foundation, supporting the youth of Oklahoma and mental health issues.

Meanwhile, Owens continues to have strong ties to the University of Oklahoma and once served as its athletics director in the 1990s. He has served as a member of the OU Centennial Committee, the OU Alumni Advisory Council, and OU Alumni and Friends of Cleveland County. He was the first chairman of the Sooner Club Fund Drive. And he served on the "O" Club board of directors and is a past president of the organization. He is a founding member of the OU Football Letterman's Association and also served on its board of directors.

He and his wife Barbara have two sons, Blake and Mike. They have one grandchild, Quincy.

The best story: In the 1960s winners of the Heisman were notified with a telephone call and then later honored at a banquet in New York. Owens's father, Olen, nicknamed "Peanut," was a hard-working truck driver who happened to be driving his rig through Dallas the day the winner was to be announced. So he pulled into a truck stop and called Owens's mother. "Did the boy win that there trophy?" he asked her. Given the response he was hoping for, he climbed back into his truck and continued on his way.

Owens almost gave up on the award himself, once 10 minutes passed the scheduled time that the winner was to receive the congratulatory phone call. He started to walk out of the OU student union when somebody hollered, "Hey, Steve, you just won the Heisman!" The Sooners still had another game to play, and in that game, against rival Oklahoma State, Owens carried 25 times in the third quarter and finished with a record 55 carries for the game. His record workload resulted in a 28–27 win over the Cowboys and was credited with saving the jobs of Fairbanks and his staff.

Billy Sims (1978)

The stats: Sims's junior year was simply amazing. He rushed for 1,896 yards and 22 touchdowns as OU rolled to an 11–1 record.

His season included four 200-yard games. Sims finished his career with 1,670 yards during his senior season, but USC's Charles White won the Heisman, while Sims finished second. Also, it is worth noting that several injuries prevented Sims from accumulating even more impressive career statistics.

The runner-up: Chuck Fusina, quarterback, Penn State

Margin of victory: 77 points

In his words: "I had no idea of what to expect about the Heisman Trophy, but Steve Owens gave me a little insight on it. Until you experience the aura and history of it, you have no idea of how big it is. It was the first time I ever bought a suit, and I even borrowed some luggage for the trip to New York. Coming from Hooks, Texas, where all we had was trees and grass and countryside, I had never seen a place with so many buildings and concrete. It was quite an event and something I will never forget. Now, more than 25 years later, 99 percent of the people I meet relate me to winning the Heisman rather than the NFL or the Detroit Lions or anything else."

From his coach: "One of the things I am most proud of Billy for is that he came back and he graduated. Not many Heisman Trophy winners graduated around his time. They were going on to pro football and forgetting about their academics. But he made a promise to his grandmother that he would graduate. And he did. I remember the joy on Billy's face with his cap and gown on and his diploma in his hand, hugging his wife and his relatives." —Barry Switzer

After Oklahoma: Sims became the top pick of the 1980 NFL Draft by the Detroit Lions, with whom he played five seasons before his career ended prematurely due to a knee injury. He rushed for 5,106 yards and 42 touchdowns. He was inducted into the National Football Foundation and College Hall of Fame in 1995. Sims fell on hard times financially following his NFL career and eventually had to sell his Heisman Trophy to help pay some of his mounting debt. Like OU's other Heisman winners, he has been honored with a bronze statue in "Heisman Park" outside of Memorial Stadium.

The best story: Before his junior season, in which he won the Heisman, Sims almost quit the Sooners team. "I was so frustrated that I really wanted to quit football," he said. "The injuries really caught up with me. I thought I would just go to class, get my degree, and then go get a job. I was frustrated. It's tough being injured. I mean, coaches who used to talk to me were not talking to me all of a sudden. It was like I wasn't adding anything to the team, so I was forgotten. Coach Switzer talked me out of quitting. He knew I had been a great player in high school, but things just weren't working out for me. He understood all of that and told me to be patient and things would work out for me eventually."

Jason White (2003)

The stats: As a junior, White set several school records while operating the Sooners' wide-open offense. He completed 278-of-451 passes (61.6 percent) for 3,846 yards and a school-record 40 touchdowns. He was intercepted 10 times. He passed for five touchdowns twice. During his senior season, White finished third in the Heisman voting, behind teammate Adrian Peterson and trophy winner Matt Leinart of USC. In 2004 he passed for 3,205 yards and 35 touchdowns, and his completion percentage increased to 65.4 percent.

The runner-up: Larry Fitzgerald, receiver, Pittsburgh

Margin of victory: 128 points

In his words: "I never thought I was going to win it. I never wrote a speech. It is still all a blur to me. Even today, I guess I don't realize what I have done. More than anything, winning it changed my life. I went from being a small-town Oklahoma boy to being interviewed on all those national TV shows."

From his coach: "Jason is one of the great stories in college football. He has shown perseverance and toughness. Jason was my first recruit when I got here. My first stop was to Jason White's house to try and convince him why he didn't want to go to Miami. Thank goodness he believed and trusted us." —Bob Stoops

After Oklahoma: White was not drafted by an NFL team, in part due to several knee injuries, but did participate in the preseason camp of the Tennessee Titans. He did not make the team and, thus, retired from football. Today, White owns and operates A Store Divided, an OU/Oklahoma State memorabilia store. He also worked with Owens in the insurance industry. The water tower in the town of Tuttle, Oklahoma, is painted with "Home of Jason White, 2003 Heisman Trophy Winner."

The best story: Like Sims, White, too, thought of quitting football because of injuries. He endured two serious knee injuries in successive seasons and had decided to quit and concentrate on getting his degree when OU quarterbacks coach Chuck Long talked him into staying. "I decided then if I sat on the bench the rest of my career, at least I could look back and say I gave it my all," White said. "I wanted to finish my career as a Sooner. I knew the way the fans and Sooner Nation treated its players was awesome, and I didn't want to give up on that. I wanted to finish as a letterman." On June 19, 2003, before what would be White's fifth season at OU, head coach Bob Stoops named him the starting quarterback. It was his 23rd birthday. That season, he won the Heisman.

Other Sooners Who Received Heisman Votes

Here are several other Sooners who finished in the top 10 in Heisman Trophy voting: Jack Mitchell, eighth, 1948; Leon Heath, seventh, 1950; J.D. Roberts, eighth, 1953; Kurt Burris, second (to winner Alan Ameche of Wisconsin), 1954; Bo Bolinger, ninth, 1955; Tommy McDonald, third, and Jerry Tubbs, fourth, 1956; Clendon Thomas, ninth, 1957; Bob Harrison, seventh, 1958; Granville Liggins, seventh, 1967; Greg Pruitt, third, and Jack Mildren, sixth, 1971; Pruitt, second (to winner Johnny Rodgers of Nebraska), 1972; Lucious Selmon, seventh, 1973; Joe Washington, third, and Rod Shoate, seventh, 1974; Washington, fifth, and Lee Roy Selmon, ninth, 1975; Billy Sims, second (to winner Charles White of USC), 1979; Brian Bosworth, fourth, 1986; Josh Heupel, second (to winner Chris Weinke of Florida State), 2000; Roy Williams, seventh, 2001; Adrian Peterson, second (to Matt Leinart of USC) and Jason White, third, 2004.

chapter 20
The Best to Wear the Crimson and Cream

Jason White, perhaps the best quarterback in Oklahoma's history, celebrates the Sooners' 12–0 win over Texas with fans in Dallas on October 9, 2004.

Ranking the greatest this or the best that of all-time is a very subjective and difficult way to categorize football players.

There really is no definitive way to rank them since the criteria vary from era to era. Are they judged by personal awards, statistics, performance, talent, or, even, was the player a significant part of a championship team?

For example, was a Heisman Trophy winner in the 1950s a better running back than a three-year starter who played in only two losing games in his career, rushed for 4,071 yards, and 39 touchdowns but did not win the Heisman?

That's the case of Billy Vessels and Joe Washington, separated by 20 years and a generation of football.

Vessels gained a little more than half of the yards gained by Washington. He rushed for 1,072 yards in his Heisman-winning season of 1952. Washington had *three* 1,000 yard seasons.

It's truly impossible to compare them, given how the game changed a thousand different ways from the early 1950s until the 1970s. In fact, the game has changed so much since World War II that statistics don't translate. A 600-yard rusher in 1945 is what a 1,200-yard rusher is today.

And when it comes to quarterbacks and passing statistics, the comparison is completely lost. The game of football was a run-oriented game through the 1970s, especially at Oklahoma where the single-wing and the wishbone were signatures. Until Bob Stoops brought a wide-open offense to Norman in 1999, Cale Gundy held the school's single-season passing record of 2,311 yards.

Stoops's quarterbacks have surpassed that mark every single season in which he has been head coach.

That is why I never liked to compare players or teams, for that matter, from one era to another. It really is apples and oranges. But I will do it here, anyway, for the sake of discussion and provoking thought of just how great the following players were.

Bear in mind, I put a large emphasis on the player's total career, not just how great he may have been in one particular season. These rankings, however, are not affected by a player's ensuing success, or lack of it, in the NFL.

So here goes…

Quarterbacks

1. Jason White (1999–2004)
2. Jack Mildren (1969–1971)
3. Josh Heupel (1999–2000)
4. Jamelle Holieway (1985–1988)
5. Steve Davis (1973–1975)

Honorable mention: Thomas Lott (1976–1978), Bobby Warmack (1966–1968), J.C. Watts (1978–1980), Jimmy Harris (1954–1956), Eddie Crowder (1950–1952), Darrell Royal (1946–1949), Cale Gundy (1990–1993), Nate Hybl (2000–2002), Jack Mitchell (1946–1948)

White holds most of OU's passing records and won the Heisman Trophy. Enough said. His 81 career touchdown passes is 28 more than No. 2 on the list—Heupel. In fact, Heupel is second in most OU career passing categories and would have been number one, but remember, he was a transfer who played only two seasons for the Sooners. Still, he holds many of OU's single-season records. Amazingly, he had 14 career 300-yard passing games and two 400-yard passing games.

The downside is that he ranks eighth on OU's career passing efficiency list (135.92) due to his 31 interceptions in 25 starts.

My personal favorite, Mildren, the "Father of the Wishbone," holds OU's single-season record for passing efficiency (199.52 in 1971).

Crowder ranks first in career passing efficiency, but he attempted only 114 passes in three seasons—a little more than White attempted in two games.

Even though he does not rank in OU's career passing categories, Holieway probably was the best Sooner ever at running the option.

It seems that all OU quarterbacks had spectacular winning records. Lott was a winner (he won 23 of 29 starts). Likewise for

Watts, who won 22 of 25 starts and improved dramatically as a passer as his career progressed.

The best winning percentage of any quarterback is owned by Jimmy Harris, who orchestrated the Sooners offense during the 47-game winning streak of the 1950s. OU won 15 of 16 games in which Royal started and 18 of 22 in which Jack Mitchell started. Davis, who was not highly recruited, won 32 of 34 starts, and isn't that what a quarterback is all about?

Running Backs

1. Billy Sims (1975–1979)
   Steve Owens (1967–1969)*t*
3. Joe Washington (1972–1975)
4. Adrian Peterson (2004–2006)
5. Greg Pruitt (1970–1972)
   Billy Vessels (1950–1952)*t*

Honorable mention: Clendon Thomas (1955–1957), Tommy McDonald (1956), Quentin Griffin (1999–2002), Stanley Wilson (1979–1982), Lydell Carr (1984–1987)

I know, I know, you may think I took the easy way out in picking both Sims and Owens as the top running backs in Sooners history. But how you can really rank one above the other? Both won Heismans.

Owens ranks first in OU history in rushing attempts (958) by more than 200, touchdowns (57), and 100-yard games (23). His seven games of 40 carries or more is one of the most amazing statistics in college football history. Did you realize he had 55- and 53-carry games in 1969? Most teams do not have that many rushing attempts per game these days. Sims ranks number one in career rushing yards (4,118) and 200-yard games (seven). He is second with 53 touchdowns and third in 100-yard games (20).

You may wonder why Peterson is fourth—behind Washington. For starters, he left with a year of eligibility remaining or he otherwise would hold most of OU's career records.

Peterson rushed for 4,045 yards and 40 touchdowns in his career and holds the single-season rushing record with 1,925 yards in 2004. Imagine what he would have done if he remained healthy and stayed for his senior season.

Simply put, Washington was spectacular. His 4,071 career rushing yards ranks slightly behind Sims. As a matter of fact, there is a case to be made for him to be ranked first even though he did not win all the national awards that Sims and Owens did.

It shows you the depth of talent the Sooners have had in the backfield over history when Pruitt, who still holds the school's single-game rushing record (294 yards against Kansas State in 1971), and Vessels rank fifth. After all, all but Peterson are members of the College Hall of Fame.

Here's a statistic that blew me away, and you get bonus points for having an extremely high Sooner IQ if you get it: Who is second on the OU career list in receptions behind Mark Clayton? Tinker Owens? No? Curtis Fagan? No.

It's running back Quentin Griffin, of all people, who finished with 169 career receptions—all out of the backfield.

Receivers

1. Mark Clayton (2001–2004)
2. Eddie Hinton (1966–1968)
3. Trent Smith (1999–2002)
4. Curtis Fagan (1999–2002)
5. Antwone Savage (1999–2002)

First of all, Keith Jackson (1984–1987) was more talented than anyone on this list, but he played tight end during the wishbone and I formation era, so I will give him an asterisk. I sure hate the fact that this list is tilted toward recent history, but how can it not be, given the wide-open offense the Sooners have operated since 1999?

Clayton set all of the OU receiving records during his career, from 2001 to 2004, finishing with 221 receptions for 3,241 yards and 31 touchdowns—which all are school records by a wide, wide margin. His 83 receptions and 1,425 receiving yards in 2003 are also single-season school records.

Naming numbers two through five on this list was the hard part, given the offensive style transformation the Sooners underwent over the years. The only major award an Oklahoma player has never won is the Fred Biletnikoff Award, which is presented annually to the nation's best receiver.

Hinton was a great, great receiver who is penalized statistically because he played in the run-first, run-second, throw-if-you-must era. He finished with 123 receptions for 1,894 yards and 12 touchdowns. He was a potent deep threat, and his 15.4-yard receiving average is higher than even Clayton's. And remember, his career statistics, like anyone who played before 1972, were accumulated in only three seasons—not four.

Hinton's senior season—64 receptions, 1,034 yards, and six touchdowns—produced then–mind-boggling numbers for 1968.

Now, as far as Jackson is concerned, he doesn't rank in the top 10 in OU history in most receiving categories except career touchdowns (his 15 ranks fourth behind Clayton, Travis Wilson, and Smith). Those numbers illustrate how Jackson was mostly used on third down and near the goal line.

Offensive Linemen

1. Tom Brahaney (1970–1972)
2. Buddy Burris* (1946–1948)
3. Anthony Phillips (1985–1988)
4. Jammal Brown (2001–2004)
5. Bill Krisher* (1955–1957)
   Jim Weatherall* (1948–1951)*t*

Honorable mention: Bob Kalsu (1965–1967), Kurt Burris (1951–1954), Wade Walker (1946–1949), J.D. Roberts* (1951–1953), Bob Harrison (1956–1958), Jerry Tubbs* (1954–1956), Wayne Lee (1960–1962), Sammy Jack Claphan*

(1976–1978), Karl Baldischwiler (1975–1977), Ralph Neely (1962–1964), Leon Cross (1960–1962), John Roush (1972–1974), Jerry Thompson* (1957–1959), Greg Roberts (1975–1978), Terry Crouch (1979–1981), Louis Oubre (1978–1980), Mark Hutson (1984–1987), Ken Mendenhall (1967–1969) (*Played both offense and defense)

Okay, there are no statistics on which to judge a linemen's career, other than the offense's yardage production, so this is a tough category, especially since Oklahoma has produced so many great offensive linemen.

A dominating center, Brahaney anchored the Sooners' best offense (1971) in school history. He was a two-time All-American.

There was no TV to show how good he was, but they say nobody was tougher than Buddy Burris, that is, during his playing days. There's the time that Darrell Royal got the better of him one night many years later, but that's another story for another time.

Burris is one of two Sooners ever to be named an All-American three times.

Consider that Tubbs, Weatherall, J.D. Roberts (Outland Trophy winner), and Brahaney are in the College Football Hall of Fame—and that Burris and Krisher should be.

Phillips is one of only three Sooners to be named all-conference in four seasons, a testament to his consistency. Walker, later the school's athletics director, was another (Darrell Reed was the third).

Brown was a massive, dominating offensive tackle who did not allow a sack during his senior season. And that's quite an accomplishment, considering the Sooners attempted 406 passes in 2004.

Defensive Linemen

1. Lee Roy Selmon (1972–1975)
2. Tommie Harris (2001–2003)
3. Tony Casillas (1982–1985)
4. Granville Liggins (1965–1967)

5. Rick Bryan (1980–1983)

Honorable mention: Darrell Reed (1984–1987), Lucious Selmon (1971–1973), Dewey Selmon (1972–1975), Dan Cody (2000–2004), Reggie Kinlaw (1975–1978), Kevin Murphy (1981–1985)

There is no doubt about who's number one on this list. Lee Roy Selmon will go down as one of the best defensive linemen in college football history.

He was nothing less than dominating and unblockable.

"I don't think anyone ever blocked him during our four years at Oklahoma," running back Joe Washington said.

Selmon and Casillas are in the College Football Hall of Fame, and I really believe Liggins deserves to be. Liggins was a classic nose guard, strong and mobile who could shed centers and guards with ease.

Harris was a two-time All-American and played the run and rushed the quarterback equally well. At times, he was dominating, despite being double-teamed, but he left early for the NFL's riches. Bryan, too, was a great, great player.

Also, I want to state that many of the offensive linemen listed above during the two-way days could be listed as defensive linemen as well. Krisher, for example, was one of OU's all-time greats as a defensive lineman. According to those he played with, he hit as hard as today's players.

Linebackers

1. Rod Shoate (1972–1974)
2. George Cumby (1975–1979)
3. Brian Bosworth (1984–1986)
4. Daryl Hunt (1975–1978)
5. Rocky Calmus (1998–2001)
    Teddy Lehman (2000–2003)*t*
Honorable mention: Jackie Shipp (1980–83)

Without a doubt, ranking this category was the most difficult, simply because the Sooners have produced so many great linebackers. The heck with Penn State—OU could be labeled "Linebacker U."

Therefore, I am sure this will be one of the most controversial categories, and I have listed the most controversial player in OU history third on this list.

Love him or loathe him, Bosworth was a great, great college linebacker. He played sideline to sideline in a rage. He won the Butkus Award twice. Still, his detractors would say that his 413 career tackles ranks only sixth on Oklahoma's all-time list. If he had stayed for his senior season, he likely would have finished atop this list.

Hunt recorded 530 career tackles and was as consistent as any player in OU history. Shoate was a three-time All-American, a talented hitting machine. Cumby, who wasn't recruited by any major program other than Oklahoma, was a diamond in the rough.

Calmus finished with 59 tackles for loss—by far the tops in OU history. That number illustrates the attacking defense that Bob Stoops brought to Norman and how defenses have changed over the years. He and Teddy Lehman (48½) are the only linebackers in the top 10 on the tackle-for-loss list because linebackers did not blitz as often pre-1980.

Surprisingly, Lehman, however, does not rank in OU's top 10 in career tackles.

If anything, perhaps I may have Shipp underrated. He had 489 career tackles, but he is penalized somewhat because the Sooners defenses simply were not that good during the 1981, '82, and '83 seasons, in which OU lost 12 games—many of them high-scoring shootouts in which the defense could not get off the field.

Hunt, Bosworth, Shoate, Cumby, Calmus, and Lehman, on the other hand, were major reasons the Sooners had great defenses during their years.

Defensive Backs

1. Rickey Dixon (1984–1987)
2. Roy Williams (1999–2001)
3. Zac Henderson (1974–1977)
4. Darrell Royal (1946–1949)
5. Randy Hughes (1972–1974)

Honorable mention: David Vickers (1984–1987), Derrick Strait (2000–2003), J.T. Thatcher (1997–2000), Darrol Ray (1976–1979), Sonny Brown (1983–1986), Scott Case (1982–1983)

Along with receivers, this is the least-honored position throughout Oklahoma history, and I think that relates more to the type of offenses the Sooners faced through the decades of the Big 8. Most Big 8 teams ran the football, or at least tried to.

Dixon finished his career with 17 interceptions, including the school's single-season record of nine in 1987.

Henderson was a two-time All-American and three-time All–Big 8.

After that, Williams, Hughes, and Dixon were All-Americans, but there hasn't been a collection of honors for OU defensive backs over the years.

Royal still holds OU's career interception record with 18, which is very surprising given the era in which he played was not exactly a pass-happy period. You would think someone would want to break that record, just to knock a converted Longhorn out of the Sooners record books.

Kickers

1. Garrett Hartley (2004–2007)
2. Tim Lashar (1983–1986)
3. Tim Duncan (1999–2001)

4. R.D. Lashar (1987–1990)
5. Uwe von Schamann (1976–1978)

Honorable mention: Trey DiCarlo (2002–2004), Scott Blanton (1991–1994), Jeremy Alexander (1994–1997), Michael Keeling (1979–1982), Tony DiRienzo (1973–1975)

Hartley ranks first on OU's percentage list, having made 47-of-58 field goals during his career. He was a Lou Groza Award finalist as a junior, but he didn't have many chances as a senior, making 13-of-15 field goals. He ranks third in scoring among kickers with 310 points. On the downside, he missed five PATs during his senior season, after making 98-of-100 as an underclassman.

Tim Lashar ranks second all-time in kick-scoring and is tied with Tim Duncan with 48 career field goals each.

R.D. Lashar made 44-of-63 field goals in his career, good for third in percentage at OU.

Von Schamann doesn't have the statistics others have on this list. He made only 33-of-51 field goals in his career, but he made arguably what was the biggest field goal in OU history—the 41-yarder that beat Ohio State 29–28 in 1977. Remarkably, he made 149-of-150 extra points.

Punters

1. Jeff Ferguson (1998–2001)
2. Jack Jacobs (1939–1941)
3. Michael Keeling (1979–1982)
4. Blake Ferguson (2002–2004)
5. Brad Reddell (1989–1992)

Honorable mention: Brian Lewis (1995–1996), Todd Thomsen (1986–1988)

First of all, a punter had to average 40-plus yards over a career to make this list. Jeff Ferguson leads in career average—at 42.48—and, remarkably, he punted 252 times, also the most in OU history.

Jacobs, nicknamed "Indian Jack," was an Oklahoma legend. He holds the single-season record with 47.84 yards per punt, set in 1940 on 31 punts.

Keeling was Oklahoma's finest punter during Barry Switzer's era of 1973 to 1988.

As far as single seasons go, Cody Freeby was spectacular in 2005 in his only season as a starter, averaging 42.31 per punt.

The Biggest Victories (In No Particular Order)

Oklahoma 17, Nebraska 7—November 21, 1987. In this colossal matchup of No. 1 versus No. 2, the Sooners came out on top in Lincoln.

Oklahoma 13, Florida State 2—January 2, 2001. A large underdog, the Sooners rode one of the greatest defensive performances in school history to shock the Seminoles to win the national championship in Bob Stoops's second season.

Oklahoma 29, Ohio State 28—September 24, 1977. It wasn't for a national championship, but it was one of the largest marquee regular-season non-conference matchups in college football history. The game went back and forth before von Schamann's 41-yard field goal on the final play ended it in grand fashion.

Oklahoma 20, Maryland 6—January 2, 1956. The Sooners capped a perfect 11–0, national championship season with a convincing win over the Terps in the Sugar Bowl. Trailing 6–0 at the half, OU went into its famous fast-break offense to score two touchdowns in the second half before Carl Dodd put the game away with an 82-yard interception return for a touchdown.

Oklahoma 31, Nebraska 14—October 28, 2000. In a matchup of unbeaten teams, the Sooners knocked off the No. 1 Cornhuskers in Norman after falling behind 14–0. The game signaled the Bob Stoops's era would be a great one and was a springboard for the national championship.

Oklahoma 25, Penn State 10—January 1, 1986. The Sooners entered this Orange Bowl ranked No. 3, but were facing the top-ranked Nittany Lions. Once No. 2 Miami lost to Tennessee in the Sugar Bowl, it opened the door for OU to claim another national title. And the Sooners did just that, as Tim Lashar kicked four field goals and the OU defense, led by Bosworth, smothered Penn State's offense.

Oklahoma 35, Nebraska 10—November 22, 1975. The Sooners entered the game ranked seventh, but demolished the No. 2 Cornhuskers in Norman.

Oklahoma 24, Oklahoma State 14—November 24, 1984. With the Sooners ranked second and the Cowboys third, this marks the highest-ranking for both teams in the state rivalry. For the record, OU is 79–16–7 against Oklahoma State all-time.

Oklahoma 14, Texas 13—October 23, 1915. Yes, this game was played before Memorial Stadium was ever built, but it was the biggest game of Bennie Owen's 22-year career as head coach of OU. The Longhorns had dominated the early years of the series, and this was the crucial victory for Oklahoma's first undefeated season and first conference championship.

Oklahoma 35, LSU 0—January 1, 1950. Capping Wilkinson's first undefeated team, the Sooners were angered by a former LSU player spying on their pre–Sugar Bowl practices.

The Most Disappointing Defeats

Notre Dame 7, Oklahoma 0—November 16, 1957. This would surely rank number one—the shocker that ended the NCAA record 47-game winning streak. Bud Wilkinson's team had not previously lost since September 26, 1953, and that, too, was to Notre Dame.

Nebraska 35, Oklahoma 31—November 25, 1971. In "The Game of the Century," which pitted the No. 1 Cornhuskers and the nation's top-ranked defense against the No. 2 Sooners and the nation's top-ranked offense, it was Heisman Trophy winner Johnny Rodgers's punt return for a touchdown that made the difference. Whoever won it surely would win the national title, and Nebraska did. The Sooners, too, rolled over their two remaining opponents to finish 11–1 and ranked No. 2. In any other year, they were plenty good enough to win the national title.

Nebraska 17, Oklahoma 14—November 11, 1978. This one kept Oklahoma from winning the national title that season, although they did exact revenge on the Cornhuskers more than a month later with a 31–24 win in a rematch in the Orange Bowl.

Miami 20, Oklahoma 14—January 1, 1988. The Sooners were poised to take home another national championship from the Orange Bowl, but the Hurricanes broke their hearts for a second-consecutive season. OU had rolled to an 11–0 record with only two close games before the season-ending defeat.

USC 55, Oklahoma 19—January 4, 2005. What was supposed to be a classic for the national championship between two unbeatens turned into a lopsided affair in the Orange Bowl. OU entered the game 12–0, having rolled over every opponent except Oklahoma State (38–35) and Texas A&M (42–35).

LSU 21, Oklahoma 14—January 4, 2004. The Sooners, who had put together what most thought was an unbeatable team on their way to a unanimous No. 1 ranking before being shocked by Kansas State 35–7 in the Big 12 Championship Game, laid another giant egg in the national championship game.

Arkansas 31, Oklahoma 6—January 2, 1978. Oklahoma was a heavy, heavy favorite in the Orange Bowl clash versus Barry Switzer's alma mater, especially with three of the key Razorbacks suspended for the game. But Lou Holtz had the Hogs motivated. Switzer called it "the most disappointing loss of my career." The loss hurt even more given the fact that Notre Dame had upset No. 1 Texas earlier that day in the Cotton Bowl, meaning that the Sooners could have captured another national title with an impressive win.

Kentucky 13, Oklahoma 7—January 1, 1951. Oklahoma had already captured its first national championship (awarded before bowl games during this era). The win by Paul "Bear" Bryant's Wildcats broke OU's 31-game winning streak.

Kansas 23, Oklahoma 3—November 8, 1975. There was no explaining this one as the No. 1–ranked Sooners fell to the unranked Jayhawks by three touchdowns—in Norman! OU could not hold onto the football that day, but did rebound to win its final three games and, after No. 1 Ohio State was upset by UCLA in the Rose Bowl, the Sooners captured the national title with a 14–6 win over Michigan in the Orange Bowl. This also was Switzer's first loss as OU head coach, after a 29–0–1 start.

West Virginia 48, Oklahoma 28—January 2, 2008. It was a game in which Stoops's Sooners were supposed to redeem themselves for the frenzied, classic 43–42 overtime loss to Boise State in the previous Fiesta Bowl. But Oklahoma appeared flat, as the underdog Mountaineers played better and faster from start to finish.

Santa Clara 20, Oklahoma 17—September 25, 1948. To begin Bud Wilkinson's second season as head coach, this three-point loss left the fans at Memorial Stadium stunned and critical of Wilkinson. The Sooners started a 31-game winning streak the following week against Texas A&M.

chapter 21
Oklahoma Traditions

The Sooner Schooner mistakenly rolled across the field during play in the second half of the Orange Bowl on January 1, 1985.

The traditions surrounding Sooners football are many and unique, from the "Sooner Schooner" to "Boomer Sooner," they have grown and matured into the hearts of all Oklahoma fans.

And lest we forget, they endure and thrive largely due to Oklahoma's tradition of success on the field.

The Sooner Schooner

This is the most recognized conestoga—or covered wagon, in laymen's terms—in the world. Or at least in the college football world.

The Schooner represents the way of travel used by pioneers who settled the Oklahoma Territory around the time of the 1889 Land Run. Powered by identical white ponies named Boomer and Sooner, the Schooner races across Owen Field after every OU score.

The Schooner was introduced in the fall of 1964 and became the official mascot of the Sooners in 1980. The RUF/NEKS, OU's all-male spirit squad, maintain and drive the Schooner.

Mick Cottom, a freshman RUF/NEK member from Liberty Mounds, Oklahoma, has the distinction of being the first person to pilot the Schooner across Owen Field in 1964. The Sooner Schooner and accompanying ponies are housed at the Bartlett Ranch in Sapulpa, Oklahoma. Charley F. "Buzz" Bartlett and his brother, Dr. M.S. Bartlett, organized the Doc and Buzz foundation in 1964.

The Schooner has made a few headlines of its own over years, as well.

Who could forget the time it crashed on its side, fumbling its occupants across the Memorial Stadium field?

It occurred in the 1993 game against Colorado after kicker Scott Blanton made a field goal. The Schooner took a corner too sharply and tipped over, sending driver Scott Gibson, flag-waver Ryan Wray, and the RUF/NEK queen, Jean Connelly, who was riding shotgun, flying through the air and onto the turf.

"We made national news for that," RUF/NEKS official Ian Schaper admitted, "because the queen wasn't wearing any underwear."

Gibson broke his arm. Otherwise, the tumble provided a good laugh and an embarrassing moment.

However, the time the Schooner was penalized for illegal procedure was serious stuff and the OU coaching staff was not laughing.

The Sooners entered the 1985 Orange Bowl ranked No. 2 with a 9-1-1 record, with a possible national championship on the line. They were gripped in a 14-14 tie with Washington when Tim Lashar nailed a 22-yard field goal early in the fourth quarter to give OU an apparent three-point lead.

On cue, the Schooner ripped across the Orange Bowl field as OU fans cheered. However, Oklahoma had been penalized for an illegal procedure on the field-goal attempt. The officials, furious that the Schooner was on the field and, specifically, driving through the Huskies' defensive huddle while the five yards were being marked off, called an unsportsmanlike penalty on OU and marked off another 15 yards.

Lashar's subsequent try from 42 yards was blocked. The momentum seemed to change dramatically, and Washington went on to win 28-17.

"The penalty really affected the outcome of the game," said longtime Sooners fan Bob Jackson. "The officials didn't want the Boomer Schooner on the field because they considered it a delay of the game."

Still, Barry Switzer was angry at the 15-yard penalty, saying, "The officials told us he could come out there after a score, and we said, 'That's all we ever do.' Hell, it's after the fact. We had scored. It was really a terrible, terrible call by the officials."

Years later, however, Switzer has softened somewhat, saying the penalty on the Schooner did not affect the outcome.

"No, Washington was better than we were that night, and they would have won the game anyway," he said. "They deserved it."

Washington, which finished 11-1, did not win the national title, either. That was the season in which Brigham Young, having defeated a 6–5 Michigan team in the Holiday Bowl, finished 13–0 to win its only national title.

And when the Sooners returned to the Orange Bowl to defeat Penn State 25–10 to win the national title a year later, the Schooner and the RUF/NEKS stayed on the sideline, as ordered by the OU administration.

It hasn't been penalized since.

The RUF/NEKS

What's in the name? It all started when some elderly fan grew disgusted at a young man during an Oklahoma–Oklahoma A&M basketball game.

She yelled, "Sit down and be quiet, you roughneck!"

The name, originally meant as an insult, stuck like flypaper.

Now, almost a century later, the RUF/NEKS are legendary. They take care of the Schooner and carry shotguns—which do not shoot real shotgun pellets, fortunately, or a few officials at the 2006 Oregon game would have resembled Swiss cheese.

"Only in Oklahoma," Schaper once said, "would they screen 75,000 fans for security when they enter the stadium—and allow 25 students in with shotguns."

The RUF/NEKS did cross the line a few times with Bob Stoops. Once, they knocked into him during a celebration. Another time, they tapped him on the rear end with a paddle as they rode by.

Memorial Stadium

Like Sooners tradition, Memorial Stadium has grown and matured over the decades.

Completed in 1925 at the urging of head coach Bennie Owen, the stadium cost a mere $293,000, which is about what Stoops earns per month these days.

However, the first game played at the site of the stadium took place two years earlier, resulting in a 62–7 win over Washington, Missouri, on October 20, 1923.

When the stands on the west side were completed, the capacity was 16,000. Another four years later, when the east-side stands were constructed, it doubled to 32,000, where it remained for two decades.

Just after World War II ended, school president George Lynn Cross—the same man who brought Bud Wilkinson to Norman—had grand designs to expand Memorial Stadium. What resulted was the removal of the running track surrounding the playing field. The field then was lowered approximately six feet, and more seats were fitted next to the field. Also, the north end of the stadium was enclosed, bringing capacity to 55,000.

In 1957 bleachers were added to the south end, raising it to 61,836. Before the '75 season, in which the Sooners won their second national championship under Switzer, the upper deck was added, and capacity reached 71,187. Today, capacity is listed at 82,112, but crowds exceed 84,000 for the big games. The Sooners ranked ninth in the country in home attendance in 2007.

And in case you were wondering just how much of an advantage the Sooners have at home, OU has a 337–78–15 record at Memorial Stadium—a .798 winning percentage.

The Sooners Name

Among all the Bears, Tigers, Lions, Trojans, and Cowboys, there are just a few unique names in college football.

For example, you know what schools are affiliated with the Crimson Tide, Fighting Irish, and the Buckeyes.

Likewise, everyone knows the "Sooners" belong to Oklahoma.

So just where and how did the name originate?

As the United States grew and the population spread to the West, the Oklahoma Territory began with a land run in 1889.

Settlers from across the country, attracted by the offer of free land, journeyed to the prairie to begin a new life.

One of the laws then was that those who claimed land had to start searching at the same time, signaled by the boom of a cannon. Those who jumped the so-called cannon were labeled as "Sooners."

For approximately 10 years at the beginning of OU's athletic program, its teams were called the "Rough Riders" or the "Boomers." By 1908, the name "Sooners" emerged.

As the years progressed, "Sooners" became very popular, and the rest is so-called history. It was a good thing, since "Boomer Rough Rider" doesn't sound right.

"Boomer Sooner"

"Boomer Sooner" has been one of the most recognizable college fight songs in the country for decades. Written in 1905 by Arthur M. Alden, a student studying history and physiology, the tune for his lyrics originated from Yale University's "Boola Boola." One year later an addition to the song was made from North Carolina's "I'm a Tar Heel Born."

However, most college football fans would recognize the tune as belonging to Oklahoma all these years later.

You probably know the words by heart, but here they are for posterity's sake:

Boomer Sooner, Boomer Sooner,   *I'm a Sooner born*
Boomer Sooner, Boomer Sooner,   *And a Sooner bred,*
Boomer Sooner, Boomer Sooner,   *And when I die*
Boomer Sooner, O-K-U!   *I'll be Sooner dead.*

Oklahoma, Oklahoma   *Rah, Oklahoma! Rah, Oklahoma!*
Oklahoma, Oklahoma   *Rah, Oklahoma! O-K-U!*
Oklahoma, Oklahoma,
Oklahoma, O-K-U

The OU Chant

The OU Chant was written in 1936 by university girls Glee Club director Jessie Lone Clarkson Gilkey. Thus, she was voted OU's Outstanding Faculty Woman the following year.

The chant's lyrics:

> *O-K-L-A-H-O-M-A*
> *Our chants roll on and on!*
> *Thousands strong*
> *Join heart and song*
> *In alma mater's praise*
> *Of campus beautiful by day and night*
> *Of colors proudly gleaming Red and White*
> *'Neath a western sky*
> *OU's chant will never die*
> *Live on University!*

When the chant is played during OU sporting events, Sooners fans stand and signal number one, symbolizing the unity between all Sooners, as well as the unity of its fans, students, and athletes.

Crimson and Cream

In 1895, when football kicked off at the University of Oklahoma, a student by the name of May Overstreet—no relation to David—was asked to chair a committee to select the official colors of the school.

The committee toyed with several combinations before selecting crimson and cream. The student body then approved, and suddenly pennants, banners, and signs colored in crimson and cream appeared throughout Norman.

Although the OU chant mentions red and white, crimson and cream are the official colors of the university.

chapter 22

The Oklahoma Sooners by the Numbers

Despite playing only two seasons for Oklahoma, Josh Heupel still holds nine major OU passing records, including single-game completions (39 against Mississippi), single-game passing attempts (58 against Colorado), and single-game passing yards (429 against Louisville)—each set during Bob Stoops's first season of 1999. Photo courtesy of University of Oklahoma.

It can be said the success of a college football program can be defined by its numbers. A higher number of wins and championships, of course, translates into a history rich in tradition and prosperity.

Here's an extensive list of numbers relating to OU football:

1: Number worn by quarterback Danny Bradley (1981–1984).

2: Three-time All-Americans (Buddy Burris, 1946–1948, and Rod Shoate, 1972–1974).

3: Sooners selected first-team all-conference four times (Wade Walker, 1946–1949; Darrell Reed, 1984–1987; Anthony Phillips, 1985–1988).

4: Heisman Trophy winners (Billy Vessels, Steve Owens, Billy Sims, Jason White).

5: Sacks by Cedric Jones against Texas Tech in 1994—OU's single-game record.

6: Rushing touchdowns by Quentin Griffin against Texas in 2000—also an OU record.

7: Associated Press national champions (1950, '55, '56, '74, '75, '86, and 2000).

8: Number worn by quarterback Nate Hybl (2000–2002).

9: Interceptions by Ricky Dixon in 1987—the OU single-season record.

10: Number worn by linebacker Torrance Marshall, who led the OU defense to a national title in 2000.

11: Number worn by Jack Mildren (1969–1971), Tinker Owens (1972–1975), and Teddy Lehman (2000–2003).

12: Conference championships under Coach Barry Switzer.

17: Number worn by the Crosswhites—Rodney (1964–1966), Leon (1970–1972), and Kenneth (1975).

18:	Interceptions by Darrell Royal from 1946 to 1949—the OU career record.
21:	The number of Sooners head coaches.
22:	Sooners named All-Americans since Bob Stoops arrived in 1999.
23.77:	Average yards per punt return in the career of Jack Mitchell (1946–1948)—an OU record.
29:	Times an OU football player has appeared on the cover of *Sports Illustrated*, as of the conclusion of the 2007 season.
30:	Seasons in which the Sooners won 10 games or more (an NCAA record).
32:	Career victories in which Steve Davis started for the Sooners (1973–1975)—the OU record for a quarterback.
37:	Sooners selected in the first round of the NFL Draft (through 2008).
38:	Number worn by Prentice Gautt from 1956 to 1959.
39:	Completions by Josh Heupel against Mississippi in 1999—the OU single-game record.
41:	Conference championships.
41:	Bowl games (OU has a 24–16–1 record following the loss to West Virginia in the 2008 Fiesta Bowl).
47:	Games comprising the NCAA-record winning streak (1953–1957).
50:	Turnovers forced by the 1955, '75, and '78 teams—tied for number one all-time.
53:	Ties in Oklahoma football history.
55:	Rushing attempts by Steve Owens versus Oklahoma State in 1969.
57:	Career rushing touchdowns by Steve Owens—the OU record.
57:	Games in which Texas has defeated the Sooners—making the Longhorns the school that has defeated OU the most times.

59.7:	Yards rushing per game allowed by the 1986 Sooners—an OU record.
60:	Yards of the longest field goal in school history, kicked by Tony DiRienzo against Kansas in 1973.
74:	Consecutive conference wins under Coach Bud Wilkinson (1946–1959).
77:	Number worn by Bob Kalsu (1965–1967), a number OU should considering retiring.
80:	Times Oklahoma has defeated Oklahoma State, making the Cowboys the school OU has defeated the most times.
79:	Games played at the Cotton Bowl between OU and Texas.
83:	Receptions by Mark Clayton in 2003—the OU single-season receiving record.
91:	Number worn by Dewey Selmon (1972–1975).
93:	Number worn by Lee Roy Selmon (1972–1975).
95:	Weeks OU ranked No.1 in the Associated Press poll (tied with Notre Dame for first in NCAA history).
98:	Number worn by Lucious Selmon (1971–1973).
113:	Seasons of Sooners football.
142:	Sooners selected first team All-Americans.
189:	Tackles by linebacker Jackie Shipp in 1981—the OU single-season record.
250:	Shutouts by Oklahoma's defense.
294:	Single-game rushing record, held by Greg Pruitt against Kansas State in 1971.
295:	Losses in Oklahoma football history.
334:	Sooners selected in the NFL Draft (through 2008).
337:	The number of Oklahoma wins at Memorial Stadium (versus 78 losses and 15 ties).
429:	Yards passing by Josh Heupel against Louisville in 1999—the OU single-game record.
438:	Sooners selected first-team all-conference.

530:            Tackles by Daryl Hunt (1975–1978)—the OU career record.

556.8:   Yards per game for the 1971 Sooners—the OU single-season record.

601:            Points scored by the 2003 Sooners—the OU single-season record.

768:            Rushing yards against Kansas State in 1988—the OU single-game record.

779:            Wins in Oklahoma football history.

829:            School record for total yards gained in a game—against Kansas State in 1988.

1895:   Year of the beginning of OU football.

1900:   Year of the first game against Texas—a 28–2 loss in Austin.

1923:   Year Memorial Stadium opened.

1939:   Year of the Sooners' first bowl game—a 17–0 loss to Tennessee in the Orange Bowl.

1952:   Year of the first televised game in Sooners history (November 8 versus Notre Dame).

4,118:   Career rushing record, held by Billy Sims (1975–1979).

7,922:   Career passing yards record, held by Jason White (1999–2004).

29,772:   Points scored by Oklahoma (1895–2007), the most for any major-college football program in NCAA history.

85,313:   The Largest crowd at Memorial Stadium (November 11, 2006).

$293,000:   The original cost of building Memorial Stadium, which consisted of 16,000 seats when it was finished in 1925.

$65 million: Price tag of the stadium's latest renovation, completed in 2003.

Bibliography

Cross, George Lynn. *Presidents Can't Punt*. Norman, OK: University of Oklahoma Press, 1977.

Dozier, Ray. *The Oklahoma Football Encyclopedia*. Champaign, IL: Sports Publishing, 2006.

Snook, Jeff. *What It Means To Be A Sooner*. Chicago: Triumph Books, 2005.

Switzer, Barry. *Bootlegger's Boy*. New York: William Morrow and Company, 1990.

Wilkinson, Jay. *Bud Wilkinson: An Intimate Portrait of an American Legend*. Champaign, IL: Sagamore Publishing, 1994.